THE SAVOY

also by Stanley Jackson

MR. JUSTICE AVORY
GUY DE MAUPASSANT
AN INDISCREET GUIDE TO SOHO
THE LIFE AND CASES OF MR. JUSTICE HUMPHREYS
THE AGA KHAN
LAUGHTER AT LAW

The Strand entrance, Coronation Year, 1911

STANLEY JACKSON

THE SAVOY

The Romance of a Great Hotel

FREDERICK MULLER LIMITED, LONDON

First published in Great Britain 1964 by
Frederick Muller Limited
Printed by Ebenezer Baylis & Son, Limited
The Trinity Press, Worcester, and London

for C. R. WILLIS

Contents

7

Illustrations

Most of the photographs used in this book came from the files of the
Hotel's Press Office and Archives Departments, but we also acknowledge the following sources for their material.

Tom Aitkens; Associated Newspapers Ltd.; Associated Press; Walter Bird; Brompton Studios; the Central Office of Information; Central Press; *Daily Express*; *Daily Sketch*; *Evening News*; *Illustrated London News*; Keystone Press Agency; London News Agency; Mirrorpic; Odham's Periodicals; Pictorial Press; Planet News; Radio Times; Hulton Picture Library; Sport and General; A. V. Swaebe; United Press.

Preface

THE YEAR 1964 marks the seventy-fifth anniversary of the Savoy Hotel, now almost as familiar a part of the London scene as the Strand and the Embankment which contain it. The best-known of all international hotels, its history reflects the social panorama of six Reigns.

Today, there are almost a hundred luxury hotels of the top rank in the world's capitals and pleasure resorts. Each sheds a subtle but quickly-detected aura of opulence and sophistication. Technical precision blends so effortlessly with a cosmopolitan suavity of style that, apart from local nuances of cuisine and décor, they are not always distinguishable except to the most habitual and discerning of patrons.

A grand hotel's true mystique stems partly from its management but even more from the clientèle who nourish and renew its prestige. There are larger, costlier and even older hostelries than the Savoy but none has provided a more glamorous setting for the round-the-clock romance, comedy and tragedy implicit in hotel life. Statesmen, princes and countless industrial and other magnates have made history at different levels in its suites and private banqueting rooms. Under its chandeliers almost every social and artistic celebrity has at some time played the rôle of host or guest, not to mention the famed restaurateurs and hoteliers who first served their apprenticeship in its kitchens.

Longevity in itself confers no special claim to distinction. As I hope to make clear, the Savoy has escaped becoming a mellow platitude. In an age of standardization when the trend is for even luxury hotels to be identified largely by their booklet matches, it has managed to preserve a sharply individual style and personality. Few hotels have so smoothly equated tradition with contemporary taste or proved less vulnerable to passing shocks. Almost a city in itself, one of the Savoy's special fascinations is a reliance on its own resources, from basement to roof.

No single volume could hope to deal exhaustively with its numerous departments, let alone the glittering house-list of guests since its doors opened for the first time on 6 August 1889. My own acquaintance with the Savoy extends over thirty years but I have, fortunately, also had access to a treasury of files, documents, relics and miscellanea of every kind preserved from the days when the scaffolding of the new hotel slowly rose on the rubble of Count Peter's ancient Palace.

For this indispensable material my thanks are due to the management who are not, however, responsible for any expressions of personal opinion or the final selection of my subject matter. I owe a special debt to Hugh Wontner, Chairman and Managing Director of the Savoy Group, for his encouragement, courtesy and patience; to Miss Bridget D'Oyly Carte for the loan of the Whistler etching reproduced facing page 33; and among many others, to directors John Hannay and G. B. Potts; Miss Olive Barnett for much assistance and liaison; Miss Mary Tweedy and her colleagues in the hotel's Press Office; and my daughter, Mrs. Tisha Browne, whose secretarial help was invaluable throughout my long but most congenial task. Finally, I must acknowledge the contribution of several members of the hotel staff, active or now in retirement, who were able to draw on personal recollections often dating back to the eve of the century.

OVER THE courtyard entrance to the Savoy Hotel in London stands the gilt figure of Peter, Count of Savoy. It towers above seven plaques which link the site with centuries of violent and quick-changing history. In 1246, Henry III presented to Count Peter, Queen Eleanor's uncle, a piece of land between London and Westminster for a nominal annual rent of three barbed arrows. This was to become 'the fayrest mannor in Europe' and, six hundred and fifty years later, London's first luxury hotel. Peter built a splendid palace where he received the gayest and loveliest of French noblewomen, many of whom married English peers. As a foreigner, however, his influence was resented and finally he crossed the Channel, never to return. Under John of Gaunt, Duke of Lancaster, who lived in the Palace for nearly twenty years, the poet Geoffrey Chaucer was granted £10 a year for life to be paid at the Manor of Savoy. The legend persists, if on little real evidence, that the *Canterbury Tales* were written or at least planned between the richly-tapestried walls of the old Palace.

When John of Gaunt's son became King, the Duchy of Lancaster was absorbed by the Crown, and to this day the precincts of the old estate, which still house the Duchy headquarters, are known as the Liberty of the Manor of the Savoy. In the fourteenth century the wealth and power of John of Gaunt created many jealousies leading inevitably to violence. The Palace was ransacked, burned down by Wat Tyler's mob and left in ruins for over a century before being rebuilt by the first Tudor King as a hospital for the needy. In 1660, Charles II ordered an ecclesiastical conference to be held in the Master's lodgings at the Savoy. It resulted after two years in the Revised Prayer Book.

While the Palace crumbled into decay, the Chapel of the Savoy managed to survive, although for over two centuries it remained an unused shell. In 1773, the Duchy of Lancaster became responsible for its maintenance; a high bailiff was appointed to administer the Manor and Liberty, and a Court Leet organized with four constables who were charged to maintain law and order and to keep out vagrants. The area did indeed need policing. The Strand was then a highway of thieves and whores, and Boswell has related with some relish how he and Dr. Johnson were accosted by a woman of the town as they passed Somerset House.

The Court Leet flourished on and off for years, concerned mainly with nuisances, defective buildings, testing weights and measures and inspecting food and drink. By the end of the nineteenth century its duties had dwindled to an annual tour of the Manor which ensured that the twelve 'marks' or boundaries were maintained in good condition. One of these, bearing the red-painted crest of the Duchy, was on the stage of the Lyceum Theatre where Sir Henry Irving always refreshed officials with cakes and wine.

The picturesque ceremony of Beating the Bounds lapsed in 1940 but was revived for the Festival of Britain and now takes place in alternate years, at Rogationtide. Eight jurymen, living and working within the Liberty of the Savoy and sporting the red rose of Lancaster, are sworn in and accompany the High Steward of the Manor (the Earl of Birkenhead) to the Savoy Chapel where a short service is held. With the bailiff, who is Chief Clerk to the Duchy of Lancaster, and a beadle, carrying a silver-tipped staff and resplendent in cocked hat and lace coat, attended by ten choirboys in purple cassocks and white surplices, the High Steward leads the procession on a tour of the 'marks'. These run from the rear wall of the Lyceum, down the Strand and past the Embankment. At two selected 'marks', one by Cleopatra's Needle and the other sunk in the lawn of the Temple Gardens, the youngest member of the choir is ceremoniously bumped ten times, head downwards on a hassock, by two of his fellows instead of being whipped as in the bad old days. The purpose of this punishment is to impress the exact location of the boundaries on the choirboys, in case of dispute.

The jury, among whom is nearly always a representative of the Savoy Hotel, are paid fifteen shillings by the beadle and report to the High Steward and his six burgesses of the Duchy that the 'marks' have been duly inspected and are in good order. The company then retires to a pleasant luncheon in the hotel, undisturbed apparently by their continuing obligation to furnish, in time of war, one hundred men to put down riots in the Strand.

Repairs to the Savoy Chapel had begun when the Duchy of Lancaster assumed responsibility, but the work was interrupted by several disastrous fires. A visit by the Prince Consort led to extensive rebuilding and it was one of the first churches in England to be lit by electricity.

Long known rather vaguely as a chapel royal, although it did not in fact become so until May 1937, the Chapel always enjoyed a social cachet; being exempt from the jurisdiction of the Archbishop of Canterbury, it also had a special attraction for divorced persons who wished for a religious service on remarriage. It is no secret that King George V frowned on this growing practice and asked the Chancellor of the Duchy to reprimand the Chaplain, himself a vice-president of the Divorce Law Reform Union.

An important change in status and prestige came with the Coronation Honours List in 1937 when the new King announced that the Chapel of the Savoy would henceforth be at the disposal of the Sovereign's private Royal Victorian Order. Extensive alterations were carried out, the cost being shared by the Order and the Duchy. A few months before the war, the title of King's (or Queen's) Chapel of the Savoy was formally granted. Today it remains the private chapel of the Sovereign in right of the Duchy of Lancaster, free and exempt from all ecclesiastical control.

A steel beam spans the forecourt of the hotel between the Savoy Theatre and the former block of residential chambers, now part of the hotel but still known by its old name, Savoy Court. The key to this apparently haphazard union of interests is Richard D'Oyly Carte. He was the son of a flautist who later became a partner in a firm which made musical instruments for the Army and first introduced the saxophone to this country. His maternal grandfather had been Chaplain to the Savoy Chapel but, beyond this coincidence, there was little to suggest that D'Oyly Carte's name would come to be associated, over six centuries later, with the ruins of Count Peter's palace on the Thames.

After leaving his father's firm the young man turned concert agent, his clients including Adelina Patti, Gounod and Matthew Arnold for whom he arranged lecture tours. Later he became manager of the Royalty Theatre, then in Soho, where his father carried on business. In his leisure he had himself written music for operettas, including a curtain-raiser for the Royalty. He now invited W. S. Gilbert to write one for him, and Arthur Sullivan agreed to compose the score. The famous partnership began with a one-act cantata with music, to follow Offenbach's *La Périchole* at the Royalty. *Trial by Jury*, which opened in March 1875, made a triumphant début for the new partnership but ended on a note of sadness. Sullivan's brother, Frederick, had played the Judge with enormous success and died only two years later, at 39. This tragedy was to inspire the very popular requiem, *The Lost Chord*.

At this time D'Oyly Carte was barely thirty, a spry little man with a lively social manner which camouflaged his shrewd commercial sense. He leased the Opéra Comique Theatre and with the help of a small syndicate of backers, including the music publisher Chappell, promoted a company to stage light opera. Their first venture was *The Sorcerer*, written by Gilbert with music by Sullivan for a fee of two hundred guineas as advance royalty against payment of six guineas a performance during the run. George Grossmith, then a light after-dinner entertainer, made his professional stage bow at three guineas a week, while Rutland

Barrington very firmly insisted on £6. They would become celebrated Savoyards.

The Sorcerer had a success but nothing like that of *H.M.S. Pinafore* which ran for nearly six hundred performances, an astonishing record at that time. The syndicate quickly developed teething troubles and D'Oyly Carte decided to form a new company with himself as business manager at £15 a week. Gilbert and Sullivan would receive a small fee for each performance of their operas, and any profits were to be divided equally between the three of them.

With *The Pirates of Penzance* and *Patience* all London flocked to the little Opéra Comique, and the partnership was making so much money that D'Oyly Carte proposed to re-invest it in a larger theatre. He bought the freehold of a plot of disused land in the old Savoy Manor, then little more than an open field and littered with rubbish, but an ideal geographical site for a theatre to accommodate audiences clamouring for more and more Gilbert and Sullivan.

The new Savoy Theatre opened its doors, in October 1881, with *Patience* which had transferred from the Opéra Comique. It was the first theatre in the world to have electric light—provided by a weird engine chugging away in a nearby shed—with gas jets at hand in case the supply failed. For the first time in theatrical history space was reserved for orderly queues to pit and gallery who were served with tea and cakes while they waited. A silk curtain replaced the old-fashioned 'drop' and, among other innovations, audiences were presented with free programmes.

Patience ran on and on, followed by other and now familiar favourites. In their first eleven years the partners split nearly £300,000 between them, but personal relationships became strained. The irascible, gouty Gilbert quibbled over small financial details and came to resent the warm friendship between his two partners. His temper was not improved when Sullivan's name was placed over his own in the programme for *Trial by Jury*. He had a malicious consolation when, with little success, Sullivan's

Ivanhoe was presented at what is now the Palace Theatre and built specially for grand opera by D'Oyly Carte. The latter managed to extricate himself very neatly from financial disaster by selling the new theatre to Sir Augustus Harris of Drury Lane.

D'Oyly Carte was already exploring a more dazzling, if even riskier, project. During his many visits to the United States over copyright problems and the huge number of pirated productions of Gilbert and Sullivan, he had quickly noticed the marked superiority of hotels like the Palace in San Francisco, and the increasing number of American tourists embarking for Europe. It seemed to him that the rich and fashionable audiences at his theatre might also be tempted to sup at an adjacent hotel.

The site was at hand between the theatre and the Embankment, with a superb view of the Thames. Building began in 1884 and took five years to complete. Whistler installed himself one day in D'Oyly Carte's office overlooking the site and made an etching of the scaffolding. "The hotel will never look so well again," was his rasping comment. Years later, like Monet, he would return to the Savoy and from a lofty terrace paint the Thames and her bridges, usually as the sun went down.

Londoners rubbed their eyes when the drapes were stripped off a seven-storey, steel-framed building in which concrete was used for the first time. A power plant in the basement provided all the hotel's electricity while a deep artesian well made it independent of any outside water supply. Completely fireproof, the new hotel was entered from Savoy Hill. In the courtyard an elegant fountain tossed spray up to balconies which glowed with artistic flower arrangements.

The first brochure proudly offered guests, 'Shaded electric lights everywhere at all hours of night and day. No gas. Large and luxurious ascending rooms (lifts) running all night. Top floor rooms equal to the lowest. All the corridors warmed night and day. Seventy bathrooms.' *Seventy bathrooms.* When Mr. Holloway, the builder, first heard of this specification, he asked D'Oyly Carte if he expected his guests to be amphibious. The Savoy's nearest rival, the recently-opened Hotel Victoria in Northumberland Avenue, had only four bathrooms for its five hundred guests. The vast majority managed with a flat bath which reposed under each bed. The bath was placed on a blanket spread on the floor and two huge cans of water, hot and cold, rounded off the Heath Robinson ensemble.

A single bedroom at the Savoy cost 7s. 6d. a day while a double room (with bath) was 12s. De luxe service came into being for the first time and guests were confidently encouraged to use the speaking-tubes in their rooms. 'Please command anything from a cup of tea to a cocktail, and it will come up in the twinkling of an Embankment lamp'.

In memory of his first and greatest love, D'Oyly Carte set aside private dining-rooms, each to be named later after a popular Gilbert and Sullivan opera. Advising him on details of interior decoration, floor service, catering and numerous other matters demanding the feminine touch was his wife, Helen, who had been his secretary and became his business manager. She was at his right hand while he was building the Savoy Theatre and studying the blueprints for the hotel.

A London University graduate and talented actress, she had an excellent and original taste in décor. Whistler was commissioned to design the library and billiard room in their house in Adelphi Terrace where they had installed the first private lift in England. Like her husband, she had paid several business visits to the United States and was equally impressed by American plumbing and engineering. She was even more emphatic that the Savoy must have its own electricity, sound-proofing, lifts and the fantastic number of bathrooms. Although slight and fragile in appearance, she had almost unlimited energy but allied to a natural sense of diplomacy. She had to keep the peace between Gilbert and her husband, and more often between librettist and composer. Numerous staff problems in the hotel's early days were also solved by her quiet intervention.

The share capital of the new Company, incorporated on 28 May 1889, was £200,000. Members of the Board, apart from D'Oyly Carte, included the faithful Sullivan, the Earl of Lathom

(Lord Chamberlain), Hwfa Williams, a leading member of the Prince of Wales's circle, and Michael Gunn, manager of the Gaiety Theatre in Dublin.

Every new hotel is in danger of becoming a nine-days' wonder and D'Oyly Carte, experienced in the theatre, had timed his opening for a brilliant London Season, with the wedding of Princess Louise to the Duke of Fife as its centrepiece. Among the foreign Royalties expected were the Shah of Persia, the new German Emperor and the King of Greece. From Londonderry House, that elegant hub of Toryism, would come leaders of the political inner circle, while Lady de Grey, *patronne* supreme of Covent Garden, promised to convoy an artistic set dazzled by Melba and the elegant De Reszke brothers.

Convinced that an hotel's balance sheet marches on its stomach, D'Oyly Carte instructed his chefs to tempt all manner of palates. While the cuisine was to be dominantly French, there would also be national dishes from many other countries, in particular American specialities like clams, terrapin, sweet corn and pumpkin pie. Significantly, the first gold sovereign taken on the opening day, Tuesday, 6 August 1889, came from Harry Rosenfeld, a guest from Chicago, for a bottle of Moët and Chandon. It remains one of the hotel's prized souvenirs.

Yet D'Oyly Carte's instinct made him nervous and uneasy; he had seen too many spectacular premières followed by chilly, half-empty houses. His hotel needed both a manager and a chef who would not only attract clients but make them return again and again. Casual-seeming enquiries confirmed that a pied piper seemed to be followed around Europe's luxury hotels by the most brilliant stars of international Society. He was César Ritz, a former Swiss waiter turned hotelier, whose taste for detail fused with a remarkable instinct for new ideas. He was backed by a chef of acknowledged genius, Auguste Escoffier, who in his time had cooked for Napoleon III and the German Emperor.

D'Oyly Carte made up his mind to approach Ritz and was encouraged to do so by Lily Langtry, one of his close friends and an early patron of the Savoy. At one time he had considered engaging Romano but Mrs. Langtry made him change his mind. "Romano is a man's man," she declared firmly. "Ritz will attract the ladies." While D'Oyly Carte was taking the cure in Baden-Baden where Ritz had already established himself in a fashionable hotel and restaurant, he noted with envy that the leaders of London Society seemed to be almost like members of Ritz's entourage and followed him from Nice, Paris, San Remo and Lucerne whenever he opened a new place. Apart from the Grand Dukes, the Rothschilds and the new South African millionaires, the Vanderbilts and Morgans from America treated Ritz as a friend. Most significant of all was the constant presence of the Prince of Wales who drove over regularly from Cannes to the Grand Hotel in Monte Carlo. For him Escoffier would create subtle magic like *poularde Derby*.

Ritz charmingly declined a handsome offer to take over the new hotel. With all his persuasiveness D'Oyly Carte enlarged upon the bright opportunities offered by London, but Ritz remained unimpressed. Moreover, even with Escoffier as kitchen bait he doubted if any English gentleman of quality would leave his club to dine out in public with his wife. He was also dismayed by reports of London's cramping restrictions over licensing hours. Finally, he explained that he had only recently opened the Hotel de Provence in Cannes which would demand his personal attention.

D'Oyly Carte persevered. Occupied more and more by theatrical business, he was desperately anxious that the new hotel should be launched successfully in those vital early months. Shiny and beautiful, his Savoy was like a new Atlantic liner without a captain. Ritz, with some reluctance, agreed at last to visit London for the opening and perhaps give the Board the benefit of his expertise. He was not a peasant's son for nothing and seemed perfectly aware that D'Oyly Carte wished to exploit the magic of his name and reputation.

He and his young wife, Marie Louise, were persuaded to spend a few days in London but only, he insisted, as a holiday. A fine suite had been reserved for them and Ritz was invited to survey the new hotel, from the kitchens upwards. He was dazzled by the electricity, gazed in wonder at the vast marble bathrooms, and seemed quite enchanted by the view over the Thames. He met Sir Arthur Sullivan and his nostrils twitched at the incense offered by the Board and all the beauties and dandies.

The new hotel had already begun to glitter with debonair and distinguished leaders of Society who expected not only princely attention but the highest standards of decorum. No lady was admitted into the restaurant with a head-dress of any kind, and those unescorted were most firmly whisked out into the Strand, while even the wife of the British Ambassador in Constantinople was not permitted to go to her table when she declined to remove her toque.

As D'Oyly Carte had anticipated, Ritz could not long content himself with remaining a guest. Soon he was noting possible improvements in the organization and particularly the cuisine, which was good yet lacked the finesse of an Escoffier. The new electric lights were bright and indeed cheerful but scarcely flattering to the ladies. The colour scheme was not to his taste and the furniture seemed to him heavy and over-opulent, although he was too gallant not to congratulate Helen D'Oyly Carte on some subtle touches. Slightly dazed by his reception, he agreed to take over as manager but insisted on six months in each year to look after his other hotels on the Continent.

A new and historic régime had opened. From Monte Carlo Ritz brought over his cashier, Agostini, and as maître d'hôtel one of the world's supreme judges of wine, Echenard, who looked like a Spanish hidalgo. And, of course, Escoffier upon whom the Kaiser had bestowed the title, 'Emperor of Cooks'.

Born near Grasse, Auguste Escoffier was just over forty when he came to London. The son of a blacksmith, he could not read or write until he was fourteen. To the end of his days he mastered no more than a few words of English and would explain jokingly that if he spoke the language he might also learn to cook in the native fashion. One of his special nightmares was the British habit of gorging tea and cakes which ruined palates for his divine dinners. He himself was a light eater and always preferred to dine alone, content with a bowl of vegetable soup lightly sprinkled with rice, with a little fruit as dessert. Particularly he deplored the growing American taste for cocktails before meals and cold water afterwards.

Short of inches, he wore high heels to enable him to see over the huge open ranges. He seldom tasted a dish in his life, relying entirely on his sense of smell. A courtier of the kitchen, he knew how to flatter his guests, creating *poularde Tosca* for Melba, *soufflé Tetrazzini* and *filet de sole Coquelin*. When Melba asked for *pêches flambées* at a dinner to be attended by the Duc d'Orléans, Escoffier asked her to give him time to consider the *entremet*. He thought, quite rightly, that something cold would prove a more palatable epilogue to what had gone before. When the time came, he presented a swan carved out of ice which was wheeled to her table in tribute to *Lohengrin*. In a cavity scooped out of its back to form a nest of spun sugar and strawberry leaves, a superb peach rested on a vanilla-flavoured ice coated lightly with strawberry jam. It was the début of *pêches Melba*. Escoffier went on to create *poires Melba* and *fraises Melba*, with less success, but the *prima donna* was consoled by the comparative lack of popularity of *poires Mary Garden*. After one strenuous American tour, she returned ill and in need of a diet. Escoffier listened gravely and prescribed the crisp austerity now universally known as *toast Melba* but originally devised for Madame Ritz who tactfully abandoned the honour and title to the celebrated singer.

Escoffier was Bernhardt's willing slave. They had been friends since the days when he was cooking at the fashionable Le Petit Moulin Rouge in Paris and she an *ingénue* at the Comédie Française. On the night when she came back exhausted to the Savoy and took an overdose of chloral, he wept outside her door until a doctor from the French Embassy brought news that the danger was over. He went to all her first nights but would hurry back to cook her favourite dish, *zéphyr du poularde Belle Hélène*, created from dainty slices of chicken's breasts on pâté de foie gras and served with asparagus salad. He gave loving care to her birthday dinners which she usually ate in her private suite with the devoted maître-chef as her only guest. One of his secret recipes was for a dish of scrambled eggs prepared in a silver skillet.

Although a master of gastronomic flattery, Escoffier never forgot his own poverty-stricken days. In his waistcoat pocket he always carried a stock of sovereigns which he handed out as rewards for good work, and rather more often to help needy kitchen servants and porters. After a lifetime of heavy earnings and great generosity, he left his name and art as a legend but only £355 in cash.

In her fascinating memoirs Madame Ritz recalled how remarkably her husband harmonized with Escoffier. Ritz was the gifted conductor for whom the chef performed dazzling solos in his kitchen, but they were good enough friends to exchange frank advice. Ritz might taste and give his opinion on a revolutionary new sauce, while Escoffier would volunteer his views on tableware and the luxury equipment which the manager ordered so liberally. For Ritz only perfection was good enough; table covers must gleam white and immaculate; the crystal had to be slender Baccarat and cutlery of the highest quality. He ransacked the civilized world for Christofle silver, rare carpets and the purest marble but did not overlook details like the efficient heating and cooling of his wine cellars. Similarly, Escoffier was a kitchen poet always conscious of the mechanics of his Muse. He was almost fanatical about machinery and used to spend many patient hours supervising the lighting over his ovens and tables.

Both men appreciated the supreme value of detail and appearance. To them a sauce boat was a thing of beauty and a tureen a joy for ever. While Ritz was a martinet over the correct wear for his staff, from managers down to the humblest *commis*, Escoffier attached as much importance to fresh rolls and specially imported a baker from Vienna.

Ritz was the first hotelier to adopt the policy that the customer is never wrong, but with one firm exception; full evening dress had to be worn in his restaurant. To keep out *demi-mondaines* and other undesirables, he also started the practice of placing 'reserved' cards over most of the best tables. He scrapped the original Savoy fittings and installed indirect lighting which was kinder to his dowagers. At their home in Golders Green his wife tells us that she often acted as model for endless experiments until he was completely satisfied with angles and watts.

Diplomacy was his speciality and he never forgot a name or a palate. If a guest committed the felony of ordering tripe and onions he made it seem like a flash of genius. Often he had to deal with rich vulgarians who did not know a Poussin from a *poussin*. Supreme tact was always needed. Glittering with jewels, Patti would make grand operatic entrances, to the disgust of Melba. Seating arrangements had to be hastily scrambled so that the *divas* did not breathe fire at too close range.

Although delicate in health and nervous, Ritz had the hotelier's natural gift of never appearing flustered. With a white carnation in the silk lapel of a flawless frock-coat, he would advance with serene dignity to greet Mrs. Langtry's carriage in the forecourt. He had his special man-of-the-world smile for Barney Barnato who had once created a sensation in the palm lounge when asked by a silly woman if it were true that he had been a clown before becoming a Rand millionaire. Without a word he took off his coat, flung it to a waiter and walked three times round the lounge on his hands.

Ritz listened with sympathy to Mark Twain who had stomach trouble and dined on a baked apple, toast Melba and a pint of draught bitter. He smiled lovingly on Lady Dudley and her pretty daughters, while there was always a bow for Lord Randolph Churchill who made an impressive entrance with his smoothly-ironed silk hat, his buttonhole and a cigarette in the inevitable amber holder.

The Prince of Wales, in too tight a frock-coat, was a familiar visitor. For him Escoffier created a new dish, *cuisses de nymphes à l'Aurore*, but Ritz was a little nervous when Marlborough House sent a note asking for the recipe. It was frogs' legs served in a cream jelly with Moselle and gently flavoured with paprika. Nobody in England had ever before served frogs' legs, and the Prince became an addict. He was followed by every snob in London until Escoffier came almost to regret his inspiration. Luckily, H.R.H. soon became a slave to quails for his supper.

The French Pretender, the Duc d'Orléans, was also one of the hotel's earliest and most favoured patrons, although his three pet lion cubs did not comfort the staff. A tallish man with a light brown beard, he was fastidious in his tastes. Every morning a selection of buttonholes had to be sent to him, and for any private party in his suite overlooking the Thames the meal was always prepared under his personal supervision.

Like most Pretenders and ex-Monarchs, he was ultra-sensitive on matters of protocol and prestige. One day he ordered a wedding breakfast for 64 distinguished guests to celebrate the marriage of his daughter to the Duke of Aosta. He had asked particularly for the immense suite of private rooms on the first floor, but it was bespoken for a Guards Club luncheon at which the Prince of Wales would be the guest of honour.

For once even Ritz's white carnation began to wither. The Prince and the French Pretender shared royal blood but little else except a pitiless mutual dislike. For an agonizing hour Ritz seemed to hover between the Tower and the Bastille, but again his genius for improvisation was to hand. He hit upon the idea of using three basement rooms normally kept for billiards and storage. The Orléans entourage was shocked at the suggestion but clearly it would have been even more humiliating to go elsewhere after having announced that the reception and wedding breakfast would be held at the Savoy. With only a few days in hand, the Duke gave a reluctant *carte blanche*. Doors and walls were promptly ripped out to provide suitable ventilation, and an army of painters soon applied the Ritz touches of elegance. Flowers and ferns sparkled from vases carved in solid ice. On all sides sprouted the tactful *fleur de lis* which adorned even the toilet seats in the Duke's country house.

For this wedding breakfast Escoffier's menu included such delights as *truite saumone royale, cailles aux feuilles de vigne, brochettes d'ortolans* and the now-famed *soufflé d'écrevisses à la Florentine*.

28

While her husband stretched his thick legs among his cronies on the first floor, the elegant Princess of Wales summoned Ritz downstairs specially to congratulate him. She then waved a flunkey aside and herself wheeled out the Duke who had hurt his knee a day or two before. The Prince sneered that the Guards luncheon was a good excuse not to eat 'in the basement', but for some time afterwards he continued to mourn over the superb Orléans menu.

Such flashes of inspiration became almost commonplace during this golden age. When the German magnate, Krupp, demanded some special novelty for a party and grandly insisted that no expense was to be spared, Ritz installed in the Winter Garden a gaily-lit fountain which gushed champagne. When Jack Joel had a fantastic run at trente-et-quarante and returned from Monte Carlo anxious to celebrate his triumph, the Savoy provided a Rouge et Noir décor. The table decorations were in both colours, the waiters wore red silk shirts and red gloves, and the winning number was cleverly fashioned in a variety of red flowers. For dessert the guests were each handed small solid gold scissors to snip their fruit from miniature vines and cherry and peach trees.

Sometimes, inevitably, even Ritz had to bear every hotelier's cross—the ignorance of clients. Already almost a legend is the bibulous client who called loudly for Vichysoise and sent it back with the complaint, "this is stone cold." Marshall Hall, the famous criminal advocate, was lunching at the Savoy when he noticed a burly and rather pompous guest arguing with the *sommelier* and brusquely waving the Burgundy aside. Ritz glided forward and called soothingly for a fresh bottle.

That night Marshall Hall again entered the hotel and Ritz invited him to join a famous gourmet and himself for dinner. It was, of course, a splendid meal and the lawyer was particularly enthusiastic about the wine. "By the way," he asked, "what was wrong with that Burgundy at luncheon?" Ritz held up his glass and studied it with affection and respect. "This is the very bottle," he sighed.

His insistence on perfect service—'a valet for each guest'—became the talk of the hotel world, and men like Hahn and Louis Sherry came over from New York to consult him on new ideas. They were particularly envious of his impeccable staff. Ritz insisted on personally interviewing the scores of applicants who were attracted by his own legend and the fast-growing reputation of the Savoy. Luigi Naintre, who would one day make the Embassy the most fashionable night club in London, never forgot his first interview with Ritz. Although only a boy fresh from Italy, he was received with the utmost courtesy which helped to soften the blow.

"You are not for the Savoy," Ritz decided sadly. "Please go away and learn English first." Luigi found a post at six shillings a week as footman to a Hampstead doctor, mastered the language and was then taken on as a *commis*. He was only one of the long line of famous restaurateurs who would serve their time at the Savoy, including Santarelli, Sovrani, Quaglino, Manetta, Ferraro, Mario of the Ivy, and very many more in other countries. One valuable lesson Luigi learned from Ritz and never forgot was the importance of seating. At the Embassy, years later, he always placed tradesmen at obscure tables, not from a sense of snobbery as he claimed disingenuously, but so that members who owed them money should not have their enjoyment spoilt.

Ritz needed all his sense of humour one morning when the special bell tinkled to announce the unexpected arrival of Royalty. This was the doormen's well-rehearsed procedure for alerting all members of the staff likely to be concerned. Managers, under-managers and others advanced to the foyer while Ritz slipped into his best frock-coat and joined the retinue, picking a fresh carnation on the way. No Royalty was in sight, not even a lady-in-waiting. Instead, and looking rather startled, a small boy was reporting *at the front* for his first day's duty as a page. By mischance, he had selected the Royal bell-push to announce his presence! Ritz recovered from the shock, and Harry Williams was not only pardoned but survived to become head enquiry clerk. He celebrated his eightieth birthday while still working in the

Records Office, and was presented with Company shares in token of almost seventy years' continuous service.

With a trio such as Ritz, Escoffier and Echenard, under the direction of Richard D'Oyly Carte and his fellow directors, the new hotel began to bloom. The legend of the Savoy had started. Henry Irving installed himself in a suite and was quickly followed by Bernhardt who had always abhorred London's hotels. "Before Ritz," she declared, "the cooking was execrable, the carpets were dirty, the menu was medieval, the service an insult." Brilliant hostesses like Lady de Grey, Lady Dudley, the Duchess of Manchester, Lady Randolph Churchill and the dazzling Consuelo Vanderbilt, Duchess of Marlborough, were among the first to give dinner-parties in the small but exquisitely-appointed restaurant whose foyer and staircase were artfully designed to set off the ladies' elegant gowns. It soon became a microcosm of fashion, politics and the arts.

Even Mr. Gladstone, who scowled at the menu and dourly ordered a hard-boiled egg, a slice of toast and iced water, could not refrain from an occasional visit although he denied himself the munificence of some of his fellow-guests. Nicholas Mockett, who started his career as butler to Richard D'Oyly Carte and was Head Porter at the Savoy for forty years, often recalled Gladstone's first tip, a grudging sixpence, but others were evidently more 'liberal'. He left nearly £40,000, a sum which surprised the directors who had given him a generous pension to free his last years from want! Mockett's happiest memory was the pleasure of stumping the Kaiser during a cricket match at Lord Northbourne's place in Kent. The German Emperor violently disagreed with the umpire's decision but had to go.

At the Diamond Jubilee, Royalties from a dozen countries swept into the capital for a succession of receptions and balls. The Savoy's visitors were delighted with the service and cuisine but Ritz knew that London's most fashionable entertainment still took place behind the heavy doors of the Mayfair mansions. He was determined to funnel these guests into the Savoy and also to attract playgoers, who continued to dine at home or hurried off after the theatre to sample oysters at Scott's in Piccadilly or sup at Romano's, the Café Royal and other bohemian rendezvous.

Men had always dined alone in their clubs or escorted ladies of the chorus and *demi-mondaines* to late-night suppers at a few raffish haunts. Ritz's achievement was to persuade them not only to dine in private parties at the Savoy but in the public restaurant with their wives, daughters and family friends. This social revolution had come about through a shrewd little stratagem. Ritz cajoled Lady de Grey, a willing accomplice, to invite some of her friends to a banquet in the restaurant. They were more or less screened from other guests who could not, however, avoid hearing sounds of music and gay laughter. It was whispered that Lady de Grey's 'private club' was enjoying a dinner party. Snobbish hostesses lost no time in proclaiming that it was now both respectable and highly fashionable to dine out at the Savoy Hotel.

The age of Victoria was ending, with Society eager to burst from the steel and whalebone of dinner parties in Mayfair and Belgravia and the gloomy round of country houses at weekends. Mrs. Langtry and Mrs. Keppel became a little less incognito, and daring young hostesses took to giving dinner parties in public. The Savoy, already endorsed by the Prince of Wales and the more stylish duchesses, soon became the centre of a new gaiety and wit. The pulse quickened at new faces from the exciting worlds of Ballet and the Opera, and suddenly the very air became tangy with cosmopolitanism.

Victorian snobs had long found amusement in caricaturing the accents and clothes of 'new-rich Yankees' but the sport was becoming more difficult in the presence of friends of the Duchess of Marlborough, Lady Randolph Churchill and the Duchess of Manchester. The peerage was also beginning to take a very practical interest in the young ladies from Boston and Baltimore who were refreshing after an unvarying native diet of pallid and affected débutantes.

César Ritz used to ride every morning over Hampstead Heath with his physician who warned him to forget, for an hour at

Richard D'Oyly Carte, impresario and hotelier, from a *Spy* cartoon

'Savoy Scaffolding', an etching by Whistler
while the hotel was being built in 1888

least, the schemes that buzzed incessantly in his head. By now the Savoy was patronized by Royalty and millionaires from as far afield as Wall Street and Kimberley. Every evening Ritz would greet his duchesses and such glamorous clients as Melba, the dandified Boni de Castellane who wore a white top hat and had his toenails painted coral, Henry Irving and Yvette Guilbert. Still dissatisfied, he took the bold and costly step of engaging Johann Strauss and his orchestra to play waltzes in the restaurant. Escoffier's reaction to music with his food is not on record, but the experiment was a commercial and publicity triumph. The restaurant was crowded night after night. As Ritz had anticipated, the diners ate more leisurely while they listened to the music and, of course, ordered extra champagne.

The licensing laws still hung like bats' wings over the gay suppers but, thanks to some energetic lobbying by, among others, Lord Randolph Churchill, editor 'Labby' and the tireless Mrs. Langtry, the shadow was at last pierced, if only slightly. People could now dine out on Sundays, and the restaurant was soon thronged with guests who might eat and drink until the naughty hour of 12.30 a.m.

On the surface all seemed well. The Morgans and Vanderbilts took back reports that no hotel was quite as modern or so dedicated to civilized comfort as the Savoy in London. In but a few years it had established an international reputation for its cuisine and the elegance of its furnishings, glass and china. Meanwhile, at the suggestion of Ritz, the Company had purchased the Grand Hotel in Rome which was to prove a good investment as well as a valuable reservoir of talented personnel.

There were other matters, however, on which the directors and Ritz were not seeing eye to eye. With increasing prestige he had become more autocratic and obsessional over trifles, but the familiar story that he abdicated over a minor staff dispute is pure fiction. For some time he had been wooed in private by a group of financiers headed by Harry Higgins, Leopold Hirsch and Baron de Gunzbourg. They offered heavy backing for new hotels which might profitably be opened in London and Paris. Assured

33 TS—C

of support by Escoffier and other lieutenants, and absolutely confident that his aristocratic clients would follow him anywhere, he lent a sympathetic ear to the syndicate. The directors of the Savoy had a series of frank but friendly talks with Ritz and it was agreed that he should leave. Taking with him the inseparable Escoffier, Echenard and Agostini, he at once transferred his energies to opening the great Paris hotel which bears his name and building the Carlton in London.

It could have proved a disaster for the Savoy had not most of its clientèle remained loyal. Habit and tradition are hard to break, but the problem of replacing such a celebrated manager and a chef of genius was obviously urgent. Fortunately, Richard D'Oyly Carte was not the man to bury his head or weep in the wilderness. Already he had the nucleus of a devoted staff, thanks largely to his own kindness and consideration. It was typical of him that, walking round the hotel, he would often give a waiter or porter a few sovereigns for a week at the seaside if he thought the man was looking ill or worn. With his wife Helen and his son Rupert, who had become his assistant and already showed the family flair for both theatrical and hotel management, he began searching for suitable men to run the Savoy and Claridge's, a small residential hotel in Mayfair which the Company had decided to purchase. The original cost of building the Savoy, then half its present size, and of acquiring Claridge's would amount to nearly one million pounds, and some shareholders were becoming impatient with an investment that had so far yielded more prestige than profit.

The directors set about putting matters right. They bought the Restaurant Marivaux in Paris with the sole purpose of bringing its famous owner to the Savoy. When the restaurant was sold again, the gilt mirrors alone fetched more than the Company had made out of it in three years, but the capture of Joseph was a shrewd move at a critical time. His sharp blue eyes, under the bushiest of brows and a shiny bald dome, had seen and mastered every side of catering, from the kitchens to the contours of a table napkin. Bernhardt and Coquelin always requested that he personally carve for them at a side-table and enthusiastically applauded a performance that was more a display of swordsmanship than a surgical act. In the kitchen he insisted on carving all the birds, laying the portions on beds of crushed ice with a full current of air passing over them until they were ready for serving.

As restaurant manager he developed a prestige of which he was perfectly aware. He used to say grandly, "There have been *three* great Josephs—Pharaoh's Joseph, Joseph Chamberlain, and myself," but did not care to be reminded that, although his parents were French, he was in fact born in Birmingham. His temper, quickly roused, was backed by a fierce mastery of *savate*, yet he could be gentle and whimsical and always nimble of wit. Leaving after dinner, a distinguished judge once thanked him for his hat and asked curiously, "How do you know it's *mine*?"

"I don't, my lord, but you gave it to me," murmured Joseph.

With him from Paris came the tall plumpish Thouraud who had been chef to President Faure and the Duc de la Rochefoucauld. He carried two thousand recipes in his head and was regarded even by Escoffier as a virtuoso. His *timbales de filets de sole* and the remarkable *poulet polonaise*, served with the juices of the liver soaked into the bird, have become part of the esperanto of gastronomy. He never prepared *crêpes Suzette* with a liqueur, which he regarded as a blasphemy. Nothing was too much trouble for this great artist. When Lady Randolph Churchill gave a dinner party, she and her guests were charmed by trout served in a silver boat carved from ice and ornamented with paper paddles and a flag at bow and stern.

Joseph and Thouraud were reinforced by the cream of talent from the Grand Hotel in Rome. Among the recruits was Menge, a clever and polished administrator soon to take charge of Claridge's which had now been entirely rebuilt. When its doors reopened in 1898 a few months after Ritz's departure, Richard D'Oyly Carte noticed, at the inaugural reception, a youngish-looking man with an air of unusual distinction and authority. He was a native of Scarborough, George Reeves-Smith, who had unhesitatingly made the hotel business his career. After leaving school at Brighton, he had travelled about France learning the finer points of viniculture and cuisine. He became secretary to Jean Calvet, the king of vintners, from whom he acquired a knowledge of claret with which few Englishmen are blessed. To this day George Reeves-Smith's initials remain carved on his old desk in Bordeaux.

A man of culture and fine personal taste, he quickly developed a business-like efficiency and exactitude which never affected his courtly good manners. He rarely wasted words or time and knew the business of running a first-class hotel, from A to Z. When a friend boasted that Reeves-Smith had no equal in Europe for his knowledge of food, wine, cigars—and mankind, D'Oyly Carte was impressed. He was not, however, looking for a maître d'hôtel. Private enquiries confirmed that this man, still on the right side of forty, had managed the Victoria Hotel in Northumberland Avenue and was now at the Berkeley as Managing Director, heading a small syndicate which had already made a success of the elegant little hotel.

D'Oyly Carte invited him to join the Board and direct the management of the Savoy and Claridge's, the Grand Hotel in Rome and the Restaurant Marivaux. Reeves-Smith declined the offer, explaining politely that he was already under contract to his syndicate. The difficulty was overcome with a bold stroke typical of D'Oyly Carte. The Savoy promptly bought the Berkeley, now one of the Company's most valued properties.

Not long afterwards Sir Arthur Sullivan died. His passing greatly upset his old friend and partner, Richard D'Oyly Carte, who had also been in failing health and followed him to the grave a few months later, still a comparatively young man. At the age of 27, Rupert D'Oyly Carte succeeded his father as Chairman of the Board, and George Reeves-Smith started his long reign as Managing Director of the Savoy Company.

THE DEATH of Queen Victoria and the ending of the Boer War brought a new gaiety to the social scene, with only mild irritations from the new trades unions and cloth-capped 'agitators' in the slums. Caruso, Melba and Chaliapin adorned the Opera, while George Edwardes was making ready to open a dashing reign at the Gaiety with charmers like Lily Elsie, Gertie Millar and the ravishing Edna May. At Court there was a welcome for the now unfailing crop of pretty débutantes from America, but less approval of King Edward's choice of friends, notably the financier Sir Ernest Cassel and Sir Thomas Lipton, who had sailed into Society on his tea caddies.

In the mahogany-panelled Savoy Restaurant with its rich gold and red ceiling, crystal lights sparkled over bare shoulders and tiaras perched on flippant curly fringes. Wally Allan, who worked at the hotel for sixty years, used to recall wistfully that his sole function as a pageboy at half a crown a week was to put out footstools for ladies who rarely tipped him less than a sovereign. Floridly handsome men drank emotionally to a glorious Empire which, Mr. Kipling assured them, would never see a sunset.

The gayer Edwardians numbered among them many bohemian guests like Phil May, the greatest black and white artist of his day, who drew cockneys with such loving humour. He was dining one night when a waiter brought over a five-pound note from a woman, a complete stranger, who demanded one of his lightning sketches. May promptly penned a witty little drawing on the back of the fiver and sent it back.

The new management had its problems. Running costs were high and the net profits for 1903 barely reached £44,000. Although shy by nature and ready to leave the hotels more and more to Reeves-Smith while he devoted himself to his theatre, Rupert D'Oyly Carte remained aware of the need for improvements. "The Savoy is always up-to-date and if possible a little ahead" was his proud boast, and one kept constantly in mind through the years. He was particularly interested in new ideas for furnishing and decoration, and all his life controlled these departments at the Savoy. Already facing competition from the Carlton and the Cecil, he knew that César Ritz's backers had bought part of the site by Walsingham House, overlooking Green Park, and planned by 1906 to build and equip their new hotel at an estimated cost of £900,000.

The Savoy Board was determined to forestall him by developing and improving the hotel, and plans were steadily prepared for spectacular changes which would cost nearly one million pounds. The Savoy would be doubled in size and extend from the river to the Strand. The main entrance was to be moved from Savoy Hill to Savoy Court, a cul-de-sac off the Strand and formerly known as Beaufort Buildings. Ancient rights of way, little used, were to be closed and the whole operation, complicated by the slope of the land to the river, would need to be accomplished in record time.

Following the policy initiated by Richard D'Oyly Carte at the turn of the century, Reeves-Smith had painstakingly acquired property after property along the Strand frontage on both sides of Beaufort Buildings. By 1903, a vast new site adjoining the Savoy had been assembled. All manner of dreary out-of-date property was demolished; unwanted shops were closed, and the Strand widened by agreement between the Westminster City Council and the directors of the hotel.

At this time the Company acquired Simpson's which had been pulled down to allow for the widening of the Strand. The famous restaurant was originally opened by a Mr. Samuel Reiss in 1828 as 'a home of chess' and before long developed into a coffee-house, almost a club, under the name of the 'Grand Cigar Divan'. Here patrons smoked, read their newspapers at leisure and played chess while reclining on divans. The main room was divided up into 'boxes', a style still preserved. When chess matches were played with other coffee-houses in the City, runners in silk hats used to carry the news of each move.

After some years Reiss was joined by a caterer, John Simpson, who provided patrons with excellent roasts and initiated service from trolleys, some of which are still in use today. Before long, the sirloins of beef and saddles of mutton, carved at the table for each individual guest, became an established attraction. The restaurant continued to prosper throughout the century and was renamed 'Simpsons-in-the-Strand' in 1904, when it was enlarged, extended and reopened by the Savoy Company.

Meanwhile, a block of residential chambers, the first service flats in England, was also built on the site and christened 'Savoy Court'. The building, one of the highest in London, was erected by a firm of New York contractors chosen by Rupert D'Oyly Carte and Reeves-Smith. Decorations were in Adam style with walls hung in rich brocade, although the colour scheme was left to a tenant's individual taste. The touch of a bell brought meals from its own kitchens apart from the services of a chiropodist, hairdresser and manicurist. The heating was thermostat-controlled, then an innovation, and each suite equipped with telephones and electrical sun baths.

Sir Thomas (later Lord) Dewar was a tenant for nearly forty years and rightly claimed that he had lived on the site longer than anyone since John of Gaunt. Lily Langtry took a suite at £50 a year with an extra £30 for the services of a maid, valet and chambermaid. At Savoy Court she sipped her usual morning glass of champagne at eleven while receiving friends and admirers like Arthur Bourchier with whom she played in *As You Like It*; Alfred de Rothschild, a hypochondriac who was never without an armoury of pills and powders; her monocled solicitor, Sir George Lewis; Oscar Wilde, who of course affected to despise the neo-Georgian decorations; and an endless procession of lovers, jockeys, spongers and fortune-tellers. With pride she spoke of her yacht, *White Lady*, which she kept at Cowes with a crew of thirty but would soon have to sell to the swindler, Hooley.

The hotel itself was, meanwhile, transformed by the addition of two hundred rooms and suites, many with roofed-in balconies overlooking the Thames. The new entrance was opened in the Strand, with a stone span dominated by Count Peter. The private forecourt beneath was paved with rubber to muffle the clatter of horses' hooves. Today, it is still the only thoroughfare in England where the traffic keeps to the right, thus leaving the entrance to the theatre clear of waiting vehicles.

A new foyer leading to the enlarged restaurant replaced the old narrow entrance. It was covered with, at that time, the largest carpet ever woven in one piece and made in Austria because no English loom was big enough to weave it. Across it strode Baden-Powell, Joe Chamberlain and the rich French eccentric who styled himself His Imperial Majesty Jacques I of the Sahara. A megalomaniac who once had two pageboys dismissed for daring to address him as "Mister", he issued edicts that "in my absence from the throne usurpers will be severely dealt with". The Savoy was so greatly to his taste that he loftily informed Reeves-Smith of his intention to start a similar place in the desert, "when I return". The management was not sorry to see him depart. Among the many complaints was one from a fellow-guest, Mr. Redding of Chicago, who protested that 'the Emperor' had stolen his coal scuttle.

The old Savoy Grill, which had begun its life as a supper-room for artists appearing at the adjacent theatre, was redecorated and now admitted ladies. Here evening dress was not essential and the Café Parisien, its new name, had a kitchen entirely self-contained and independent of the restaurant. It was under the direction of Gustave Seggletz, later to become the Savoy's General Manager. Less formal and rather more gay in tone, it became at once the rendezvous of the theatrical, business and literary worlds. Among regular clients was Elinor Glyn who would call on her publishers in Henrietta Street and keep a hansom waiting while she read page after page of her latest novel to patient Gerald Duckworth. Exhausted, he would then escort her to the Savoy where she always made a hearty lunch of steak, fried onions and boiled lettuce before resuming her reading aloud.

Pure drinking water was pumped into the hotel from an artesian well sunk to a depth of four hundred feet. Gigantic engines supplied power for lighting and the vast ultra-modern refrigeration plant. The first American mail-chute boxes in England were installed on each floor, and Otis lifts started running day and night.

All these amenities proved an attraction not only to London Society, which had now taken emphatically to 'dining-out', but for the hundreds of American visitors who had previously missed England out altogether or spent an uncomfortable night in the capital before moving hurriedly on to Paris and the Côte d'Azur.

There were some, however, who complained angrily that the staff was being spoilt by $100 tips and the blandishments of American millionaires. Thouraud was engaged with eight assistants to go to the United States and prepare a single banquet for a railroad magnate. There he was wooed into the service of William K. Vanderbilt, who, apart from being most unpunctual for meals, continually demanded corned beef and cabbage. This was too much for the *maître* who exclaimed angrily, "You do not need a chef, m'sieu, but a gardener." He then packed his bags and returned to the Old World.

Thouraud, like Escoffier, took no steps to learn English. On one occasion he was borrowed by a duke who was entertaining Lord Kitchener at his country seat. After a magnificent banquet, attended by house guests and tenants, His Grace demanded three rousing cheers for Kitchener. To everyone's surprise, Thouraud stepped forward and thanked them gracefully in French. He thought the duke was acclaiming the *cuisinier* and nobody dared to disillusion him.

The Savoy's traditional link with America goes back to its earliest days. One July morning in 1902, on the eve of King Edward's Coronation when the capital was crowded with visitors, Sir William Goode and two American friends, George Wilson and Lindsay Russell, met in the smoking-room of the Carlton Hotel and decided to form a small club. In the words of Wilson, "It will be composed of Americans like ourselves who have made the pilgrimage over here and have received and appreciated British hospitality, and there will be English members who have made the pilgrimage and have discovered that we are not all Red Indians."

Harry (later, Sir Harry) Brittain, one of the founders and Hon. Secretary for many years, invited to the first dinner at the Carlton speakers like Sir Edward Clarke, K.C., the American Ambassador Joseph Choate, General 'Hellfire Joe' Wheeler of the Confederate Cavalry, and the first President, Lord Roberts, with Lord Kinnaird in the chair. A huge centrepiece in ice represented the American eagle. Thus was born The Pilgrims' Society of Great Britain, with headquarters in the Savoy, and soon afterwards its sister society, The Pilgrims of the United States, which holds its dinners at the Waldorf-Astoria in New York.

At the London banquets a new British Ambassador appointed to the United States traditionally makes his first public speech, as does the newly-appointed American Envoy to St. James's. By authority first given by King Edward VII and President Theodore Roosevelt, a combined Anglo-American Loyal Toast is always proposed to both Heads of State. Later, the Society adopted the Colonial Secretary's suggestion that The Pilgrims should also welcome visiting Dominion Prime Ministers at their dinners.

The banquets take place once or twice a year in the Lancaster Room where a symbolic picture hangs. It portrays the sailing of the *Mayflower* and was painted by A. Forester to commemorate the Tercentenary. At the Savoy all the organization is conducted from a small two-roomed suite where a card-index is kept of the six hundred members and a much bulkier file for would-be members. Here also are preserved copies of historic speeches by guests like Sir Winston Churchill, Frank Kellogg, John G. Winant, Field-Marshal Lord Smuts and Lewis Douglas, and the Minutes encase sixty years of Anglo-American friendship.

No women are present at these dinners except the secretary and her assistant who used to sit at a far corner of the dining-room behind a screen but are now 'concealed' only by a huge vase of flowers. A rare and memorable exception was the banquet to Mrs. Eleanor Roosevelt to commemorate the unveiling of the Memorial Statue to her husband. It was attended by the Queen, then Princess Elizabeth, and the wives of Pilgrims.

The gatherings have not all been formal or pregnant with high policy. One of the first guests of honour was Mark Twain who confessed that on arriving in England he was startled to see newspaper posters announcing, 'Mark Twain Arrives Gold Cup Stolen'. He turned solemnly to his hosts and declared, "I have never seen the Cup. I haven't got the Cup. I did not have a chance to get it." The menu showed a steamboat on the Mississippi and, in the foreground, Twain dressed as a Pilgrim Father with a huge quill as his staff and a jumping frog on a leash.

Five years later, The Pilgrims entertained Commander Peary in honour of his expedition to the North Pole. Among the distinguished company were Captain Scott and J. Pierpont Morgan. There was a realistic representation of the Polar Sea, and a model of Peary's ship *Roosevelt* hemmed in by icebergs on which perched lifelike penguins and polar bears. The waiters were robed in white furs and parkas, while on each table stood bowers of roses with the Stars and Stripes picked out in tiny electric bulbs.

Not to be outshone, the champagne millionaire and Wall Street financier, George A. Kessler, also arranged a Christmas dinner in the Winter Garden in tribute to Peary. Plaster snow covered the entire floor and the walls were decorated with huge snow-white chrysanthemums. The Pole was represented by an enormous nail from which hung a menu of delicacies like *caviare des Sibériens, truffes du Périgord North Pole* and *bombe des esquimaux*. Gay little snowmen held the place cards, and each lady was handed a spray of white gardenias. Well over four hundred Christmas gifts had been sent from Paris for the thirty-four guests, including gold cigarette cases from Cartier for the men and diamond brooches from the Rue de Rivoli for their partners.

This party cost Kessler £2,000 but seems a quiet and informal affair compared with the famous Gondola Dinner which he gave in July 1905 to celebrate his birthday. A tall man with a pointed imperial beard and gold-rimmed glasses, he looked severe and had an uncertain temper. His appearance by no means suggested the gastronomic playboy and party-giver but his eccentric dinners had made history long before he came over to dazzle Europe.

In America he had presided over a Hobo Dinner at which his guests were commanded to wear rags and leaky boots. They had to carry their keys and loose change in gaudy knotted handkerchiefs. Some of them looked so realistic that they had difficulty in passing the flunkeys at the door. They were rewarded with the most delicious food which, however, had to be eaten from tins, with coffee served from billycans and heated over an open fire.

At another banquet his guests braved indigestion by charging through twenty courses on horseback. The waiters were dressed as grooms and made their way from the kitchens through specially erected horse-boxes. For a Jungle Dinner in New York, Kessler transformed a banqueting hall into a tropical glade lined by real orange trees from Florida and coconut palms shipped from Bermuda. Another novelty was his *fête champêtre*, decorated by Corot reproductions. During the dinner, startled pigs and chickens ran about among the guests. Even more nerve-racking for his friends was an invitation to dine with him over the Atlantic in a chartered airship.

But this 'Diamond Jim' Brady character achieved true magnificence and perhaps immortality with his Gondola Dinner at the Savoy which he modestly described later as, "the most novel little party I have yet given". Venice was to be the motif and all the arrangements were left to Reeves-Smith, his Banqueting Manager and the inspired Thouraud. As usual with Kessler, notice was short and with no limit on the budget.

The old forecourt of the Savoy was flooded to a depth of some feet of water and a small army of painters erected reproductions of St. Mark's, the Doge's Palazzo and other landmarks. The court-yard was lit by four hundred Venetian lamps, the centrepiece a vast silk-lined gondola to seat the two dozen guests who included the French actress, Réjane, and Edna May, 'the Belle of New York'. It was decorated with twelve thousand fresh carnations and even more roses. A hundred white doves fluttered over the company but the plan misfired to include swans gliding around gracefully. The chemical used to dye the water blue killed the luckless birds who floated about, feet up, until they were removed.

The food was prepared by fifteen special cooks and served by waiters dressed as gondoliers. The three great Lions of Venice, sculpted in ice, bore trays of peaches and the most elegantly contrived glacé fruits. Thouraud had created a banquet which rivalled in splendour anything prepared even for the Doges. Among the many delicacies was *filets de sole en coupe à la Véni-tienne*, cooked in transparent paper boxes bearing the city's coat of arms and illuminated by concealed electric lights.

As the curtain fell on this banquet, a baby elephant plodded sedately over the gangplank and on to the gondola. On its back rested an enormous candle-lit birthday cake, five feet high. Rising to toast their host, the guests saw him suddenly surrounded by a bevy of Gaiety Girls who were quaffing glasses of Moët and Chandon 1898. Kessler had not entirely forgotten his business interests or the sweet uses of publicity.

Then came a superb piece of stage management. The lights went down and a melon-like hotel moon beamed on the magnificent scene as Caruso parted the heavy brocade curtains. He was paid £450 to sing his arias, a minor item in a celebration which had cost Kessler £3,000. Never a mean man, he also tipped the staff £1,000 in appreciation, but like so many other multi-millionaires had his weaknesses over money. He loved London and in particular the Savoy but nothing incensed him more than the English practice of charging for a programme and a cloakroom ticket at the theatre. He regarded this toll as licensed

45

grand larceny and could never reconcile himself to it. One night he stumped out of a play and handed the commissionaire a shilling. "Give this to the management," he exploded. "I just walked down a strip of carpet which I haven't paid for yet."

These were small irritations compared with the attractions which most visitors found at the Savoy. It was already almost an American colony with the guest list crowded year after year with familiar names like the Vanderbilts and Stuyvesants, Governor and Mrs. Orlando Manning of New York, Charles Crane from Massachusetts, the Governor of Arizona and the Guggenheims. That exuberant gambler, John W. ('Bet-you-a-Million') Gates, once paid for a £20 dinner with £200 in five-pound notes and grandly waived the change. There were gay parties for the Fourth of July, the American Fleet was always lavishly welcomed, and The Pilgrims honoured athletic teams from Harvard, Yale and Princeton. Theodore and Mrs. Roosevelt lunched with the King at Marlborough House and that night joined a dinner party in the restaurant. A transatlantic chess match was played by cable between a team in Brooklyn and one at the Savoy, with the Baron de Rothschild as referee in Vienna. The one-way tourist traffic had become so much the vogue that a 'See America First' campaign was started in Washington, but with little effect.

Edwardian elegance and glitter was an irresistible attraction in those gay days preceding the First World War. Réjane came bowling down the Strand in a victoria drawn by snow-white mules given her by the King of Portugal. In explosively broken English she expressed horror at the new motor-car brought over from America by Edna May, but could not tolerate being considered old-fashioned and soon became inseparable from her vast mustard-coloured limousine.

At dinner one saw Joseph Chamberlain pontificating to his son Austen through a cloud of Havana smoke; Marshall Field and his lovely bride over from Claridge's and supping together in the more frivolous atmosphere of the Savoy; Henry Irving handing Ellen Terry into her brougham; supper parties presided over by the Sultan of Zanzibar, Prince Henry of Pless and dukes and princelings from a dozen countries; Sir Thomas Lipton and Sir Alfred Harmsworth with their heads together; the Sultan of Johore acknowledging a respectful bow from the young Aga Khan who was in residence at the Ritz but found supper at the Savoy less sedate and more to his taste.

Here a whisper was a command. When twelve princes from Siam gave a dinner party in the restaurant the table was decorated with flowers in their national colours. Next morning, serving one of the princes breakfast in his suite, a bewildered waiter was courteously thanked for his kindness and presented with the Order of the White Elephant. Another guest from the Orient demanded bird's nest soup which defeated even Thouraud until Reeves-Smith telephoned a friend at the Chinese Embassy and soon afterwards despatched a page for the recipe and materials.

The hotel prided itself on being able to provide, at the shortest notice, a banquet unexcelled in Europe. Wishing to entertain ten old friends at a private stag dinner, one London businessman left both the meal and the price to the Banqueting Department. They were offered *hors d'œuvres à la Russe, cantaloupe, potage aux nids d'hirondelles, bortsch, carpes à la Lucullus, poularde Royale, noisettes d'agneau, ortolans, mousse, soufflés* and, of course, the finest wines and liqueurs. The bill was £15 a head (at a time when the sovereign was worth twenty good shillings).

Yet it was possible to eat frugally even at the Savoy. The cover charge in the early days of the century was a modest threepence, hors d'œuvres cost a shilling, *sole bonne femme* (for two people) half a crown, while an 1889 Mille Secousses proved rewarding at three shillings a bottle. And a lonely bachelor guest could always make his way into the kitchens at neighbouring Simpson's and watch the joints of venison, beef and poultry roasting on the spit over a huge open range.

Every night was already like a first night at the theatre. On a typical Sunday evening the restaurant was so full that twenty or more tables spilled out into the palm lounge and Leslie Stuart, Kate Cutler and Gerald du Maurier had to wait patiently for others to leave. Even the mighty and eccentric Duke of Westminster was unable to find a small table to himself and stumped huffily off to the Cecil down the Strand. As usual he went bareheaded. Although one of the richest men in England, he boasted of saving £300 a year by going about without a hat.

Puccini entertained a supper party with Melba as one of his guests after a gala performance of *Manon* at the Garden. Leoncavallo stayed at the hotel while busily arranging for the opening of his new opera, *I Zingari*. Mascagni registered and at once enquired anxiously about his missing trunk which contained a staggering number of shirts and exactly 176 collars. When travelling he always preferred to await deliveries from his favourite laundry in Leghorn. Only they, apparently, could make his linen look stiff but still flexible enough to allow for his energetic conducting.

Franz Lehár entered in a flood of happy tears after the tumultuous first night of *The Merry Widow* at Daly's. Joining him for a celebration supper were the enchanting star, Lily Elsie, and George Graves who had triumphed as 'Baron Popoff'. As the evening wore on, Lehár became more and more sentimental over his Tokay. With tears running down his cheeks, he recalled that all his life he had really wanted to be a concert violinist until, one day, his great friend Dvorak listened to him scraping away and said gravely, "Nail your fiddle to the wall and try to become a composer."

Ritz had meanwhile established his new hotel but was not having too easy a passage or too friendly a neighbour in autocratic Lord Wimborne who was rich enough to have even his housemaids' uniforms designed by Worth. When Ritz's backer, the fashionable solicitor Harry Higgins, once asked Wimborne if he would consider selling his house, the peer replied off-handedly, "Why?" "Because we are thinking of enlarging the new hotel." "And I'm thinking of enlarging my garden," growled Wimborne. "How much will you take for the Ritz?"

The new hotel had social distinction and the gracious atmosphere which Ritz seemed to invest always with his own magic.

Sir George Reeves-Smith, Managing Director of the Company for forty years

W. A. 'Willy' Hofflin,
General Manager, 1941-61

Autori's caricature of department heads used by Arnold Bennett as models in *Imperial Palace*. From left to right, A. Gilles, Victor, Santarelli, Latry, Manetta, Virlogeux and Zavattoni

From the gleaming candle sconces to the crystal chandeliers and silver inkstands, it had an elegance suited to the monarchs and shy millionaires who wished to remain incognito. It was a small hotel compared with the mighty Savoy, and the two establishments have remained different in size and character ever since.

It is fascinating if unprofitable to speculate on what might have happened had Ritz not had his breakdown in health within a short time of opening the hotel that bears his proud name. Before the end of the Great War, this king of hosts and host to kings was to die in a Swiss clinic, helpless and docile as a child, the fine brain crushed by years of strain and overwork. Born the thirteenth son, he was superstitious and always convinced that he would have a tragic end. A confirmed Edwardian by instinct, it is difficult to associate him, even in conjecture, with the smooth but swift-moving progress of the Savoy. One can see him engaging Johann Strauss, if not Carroll Gibbons. He might have found himself at home at the Ritz of today but lost in the complexities of the modern Savoy.

The personality of Reeves-Smith, backed by the faith of an enterprising Board, urged the Savoy ahead of all competitors without lowering its sights on luxury and elegance. He had unique gifts, not the least an eagerness to understand the background of others. To converse more easily with the staff of the Grand Hotel, he acquired a working knowledge of Italian which he jokingly claimed to have mastered painfully during his many long train journeys between London and Rome. He resorted always to reason and diplomacy. Although a martinet over the smallest flaw in service or even a minor breach of honesty, he could forgive a genuine mistake. More than one Savoy employee would complete half a century of service after being given 'another chance' by the Managing Director.

Invariably he wore a morning coat and high collar under his silk hat when leaving the Berkeley after riding, as he did early every morning, in Hyde Park. He would walk to the Savoy through Green Park, across the foot of Whitehall where a friendly policeman held up the traffic for him, and along the Embankment, almost the whole way with grass on either side. Many years later he made his home at Claridge's and travelled by car, replacing his lost walk with exercises in his room and regular massage. At the Berkeley his collection of books became so vast that, it is said, he bought the Esplanade Hotel at Seaford mainly to take the overflow, but also to provide a holiday home for his children.

One part of his nature was quiet, cultured and scholarly, almost donnish, but nobody mistook the practical gifts he brought to his work. He could discuss philosophy or the writings of Walter Bagehot but also knew the day-to-day market prices of a thousand and one items of food and equipment. While he could argue knowledgeably and in fluent French with his chefs and the grand viziers who bought the meat, vegetables and all the other victuals for the three hotels, he had also mastered the technicalities of finance, and was of course a famed authority on wine. His card-index type of mind seemed to move with almost surgical precision through the mass of routine detail upon which a smoothly-working hotel is based. Before he became the head of the Berkeley, his long years of training, particularly in systems of control, had given him a valuable foundation. Except through illness he would rarely miss a working day. He never seemed ruffled, a quality of mind due perhaps to his deep interest in philosophy, the game of chess and a lifelong taste for fishing on the Test.

He did not care for innovation for its own sake but would encourage his staff to initiate new ideas which he always welcomed. He listened thoughtfully when his General Manager, the volatile Pruger, approached him excitedly with blueprints for a decoration to grace the hotel's New Year's Eve gala dinner for 1906. This was to be an 'aeromobile', a hybrid of motor-car and aeroplane, circling over the heads of a thousand diners who had reserved tables weeks in advance. On a set of rails fitted to the roof of the vast foyer, the seven-foot machine started its run at 11.58 p.m. Its passengers were two lovely ladies symbolic of the New Year. On the stroke of midnight, the machine landed and ran between the diners while the ladies showered souvenir gifts on the guests. An old four-wheeler, the spirit of the Old Year, then wheezed off into the shadows. Reeves-Smith's approval of the idea gave the hotel almost as much publicity as the famous Gondola Dinner.

After a series of brief morning meetings with his General Managers at Claridge's, the Berkeley and finally the Savoy, always held at exactly the same time every day, and occasionally with the heads of the banqueting, reception and other departments including the kitchens, he would walk to his usual table in the Savoy Restaurant like a dignified Roman Senator, apparently aloof but with an acute eye for even the tiniest of blemishes, from a waiter's badly-tied bow to a carpet or curtain which looked short of perfection. Ramrod straight, with a cigar made to his own specification in Havana elegantly poised between his fingers, he seemed the embodiment of the courteous old-world diplomat, but there was nothing flowery in his style. He was clear and incisive in speech like a judge anxious to dispense justice after some florid addresses from the Bar.

Outside the world of hotels his mind turned on many things. He was responsible for building the British Sanatorium at Montana in Switzerland. Medicine fascinated him and he was delighted when his daughter took up the subject. She all but qualified and later married a doctor. In the years to come, Lord Horder would be his favourite table guest at the Savoy.

Looking about him, the Managing Director had some cause for pride. Rich snobs, humbugs and poseurs are inevitable in all grand hotels, but he preferred to think of the more congenial and celebrated guests with whom he exchanged bows. The Green Room pulse beat a little faster when Irving made an entrance, sardonic and sombre, his hat tilted at an angle and smoking a cigar with an air that nobody else could quite equal, even when he was already a dying man and crippled by debts. Mrs. Pat Campbell fondled her pet griffon, Pinkie-Ponkie-Poo, while Gaby Deslys held court and passed a critical eye over beautiful Gladys Cooper and the loveliest débutante in London, Lady Diana Manners.

Lord Northcliffe presented a blushing Blériot, fresh from the first-ever flight across the English Channel, with a cheque for £1,000 in the presence of Major Baden-Powell and Lieut. Shackleton. After the banquet the aviator summoned the red-bearded General Manager, Gustave, and gave him a propeller blade from the historic aeroplane as a souvenir. Lloyd George ate Irish stew and laughingly recalled being once turned away from the restaurant because he was not in evening dress. Reeves-Smith had waived the formality when Ll.G. apologized for his frock-coat and explained that he had come straight from the House.

Margot Asquith's corkscrew curls danced as she shook her sparkling cocktail of wit and malice. Her nose, broken in a hunting accident, and the long talon-like fingers helped to make her a fascinating if formidable character. The Prime Minister lacked his wife's talent for the quick cruel thrust. At one Savoy banquet he suffered a most embarrassing experience when two suffragettes, in full evening toilette, charged in. One of them grasped the tablecloth while another pinioned him to his chair and asked what he intended to do about their colleagues martyred in Holloway. White with anger, Asquith countered weakly by asking what *they* intended to do. "Wait and see," they replied grimly before being marched out.

From the stuffy Law Courts, their long wrangles forgotten, Rufus Isaacs supped with learned brethren like Carson and Charles Russell and watched the hotel lights shimmering in the Thames as the barges waddled through the night. Already tasting success as barrister and politician, F. E. Smith cut a figure with his pleated evening shirt, cigar and carnation, an inseparable pet dog under his arm. He was enjoying a weekend at Oxford when a telegram arrived asking him to return at once to give his opinion on an important legal matter. It appeared that Mr. Lever (afterwards Lord Leverhulme) had been accused by the *Daily Mail* of creating a 'soap trust' monopoly.

'F.E.' reached the Savoy that evening to hear that he must give his views by 9 a.m. the following day. Awaiting him in his suite was a mass of documents standing nearly four-foot high on the table. He picked up the telephone and ordered a bottle of Bollinger and two dozen oysters to sustain him through the night. By 8.30 next morning, still looking as if he could go on for another twenty-four hours, he jotted down a brief but decisive opinion. "There is no answer to this action for libel, and the damages must be enormous." Mr. Lever promptly sued Northcliffe Press who finally agreed to pay £50,000 in damages, apart from a vast bill of costs.

Winston Churchill was one of Smith's closest friends, and they would often meet to talk over their many interests in common, particularly politics, horses and books. After one Christmas together with their families at Blenheim Palace, they decided to form an exclusive little club that is still very much alive. An expert draftsman, Smith jotted down the details of a constitution which has remained unchanged for over half a century.

The Other Club, founded at the Savoy in 1911, would gather every other Thursday while Parliament was in session and probably owed its name to the members' need for another meeting-place outside the larger and less private 'club' at Westminster. Members took the chair on a rotation basis. Originally it had an equal number of Liberal and Conservative M.P.s who could be 'paired', but political history disturbed that amiable balance without, however, bringing more than a handful of Socialists, like Lord Shawcross, into the club. Membership was also gradually extended to include eminent representatives of the Services and the Arts, but not the Church.

The principal object was 'to dine', and nothing in the intercourse of members would be allowed to interfere with the full asperities of Party politics. It is known that Sir Winston once met and chatted with a club member at dinner in the Pinafore Room when they were not on speaking terms outside. The names of the executive were to be 'wrapped in impenetrable mystery' and there was some embarrassment when, years later, a gossip-writer disclosed that Lloyd George had been appointed Chairman of the Wine Committee. No speeches are permitted but the rule was relaxed, by common consent, when Sir Winston acknowledged the generosity of his old friend, Brendan Bracken, who had left a bequest to the Club for a series of dinners.

There were numerous other banquets to arrange at the hotel. Older even than The Other was The Shikar Club, founded in 1907 by Sir Winston's cousin, Captain George Spencer Churchill, and other sportsmen who had 'pursued Big Game with a rifle outside the British Isles'. It meets to this day for its annual dinner at the Savoy although the 'shop' talk is now more concerned with camera guns than the double-barrelled variety, and its members show as much concern for wild life preservation as its destruction. Quite different, but even more exclusive, was the club with the motto, 'It's good to be alive!' The members had all 'died' and lived again after their hearts had stopped beating. Thanks to modern surgery, membership has greatly increased with the years.

Reeves-Smith was gratified by a boom in custom reflected in the hotel's wine cellars, already by far the largest and most lovingly stocked of any hotel in the world. Often in the early days he visited the vineyards and personally tasted every wine and liqueur before making his sage choice. On one visit alone he invested £30,000 in Champagne 1900, a figure to be much increased in later years.

To celebrate the Savoy's coming of age in 1910, the Company had refronted the entire façade overlooking the Embankment and added two completely new storeys. The old-fashioned balconies were dismantled, the rooms enlarged and many more bathrooms built. The suites over the Thames were redecorated and lavishly furnished, a remarkable feat of organization and construction completed in exactly two months without closing the hotel or indeed any part of it for a single day. To achieve this, Reeves-Smith had rented a vacant site in the Aldwych and there pre-assembled everything needed before operations began. By now the hotel had 244 bathrooms, and its three deep-sunk artesian wells pumped London's softest and purest water.

One night in 1911, two diners got up in the restaurant and daringly began to dance to a string orchestra. Others followed and a small space was soon cleared between the tables. Before long the pocket-handkerchief dance floor had expanded into a new ball-room and banqueting-hall in which two thousand guests would link arms and chant *Auld Lang Syne* on New Year's Eve. That sprung floor would see the rise and fall of many dance fashions. Gay Bostons began to alternate with the more stately waltz which remained popular although most of the dancers tactfully avoided reversing, a movement that had earned the displeasure of King Edward, perhaps because of his girth. Ragtime quickly became fashionable and even more in demand than the waltz, and Irving Berlin, who had once played the piano in a Bowery saloon, seemed a little bewildered when he first saw wasp-waisted duchesses in tiaras jigging to *Alexander's Ragtime Band* and *Everybody's Doin' It*. He used to be greeted like visiting Royalty by other guests and could never resist sitting down at the piano and leading the choruses.

For King George V's Coronation, princes and multi-millionaires crowded into the capital, and the hotel was besieged by visitors some of whom had to be content with a bed in the suburbs. In the Restaurant, recently redecorated and gay with mirrors, huge parties supped off quail, lobster and strawberries. The ballroom was jammed with dancers over whom iced cylinders of ozone had to be sprayed in that very hot summer.

Coronation Week opened with a magnificent fancy dress ball. A Russian orchestra played in the ballroom decorated in white and gold and sparkling with rare blooms arranged by seven London florists. Lady Diana Manners was among those who made graceful curtsies and presented sheaves of orchids to Prince and Princess Alexander of Teck and other Royal patrons. From his side-table Reeves-Smith watched a brilliant company which included the Radziwills, the Duke and Duchess of Wellington, F. E. Smith, Admiral Dewey's daughter-in-law, and Winston

Churchill's beautiful mother, Mrs. George Cornwallis-West, who came as the Empress Theodora. Mr. Churchill, chubby but dancing energetically, appeared in a red domino with a cowl over his already thinning hair, but the first prize of a diamond pendant from Cartier went to Lady Diana as a ravishing Velasquez Infanta. The 'cabaret' was provided by Pavlova, followed by artistes from popular successes like *The Quaker Girl*, *The Arcadians* and *The Chocolate Soldier*.

The Coronation Season had boomed the Company's trading profits to a record figure of £166,000. The most exotic delicacies pandered to gourmets and others. One American lady, asked to select a dessert, demanded "any fruit not in season". Fancy dress became ever more elaborate. At one charity ball a picturesque gavotte was danced by over eighty guests in Louis Seize costume. Lady Diana Manners, dressed as Lely's 'Picture of a Lady', inevitably won first prize, and among many pompadours were Mrs. Keppel, Lady Tree and the tireless Mrs. Patrick Campbell. Their partners in long silk coats over knee-breeches included Count von Bülow and a shy new literary lion, W. Somerset Maugham.

It was a period of brilliant dinner-parties. A. J. Balfour was in the chair at The Pilgrims' Coronation Dinner when the guests included the American Ambassador, Winston Churchill and General Sir John French. In the restaurant one table sagged with talents like the Fabian Webbs and red-bearded G.B.S.; John Galsworthy, stiff-backed and remote, looked helplessly for escape from these earnest neighbours, while shy H. G. Wells lent only half an ear to R. S. Hichens to whom the Savoy always seemed another Garden of Allah.

Melba presided at a supper party attended by many guests who had come on from the State Ball at Buckingham Palace. A dinner in honour of Anatole France brought together Mrs. Humphry Ward, Will Rothenstein, T. P. O'Connor, Jerome K. Jerome, W. W. Jacobs and W. J. Locke, but Thomas Hardy pleaded illness and stayed away. Hall Caine, who enjoyed the fleshpots, liked to excuse his constant presence at literary dinners by claiming that they provided him with mental fodder. This failed to impress Max Beerbohm who once reminded him that "the proper study of Manx kind is the Isle of Man".

Like a temperance preacher seeking converts in a gin palace, Sandow touted the Savoy with his muscles. Among the ten-course trenchermen he hoped optimistically to find patrons for his new physical culture establishment in Southwark. To a lethargic after-dinner audience he lectured on a new health-giving baking powder which he was putting on the market. His thunder was rather stolen by Annette Kellermann, 'the Perfect Woman', who was being entertained next door by fifty jovial admirers.

Rouged and raddled Bernhardt did not claim to be a perfect woman in any sense, but even with one leg her personal magnetism proved more than a match for Miss Kellermann's ripe curves. At a party to celebrate her sixty-ninth birthday, she appeared in a robe of white satin and sable to receive homage from theatregoers all over the world. The handsome volume of 100,000 signatures and messages was presented by Beerbohm Tree.

Marconi also gave lavish parties at this time. To assist him with his experiments, his suite was made soundproof by heavy screens in the corridor and several layers of felt under the carpet. He could be a severe trial to the staff. He would never allow a towel round his neck while his hair was being cut, but became indignant if any loose locks fell on his clothes. His food had always to be cut up into minute portions. Among his special dislikes were the hotel lifts and he would hop with impatience if one did not arrive almost before his finger was off the button.

His countryman, Caruso, was much less aloof. After a concert he would return to the Savoy and smoke one cigarette after another, mainly to bait his manager who disapproved of the habit and suffered nightmares over cancelled engagements. After a mammoth supper, Caruso liked to entertain the waiters with his favourite party trick of trying to move a piano by inflating his barrel chest against it.

The social tempo was varied and quick-changing. In the grill-room Horatio Bottomley would expound his plan for a

'Business Government' but find time to bow to Edna May, Pauline Chase and Gladys Cooper. Soon to go bankrupt through gambling, Melville Gideon signed autographs for admirers who could not stop humming *Yip-i-addy-i-ay*. Albert de Courville married his lovely American star, Shirley Kellogg, and celebrated with a gay wedding breakfast.

One would have liked to be in the ballroom when Max and Moritz were guests of honour. The antics of these almost human chimpanzees had made them a music-hall sensation and they were regarded as so near to *homo sapiens* that Sir William Crookes and Sir William Ramsay agreed at last to give them a public examination. The solemnity of the experiment suffered a little when Crookes felt Max's pulse and then tried to examine his teeth. This was too much for the patient who retaliated by pulling out Sir William's tie while Moritz showed a lively interest in the great man's back-braces.

Undismayed by the tragic maiden voyage of the *Titanic*, American visitors were coming over by every liner. Many of them toured London in cabs seeking rooms, but regular patrons like Charles M. Schwab of Bethlehem Steel and Otto Kahn found sanctuary in their usual river suites at the Savoy. The new American Ambassador, Walter Hines Page, was welcomed by The Pilgrims, while stocky square-jawed William J. Burns, the famous detective, slipped out of his room with expected stealth to investigate an international network of bank swindlers.

Nobody seemed alarmed by the threat of war. The anglophile German Ambassador, Prince Lichnowsky, continued to express undying love for England and Sir Edward Grey; handsome Georges Carpentier was concerned only with his personal war against Bombardier Billy Wells; the visiting New York Giants and the Chicago White Sox ate waffles and flapjacks after their game at Stamford Bridge; and Ascot Week was the most brilliant in its fashionable history.

The Fourth of July banquet twanged like a gay banjo. Harvard triumphed at Henley but England won the polo. For a Midnight Ball tickets reached the dizzy price of ten guineas each and raffle prizes included diamond pendants, new Daimler limousines and a painting by Lavery. Among the dancers in elaborate fancy dress were Lord Lonsdale, Ethel Levey, Marie Tempest and Lily Elsie. And, of course, everyone pooh-poohed the vulgar war scares.

Within a few weeks the hotel had become the headquarters of the American Citizens' Committee which had to deal with twenty thousand stranded tourists, many arriving from the Continent with only the clothes they stood up in. The White Room was turned into an office to deal with anxious last-second bookings homeward, and the Bank Trust of New York cabled a deposit of £60,000 to meet urgent drawings.

The usual spy scares swept the hotel, and a few startled German and Austrian waiters and cooks were sacked or interviewed by the police. Reeves-Smith called in his department heads and made a cool appraisal of the 'emergency' which, like everyone else, he considered would be brief. While the fullest attention was to be paid to government regulations, he proclaimed, there would be no slackness in service or any falling-off in the high standards expected of the staff. Above all, there must be no gloom or alarmist tittle-tattle.

Soon afterwards, he was summoned to the War Office by the G.O.C., London District, a peppery little man with a complexion matching his tabs. He complained that the Savoy was at fault in permitting dancing at such a time. Reeves-Smith picked up his silk hat and gloves and said quietly, "In my opinion, wars have never been won with sackcloth and ashes."

THE DAPPER young subalterns marched off smartly like the chorus of an operetta which, some thought, was rather inconsiderately being staged across the Channel. Few saw anything ahead but a short and glorious run. As yet there were no shortages at the Savoy where the Grand Duke Michael and many others gave entertaining parties. Early in the war, the *thé dansant* was started, soon to be taken up by many restaurants and clubs, while at supper the Canadian officers were always among the liveliest of the one-steppers.

On the Home Front the brilliant, birdlike Lady Cunard swore to die with Tommy Beecham if Covent Garden were hit by Zeppelin bombs. That confirmed pacifist, John Morley, was sipping a glass of hock in the grill-room when two Tory opponents stopped at his table. "I see you like everything German," one of them sneered. "I'm interning it," pointed out Morley, calmly draining his glass.

In her suite, stiff-backed in a wheelchair, Sarah Bernhardt wrote to Kitchener asking official permission to cross to France by way of Boulogne instead of Le Havre. Her letter, heavily perfumed, was passed on with many grins before reaching the C.-in-C. Through a private secretary he politely informed Bernhardt that in his view it would be dangerous to go via Boulogne. This was little short of nectar to the tragedienne.

"*Mais alors, c'est une question de mourir avec les soldats,*" she sighed in ecstasy. "*Quelle gloire!*"

The first leaves from the Front had a desperate gaiety, and the jazz sounded louder. Country mansions became hospitals and knitting needles clicked feverishly. Lord Castlerosse, one of the first to be invalided home, drank vast quantities of Bollinger but showed little patience with twittering dowagers. Wounded men in blue suits and red ties supped sadly with young women who cycled into the forecourt, chain-smoking Gold Flake.

At this long interval, life during the Kaiser's War flickers like a jerky, speeded-up newsreel of the silent era. Kitchener's recruiting poster appears beside an advertisement for a permanent wave ('Don't let a Zeppelin catch you in Curlers'). Bernhard recites her dramatic war poems at the Coliseum while Ivor Novello' *Keep the Home Fires Burning* is sung and wept over a thousand times. *The Maid of the Mountains* by Freddie Lonsdale opens a Daly's and stays three years and more, with José Collins a dazzling Teresa and Arthur Wontner as Baldasarre. In her suite at the Savoy, José gives her dresses away to friends and when someone admires her wild ranch mink, promptly cuts it up, reserving a nice snippet for the chambermaid. More restrained is young Gracie Fields who has hit London like a bomb in *Mr. Tower Of London* which will run for over four thousand performances. Taken out for a celebration supper in the restaurant, she is asked what she would like to drink. "A port and lemon, luv," she tells the *sommelier* who nearly trips over his silver chain.

Determined to keep sackcloth and ashes out of his hotel, Reeves-Smith worked tirelessly to bring some cheer to guests anxious to forget the horrors and carnage. Saxophones sobbed defiance and even silly ragtime lyrics breathed a poignant significance for the officers who danced, drank and flirted on the too-short nights before their trains left Victoria. In the men's cloakroom nailbrushes were tactfully fixed over the wash basins so that 'soldiers who have lost an arm or hand can scrub the other hand quite easily'.

Kidneys and mushrooms slipped from the breakfast menu. In the huge, half-empty kitchen with a skeleton staff of clumsy boys and tired old men, the maître-chef cursed the Boche and tried somehow to camouflage his rissoles. War restrictions had laid strain and hardship on all establishments, large and small, and Reeves-Smith found himself the envoy and spokesman of the catering trade in many delicate approaches to the government. As a tribute, the Hotels and Restaurants Association presented him with a silver cigar box before the end of the war. It is traditionally placed to this day before the Chairman of the Association at all Council meetings.

There were some memorable and historic moments before the Armistice was at last signed. Mr. Hoover's various Relief Committees used the Savoy as their headquarters, and when members of the American Society in London celebrated their country's entry into the war with a passionate speech by Ambassador Walter Hines Page, he was followed by Winston Churchill's appeal for "supreme intensity of effort" by the Allies. It was held in the Mirror Room, later to be renamed the Abraham Lincoln Room, when a bust of the immortal President, presented by T. P. O'Connor, was unveiled by the Foreign Secretary, Lord Curzon.

The usual war profiteers appeared in all the prominent hotels. A South American multi-millionaire asked the very impressive Head Porter of the Savoy what was the largest tip he had ever received. "£20, sir." The Argentine promptly peeled off eight crackling £5 notes and said joyfully, "Well, now I have made the record." The Head Porter tactfully forgot to remind him that he was himself the benefactor only a week before.

At last the nightmare was over. During the wild Victory Ball, some R.F.C. pilots decided to 'take off' and swung like trapeze artistes from the chandeliers. That night alone, 2,700 glasses were smashed. The festive air soon chilled with the shortage of American tourists held back by a lack of shipping. With business in a lull, several junior waiters in the Café Parisien downed napkins and asked for a larger share of the *tronc*.

The depression was only temporary. The Pilgrims gave a farewell banquet to Admiral Sims who had commanded the U.S. Navy in Europe since April 1917. As a souvenir he was presented with a piece of oak from Nelson's *Victory*. Alcock and Brown flew the Atlantic and were handed the *Daily Mail*'s cheque for

£10,000 by Mr. Churchill who was already giving warnings of the menace of Bolshevik Russia. At one dinner he thrust out his cigar like a torpedo and growled, "No one knows what is going on in Russia or what will come out of Russia, except that it will be something extremely formidable and menacing to the world."

After four years of a crippling war, life looked too splendid for anyone to worry about such gloomy prophecies. The crusading Prohibitionist, 'Pussyfoot' Johnson, went home after his disappointing attempt to talk England dry. Armadas of thirsty Americans, many of them refugees from the Eighteenth Amendment, were soon sailing across the Big Pond. Harry Craddock was brought over to take charge of the new American Bar, so called because it was the first in Europe to chill the Martinis. Here he once mixed a thousand drinks in five hectic hours. He had begun his career at Cleveland's Hollendon Hotel and moved on to the Hoffman House in New York where he shook cocktails for 'Teddy' Roosevelt and often served John L. Sullivan with quarts of 'bubbly'. He remained a teetotaller himself, tasting but never swallowing the fruits of his genius which included the creation of White Lady.

A notable absentee from the American Bar was Scott Fitzgerald who had come over for the publication of *This Side of Paradise*, already a dazzling success in the United States. His guide and friend, saffron-kilted Shane Leslie, had given him such stern warnings that Fitzgerald was on his best behaviour when he met Galsworthy and St. John Ervine who were enchanted by his charm and boyishness. Even his exuberant wife, Zelda, who described the Changing of the Guard at Buckingham Palace as "the Town Hall with the Redskins walking around it", proved for once a model of decorum. Intimidated possibly by the Mountbattens and other noble friends, she refrained from her usual practice of tying up the handle of the hotel lift to ensure its exclusive use.

Fitzgerald's friend, John Barrymore, rarely suffered any such inhibitions. Having already given the Ritz management several nightmares, he moved to the Savoy where Sir Gerald du Maurier

63

rashly promised to be surety for his good conduct. One evening he went up to the room of Richard Bennett, the handsome sire of Joan, Constance and Barbara. Over a bottle or two of Scotch they declaimed verse at each other until a very late hour, when Barrymore suddenly disappeared. Next morning Bennett rang the switchboard and asked to be put through to Barrymore's suite. They had a long and amiable chat before Barrymore crawled out from under Bennett's bed where he had spent the night. He had no difficulty in reproducing a telephone voice, complete with acoustics.

Apart from American tourists starved of Europe, there were champion golfers like Walter Hagen who came over on his honeymoon trip. He celebrated his arrival by going up on the roof of the Savoy and hitting ball after ball into a coal barge moored in the river three hundred yards below. It started a famous tradition, followed by Bobby Jones and Gene Sarazen, of 'playing oneself into the Savoy'.

Sensing the change in taste which would follow the end of the war and easier licensing laws, Reeves-Smith began to consider a revival of supper dancing with special cabaret performers, a revolutionary thought at that time. Meanwhile he plucked Gelardi from Claridge's and appointed him General Manager of the Savoy. The Board also decided at this time to sell the Grand Hotel in Rome and concentrate on the triumvirate of the Savoy, Claridge's and the Berkeley.

The hotel was bursting its elegant seams. The Russian Ballet had arrived in London soon after the war and Diaghilev installed himself at the Savoy where he was joined by Picasso and his recent bride, the dancer Olga Koklova. Lured from his Paris studio by Cocteau, the painter was quickly infected by Diaghilev's enthusiasm and worked feverishly on the scenery and costumes for a new ballet, *The Three-Cornered Hat*, which opened in triumph at the Alhambra in Leicester Square. Karsavina was particularly enchanted by her costume of pink silk and black lace. Under the influence of his wife, the daughter of a Tsarist general, Picasso ordered suits from London's most exclusive tailors and looked almost foppish when he entered the restaurant in stylishly cut evening clothes, always with a flower in his lapel. He worked hard during rehearsals, making drawings of Massine and the other dancers, but liked best to relax in the hotel at late-night parties with Clive Bell, bearded Lytton Strachey and Maynard Keynes who fell in love with and married Olga's friend, Lydia Lopokova.

The veteran Atlantic-crosser, Charles M. Schwab, led a gold rush of tourists, crack polo-players and millionaire playboys. A Cambridge college girl had to be specially engaged to do Christmas shopping for busy guests, one of whom chose a pair of emerald ear-rings for £700. Another visitor broke her valuable necklace during dinner and, while the waiters scrambled to look for stray pearls, remarked indifferently, "Don't bother, I can easily get another. I don't want to miss the first act at the theatre." Far less casual over his property was an elderly peer who departed without his toothbrush, valued at about a shilling, when new. Nevertheless, he sent a long and costly telegram to the manager, demanding that it be forwarded to his home in the country *without delay*.

After some lavish Christmas shopping in Bond Street and the Burlington Arcade, a party of five tourists suddenly decided to depart and made a last-minute dash for the Golden Arrow. A chambermaid, polishing the fire grate in their suite that evening, pulled out the ashpan and found tiaras, watches, rings and several hundred-dollar bills neatly wrapped in two silk handkerchiefs. A wire from Paris arrived an hour later. "Left something in fireplace. Please hold till we return. Advise if found." The story had a happy ending. Annie Farrell met the family, was engaged as maid to the daughter, the guilty party, and left with them for Detroit.

Security has often been a trial to the management. Some clients are neglectful of their property, while others prefer their private safety measures to the hotel's steel safes. A certain Belgian diamond merchant wore a bulky money-belt and always carried a loaded revolver. One day he left his belt in the bathroom and a maid tossed it into the litter basket. It contained £100,000 in unset diamonds. Thereafter, he used the safe. The Indian merchant prince, Mr. Lal, used to walk about the hotel with at least half a million pounds' worth of precious stones in his waistcoat pocket. His collection included the famous Taj Mahal diamond which he had brought to London to show to King George and Queen Mary at Buckingham Palace. He declined all protection from the hotel staff or the police, preferring to rely on a personal body-guard of four massive native servants, each armed with a vicious ruby-studded dagger.

The 'twenties were days of magnificence but with more than a touch of vulgarity and ostentation. One vandal in the Grill insisted on having a huge fresh peach served with mayonnaise. A millionaire demanded woodcock, *bécasse au fumet*, and the silver platter was wheeled to his table on a trolley. Parts were chipped off, sieved, reverently anointed with brandy and served *flambé*. The guest waved it all away. "I'm not hungry," he shrugged, "but I loved the show."

Savoy maîtres d'hôtel are not easily shocked but one of them was almost paralysed when serving Tex Austin in the grill-room. The great impresario of rodeos had the subtlety of a blow-lamp. When asked how he would like his steak prepared, he said bluntly, "Get a bullock, wound it slightly and drive it in."

With cosmopolitan taste and a shrewd sense of publicity, the managers of the restaurant and grill-room wooed both gourmets and gourmands. For a Christmas dinner in 1921, the menu was designed by Edmund Dulac and bear's ham was sent from Finland, by way of Holland. Snails crossed the Channel and Hall Caine made a scene, as usual, when supplies ran out. Frogs' legs were also in great demand, a taste picked up by officers serving in France. The first Russian caviare since the war was solemnly received by a Savoy representative in France and brought to London. Plovers' eggs slid down at a guinea each but the host at one party was startled to learn that out-of-season strawberries were available at 25s. a dozen. "In that case," he was heard to mutter, "we'll have one each."

At a memorable Brillat-Savarin centenary luncheon in honour

of the immortal author of *The Physiology of Taste*, epicures present, correct and in good appetite included stalwarts like Belloc, Augustine Birrell, Conan Doyle and Sir Squire Bancroft. Even Marconi, the smallest eater in the room, could not resist Latry's inspirations. One was composed of crayfish with foie gras imported from Brillat-Savarin's native village of Belley. Eggs were lovingly prepared with Périgord truffles, while fresh-water fish was poached in old Burgundy and caressed by a charcoal fire. The wines included such masterpieces as Montrachet 1911 followed by Château Latour 1921, while the Château Yquem was laid to rest by a rare champagne of noble lineage. There were no speeches and of course no cocktails, the occasion altogether worthy of Brillat-Savarin's famous maxim, "Beasts feed, Man eats, but only the man of intelligence and true perceptiveness really *dines.*"

A worthy successor to Escoffier, Latry prepared another banquet at which he was presented with a gold medal on behalf of the three hundred guests, who included leading chefs and gastronomes, who had come from America and every capital in Europe. Among the rare delicacies were golden pheasant stuffed with oysters, and tiny grapes sent from Chablis. The occasion was marked by the birth of *neige au Cliquot*, a new sorbet assembled from cream and 1906 champagne.

To this vintage period belongs also the famous millionaires' banquet given by two hundred of the world's most opulent gourmets in honour of the departing Chilean Minister in London, Don Augustin Edwards. The capital represented at this feast, presided over by Lionel de Rothschild, was estimated at that time to be in the neighbourhood of £200,000,000. Apart from the whole of the diplomatic colony, British guests included Lord Cowdray, Sir William Waterlow and Sir Harry McGowan. Latry imported plump quails from Egypt and stuffed them with truffles. His foie gras was braised and served up with tiny button mushrooms on solid silver dishes each in itself a collector's piece and rarely put on show except for the most discriminating guests.

Walking through Richmond Park one Sunday morning, Latry noticed some fallen oaks and next day started experimenting in his kitchens. Soon afterwards he was roasting all game on oak logs which he discovered improved the flavour. When Santarelli, prince of restaurant managers and the most charming of them all, once requested something special for a Twelfth Night dinner, Latry closeted himself in his white-tiled office for over an hour, shutting off all the telephones and his loudspeaker. He emerged with detailed instructions for a huge cygnet pie based on a royal recipe over five centuries old.

One morning he received an urgent appeal to send a chef up to Glasgow to prepare a special sauce for King George and Queen Mary who were on their way to open the Empire Exhibition. He briefed a *sous-chef* who left by the next train. Their Majesties proclaimed the sauce magnificent, quite unaware of the emergency arrangements made in their honour.

Latry was not only a creative artist but a man of warm heart who regarded many guests as his friends and spoilt them a little if they truly reverenced his cooking. When one of his favourites, Queen Marie of Yugoslavia, went home after a long visit he worried that she might be missing some of her best-loved dishes. He went up to see Gilles, the General Manager, and persuaded him to send a smoked turkey and a salmon out to Belgrade with the compliments of the management. The Queen was touched by the gesture and remained so nostalgic for the Savoy that she sent her palace chef, Gredinger, to take a three-months' refresher course under Latry who passed on his secrets for preparing roast beef and Yorkshire pudding, saddle of mutton and other English fare.

American tastes were not forgotten. In one week-end alone over twelve thousand visitors crossed the Atlantic and many were turned away by the Reception. Dinner bookings for July 4 could almost have filled Times Square. The menu included Washington melon, Bunker's Hill soup, Liberty soles, Maryland chicken, Independence salad and Harding meringue. The turkeys and sweet potatoes were specially imported from the United States. For the soup alone the turtle weighed over 600 lbs. Mindful of his old friends enduring a Prohibition Christmas, Latry arranged to make and send over several hundred puddings, each soaked lavishly in brandy and stout. Always now on the menu were waffles, girdle cakes and planked shad. Blue Points and Great Lakes trout crossed the ocean in special tanks. To make the visitors feel even more at home there were frivolous stunts like shipping over Billy B. and Silent Cal., the finalists in the famous Terrapin Derby 'run' outside Baltimore. These were carefully prepared and devoured by their countrymen.

The kitchens were under great pressure during the very hot summer of 1923 when the happiest man in the hotel seemed to be Herbert Harris, working in the ice vaults at 17 below zero in fur overcoat, thermal underwear and thigh boots. To keep cool, American visitors panted for iced water and strawberry shortcake, the Japanese ate hot curries, and a party of Brazilians demanded so many daiquiris that the rum stocks began to run dry.

A heat-wave or an abnormally cold spell has rarely dislocated the kitchens, but mistakes can happen even at the Savoy. The usual immense haggis once arrived for a St. Andrew's Night dinner. A heathen Sassenach maid thought it was a consignment of soap and sent it on to the hotel's laundry at Clapham.

AT NO time in the history of the Savoy was its tempo faster or the mood more inflationary than in the 'twenties. Hopping tables in Restaurant and grill-room, one has a sense of paradox; a new-rich ostentation jostles the remains of Edwardian magnificence; the Jazz Age carries its hip-flask in imitation of Scott Fitzgerald and with more time for Colette than *St. Joan*; and the landed gentry seems cushioned against crumbling estates, strikes, unemployment and even Mr. Ramsay MacDonald.

During this frivolous, brilliant and feverish era the Savoy not only enlarged its personality but mellowed in the process. There was no magic formula by which its atmosphere suddenly became *exciting* after so many years of comfort and an easy cosmopolitanism. Good planning by the management took care of the setting, but the guests themselves provided the colour and individuality. Overnight, the hotel became a fast-rotating stage for a company of international stars.

With a resident chorus of toothpick-thin flappers in bustless and hipless beaded tunics, the grill-room looks like a Cochran front row of chalk-white faces under bingles. One bows to Grand Opera with Tetrazzini and Chaliapin. Champion pugilists take us to the ringside of Madison Square Garden, while the incense and curry of princely India float behind a Maharajah and his retinue. From the ballroom throbs the brash rhythm of Tin Pan Alley, tamed and civilized by the Savoy Orpheans.

Through the swing-doors squeezes poor Fatty Arbuckle, so soon to be ruined by scandal. Lillian and Dorothy Gish preach earnest sermons on the true moral of *Way Down East*. Ellen Terry, with snow-white curls, is failing in sight and very deaf but smiles graciously as she is led out of the Restaurant by her god-daughter Pauline Chase, perhaps the greatest of all Peter Pans. Another young veteran of sixty is Fanny Ward who lunches on half a cup of clear soup followed by a jug of iced water. Willie Clarkson runs back and forth in quest of a wire-haired terrier to keep Bernhardt company. Fresh from a New York triumph in *Rain*, Jeanne Engels becomes hysterical over her harsh treatment by the Customs men at Southampton. H. G. Wells wanders nervously into the Palm Lounge where they are shooting a scene for *Kipps* but is too shy to protest when someone hands him a 'prop' Martini and seats him firmly at a table among the film extras. The Chancellor of the Exchequer, wearing a huge buttonhole, is sampling the first of the season's Whitstables with Mrs. Churchill.

In a modest suite high above the Thames, Ivar Kreuger works feverishly with secretaries who send relays of cables and make endless long-distance telephone calls. The Swedish match magnate, later to shoot himself in a Paris hotel bedroom, rarely goes down to the Restaurant. His meals are sent up and usually left untouched on his desk. Silent and forbidding, he slips out of the hotel's side-entrance for a solitary walk along the Embankment before returning to work into the small hours.

Briand arrives from Paris and nods distantly to rival Turkish delegations who are meeting behind locked doors to discuss Greek demands for Reparations. The members of the first Ulster Government confer in the suite of the Prime Minister, Sir James Craig, to decide their future policy. The German Delegation weep in public over the damage done by Zeppelins and tip the staff ten per cent of their bill for £5,000, but Reeves-Smith remains unimpressed and orders that the ex-enemy flag shall not be flown over the Savoy while they are in residence.

Pavlova dances in the ballroom at midnight to music by her own orchestra, and little Irving Berlin is giving big parties. From Hollywood come moguls like Marcus Loew and Goldwyn who are opening cinemas and digging into the fertile European

71

market. Harry Warner tries to buy film rights from Shaw who professes a distaste for celluloid and will yield ultimately only to Gabriel Pascal's persuasive tongue. Attended by his personal physician from New York, Carl Laemmle recuperates slowly in his suite after being given a blood transfusion in the *Berengaria*. Over a luncheon in the Grill the Fox Film Company is formed. Joe Schenck is working at high-pressure deals, nursing a heavy cold and filling his suite with Christmas presents for his wife, Norma Talmadge, and apparently half the population of Broadway and Hollywood.

The Savoy has become the Forty-Ninth State, and at least sixty per cent of the house list is American. Big Business is gnawed over at meals, in the foyer, the American Bar and in practically every other suite. Round the clock the hotel's stenographers are tapping out film scripts, plays, agreements and memoranda on numerous highly confidential deals. A new ticker-tape at the entrance of the grill-room keeps guests in touch with Wall Street.

The switchboard rattles like castanets. The hotel's telephone library now covers names and numbers all over the world, except the Soviet Union. The transatlantic service is always busy but callers may have to wait two days or more because of atmospherics. Floyd B. Odlum, the financier, takes advantage of a fairly clear line and talks to an associate in New York for ninety-five minutes, which costs him £285. Once or twice a week he telephones his future wife, Jacqueline Cochran, who will make history as the first woman to fly a bomber across the Atlantic and later crash the sound barrier.

William Hayball, who retired not long ago as Chief Telephone Clerk, recalls being put in charge of the hotel's two public telephones when he joined as a pageboy in 1905. He was paid ten shillings a month but there was only half a crown in his first pay envelope. He had been fined for taking part in a pillow-fight in the staff dormitory then located over Simpson's-in-the-Strand. His pillow sailed through a window and knocked off a doorman's dignified topper.

At an after-theatre supper, professionals promenade down the red-carpeted aisle in a 'refined exhibition' of the Tango

A contemporary artist's view of the Savoy in 1911. To celebrate the hotel's coming-of-age the whole façade on the river side was refronted and two new storeys were added; three deep-sunk

wells pumped soft water to the two hundred and forty four bathrooms, and the new ballroom and banqueting hall accommodated two thousand guests

Above, Debroy Somers rehearsing the Savoy Orpheans, pioneers of late night music over the air. Leaning on the piano is Carroll Gibbons who later took over the band. *Below*, Geraldo and his Gauchos run through an arrangement on the hotel roof. Their Latin-American music was vastly popular with guests and radio fans

A few years later during the Great War, Hayball's status soars when, for three unforgettable months, he is Staff Sergeant to Sir Sam Hughes, commander of the Canadian forces in Europe. The general occupies a suite on the third floor of the Savoy and Sergeant Hayball has his own room and full service. "I loved every minute of it," he chuckles.

Among the earliest users of the transatlantic telephone line is the excitable impresario, Charles Frohman, the last man to be imprisoned in a jammed lift between floors. He emerges several hours later with a smile, and surprisingly thanks the management for giving him his first holiday in years. Today, there is a small brass plaque over the table in the Grill where he used to sit for hours with J. M. Barrie, doodling designs for stage sets on the cloth.

The hairdressing salon sends up barbers and manicurists to guests who may want attention at the most unlikely hours, and M. Adolphe once beats his own record by giving a perfect haircut in exactly four minutes. Even he is surprised by a silent magnate who rarely says a word and has his hair trimmed round the hat which he never removes. The girls in the flower shop float among mimosa and carnations arriving daily from the Riviera. They work ten hours or more a day making up bouquets and wiring corsages. Hundreds of rich Americans travel 6,000 miles for a weekend trip which includes special flights to Aintree for the Grand National.

All the millionaires, Cyrus McCormick, Beman Dawes, Lucius Boomer, William K. Vanderbilt and Jay Gould, seem to have one habit in common; they are early risers and rarely order breakfast later than 6.30 a.m. Not all are business slaves; Cartier sends morning-coated salesmen with priceless necklaces for inspection, while from Savile Row flows an endless wave of tailors, cutters and fitters with clothes for Ascot, Cowes and the grouse moors. Poor Ernest, the hotel's goldfish whose favourite party trick is to leapfrog over a floating cork, succumbs from too much cigar ash.

Many of the Americans brought daring touches of informality to the social scene. Some ultra-prickly critics in the United States

73

were becoming so angry about the cocked-hat and gold braid regalia worn at Court that General Dawes, the Ambassador, asked King George V's special permission to wear trousers instead of knee-breeches. Even more bold perhaps was his gesture in lighting a pipe after a formal dinner at the Savoy, a privilege which until then had only been enjoyed by Mr. Baldwin when Prime Minister. There was a short anxious pause before Sir Patrick Hastings stubbed his cigar and pulled out his briar, others quickly following suit. Reeves-Smith was not amused but tactfully turned a blind eye since the crime had not been committed in one of his public rooms.

Henry S. Widener was so fastidious about the appearance and style of his evening clothes that he always kept a dress-suit of English cut in reserve at the Savoy, while at the Adlon in Berlin hung tails in the latest German fashion. Another guest, Dr. Van Allen from New York, amused himself and Londoners by offering a gold watch to the workman who would re-lay the most wooden blocks in a single day on a section of the Strand then under repair. Chick Evans arrived with his mother on his way to captain the Ryder Cup team at Hoylake. Dempsey sailed over with the Dolly Sisters and Jack Kearns, took a suite of six rooms and at once made for Mayfair to order a dozen suits and scores of ties. Back at the hotel he approved the accommodation but demanded a full-length mirror and specially soft pillows for his extra-wide double bed. He gave lunch to a hundred friends, among them Kid Lewis, Gilbert Frankau, Carl Brisson and Bombardier Billy Wells. Women mobbed him and tried to steal kisses which infuriated Marconi who complained that the noise was disturbing his experiments. High above the Thames, the champion skipped, clowned and sparred with some delighted pageboys. Much more reserved was his conqueror, Gene Tunney, who later took over a Maharajah's suite but kept very much to himself and accepted telephone calls only from G.B.S. and Hugh Walpole. Trapped by an unexpected dinner invitation, he had to issue an S.O.S. to hire a dress-suit. Handsome Georges Carpentier arrived soon afterwards and was quickly on the telephone to his wife in Paris; he had forgotten to pack his favourite after-shave powder. In a neighbouring suite his countryman, Patou, was displaying a new collection at one of the first of many dress shows to be held at the Savoy.

Stephen Leacock registers and seems more the retiring professor than a humorist, but Ring Lardner lives up to his reputation. Before going off to Stamford Bridge where they are hopefully trying to make the British public baseball-conscious, he gives his views on the climate. "I came to England because I might die any time and I haven't seen it yet. In Spain they have the bull-fighting. Here you've got your weather. You Britishers are very proud of being the people upon whom the sun never sets. I think you ought to say it never rises." H. L. Mencken quaffs English ale, smokes his corncob and puffs acridly at his usual targets; women, Babbitts and clergymen. He admits sourly that he is known as "Broadway's eighth deadly sin", and soon departs for home and real sea-food. A kindlier critic from San Francisco is Fred Dohrmann, an authority on furnishing ships and hotels, who cannot fault the Savoy's service and tells Reeves-Smith that he is enthusiastic about everything except the climate and the price of a good cigar.

George Doran, over from New York and talent-scouting for British authors, has eyes only for Compton Mackenzie, Michael Arlen and Arnold Bennett. The Grill manager, Manetta, serves Omelette Arnold Bennett, a Savoy creation of eggs and haddock with a sprinkling of Gruyère; the touch of showmanship is lost on neither publisher nor his author, although Bennett rounds off the meal with his usual rice pudding smothered by spoonfuls of salt. Doran departs to distribute hundreds of new books among the staff, not forgetting the pageboys. Glossy and always tempted to wear a pearl pin even in his public school tie, Arlen cannot resist counting the number of green felt hats worn by his devoted readers but smiles bravely when Lady Cunard introduces him as "the only Armenian who has not been massacred". She swoops on the baroque Sitwells, pecks Cecil Beaton and Oliver Messel before finally landing at the table of Syrie Maugham who would dearly love to redecorate and refurnish the grill-room in stark white which she has made the latest craze.

Will Rogers chews on his toothpick and achieves the distinction of being the only man in town who can talk down that virtuoso of the monologue, Hannen Swaffer, even though it takes him until five next morning. Still fresh, he later attends a Thanksgiving Day dinner and hears the Prince of Wales proclaim him, "My favourite American: he makes me laugh and I like playing polo with him."

Hundreds of American clients cancel their bookings because of the General Strike, but not Rogers who enjoys it all. "If this had happened in America there'd have been a thousand deaths by now. We've got only one man in America who could take a national strike like you English. I guess he must have English blood in him. Coolidge, the President, is the man I mean. He'd never miss a meal whatever happened, and that's what England has done."

Other visitors scarcely added to the gaiety of nations. Aimée Semple McPherson opened her hot gospel mission from an air-conditioned luxury suite at the Savoy and shocked people by saying that "Heaven is like Washington. All its roads converge on to the throne." With her dyed hair and eagerness to be photographed with Tallulah Bankhead, Bea Lillie and other actresses whom she bombarded with sermons and Bibles, poor Sister Aimée had rather a bad time in London.

As guest of honour at a dinner by The American Society, Henry Ford drank iced water, declined to smoke and gazed coldly at speakers who made the familiar jokes about his Tin Lizzie. When a gushing woman jumped forward and shook him by the hand, he said damply, "I don't know *you*." "But I know your *car*, Mr. Ford," said the lady, quite unabashed. That was the only time he smiled throughout his stay in England.

Far less inhibited was little Jackie Coogan, 'The Kid', who stood at the window of his river suite and waved regally to the huge adoring crowds. Dressed in a sailor suit, he begged to be allowed to conduct the Orpheans in one of their numbers. Debroy

Somers commented afterwards with some feeling, "He's no Mozart."

On the roof Bobby Jones practised chip shots, and André Citroen flew over from Paris for a light lunch and orange juice, returning the same afternoon. Not long afterwards the Master of Sempill flew his 80 h.p. Bluebird seaplane from the Welsh Harp to Waterloo Bridge and taxied upstream with his passenger, the Dowager Lady Swaythling. They arrived at the hotel by motor-launch. A Bentley which had survived a crash and gone thundering on for another seventeen hours to win the race at Le Mans, lumbered into the Savoy Restaurant, its exhaust roaring and with one headlight blazing like the defiant eye of a Cyclops.

The hotel's fourteen private banqueting rooms were continuously booked for an endless series of luncheons and dinners. Many a familiar name leaps to the eye from those signed menus of the 'twenties. There were banquets for ski-champions, lawyers, doctors and jockeys, apart from standard occasions like The Pilgrim Dinners, the meetings of The Other Club, and the sprightly festivities of The Savages. In tribute to his three thousand runs of the season, the master batsman, Jack Hobbs, was honoured by fellow-cricketers, Herbert Strudwick, 'Plum' Warner and Percy Fender and old admirers like 'Solly' Joel, who made a spectacular fortune during the early boom years in Kimberley and became one of England's most successful racing owners. He started the Fortnightly Luncheon Club which met in a private room at the Savoy, decorated in his stable colours, and attended by a gay, hard-drinking crowd of 'stags' who always included F. E. Smith and the financier, James White. The Club had originated when White, in a rash and barely sober moment, challenged Solly's son, Stanhope, to a swimming race over twelve lengths of the Joels' marble bathing-pool at Maiden Erlegh. As he failed to appear, White's forfeit was to pay the luncheon bill for twenty-four friends at the Savoy.

Solly Joel liked to make fantastic bets and always enjoyed practical jokes. Just after his second marriage, he gave a New Year's Eve party in the restaurant for his family and several

77

friends but could not be found at midnight when *Auld Lang Syne* was sung. His wife looked angry but was consoled when the 'Hungarian violinist' stepped from the platform and gave her a resounding kiss. It was Solly, who had changed places with the musician and dressed up in gipsy costume, fierce moustache and ear-rings.

The seventh anniversary of Fascism was celebrated by a party of Italian residents in London. Boys in black shirts and pretty girls wearing the national colours kissed and hugged with patriotic hysteria under a huge portrait of Mussolini, whom Pirandello saluted as 'a genius'. The Prince of Wales attended a dinner of wild boar hunters at which the two hundred guests wore buttonholes of hog bristles flown over from India. Trophies adorned the walls and Zavattoni, the Banqueting Manager, added one of his characteristic touches by decorating the room with scores of lances shaped like fans.

Shy, curly-haired Lindbergh was guest of honour in the Abraham Lincoln Room after crossing the Atlantic in *The Spirit of St. Louis* but offended admirers by refusing to sign any autographs. In another suite King Fuad dined with the Governors of the Bank of Egypt, while next door Lord Balfour was guest of honour at a gathering of prominent Zionists headed by James de Rothschild, Lord Reading, Herbert Samuel, Alfred Mond and Bernhard Baron. Under the same roof that night John Buchan presided at a dinner to launch the new film, *Tell England*, inspiring Zavattoni to adorn each table with bas-reliefs of the Gallipoli landings. In the grill-room and wearing one of his enormous collection of dazzling waistcoats, Valentine Castlerosse again proved his prodigious appetite for food and alcohol, quite insensitive to his abstemious host and benefactor, Lord Beaverbrook, who contented himself with chicken and a little fruit.

When Laddie Sanford won £60,000 on the Grand National, he arranged a lavish stag dinner party for fifty guests who included the Prince of Wales and his brothers, Henry and George. Both joined in the chorus of *I'm tickled to death I'm single* which

Melville Gideonsang at the piano. On Gold Cup or Derby Days, the small electric lifts in the gentlemen's cloakroom would shoot over a thousand silk or dove-grey toppers up to the store-room where they would be brushed, tiny stains removed and a miniature valeting service performed, often unknown to the owners. And rarely would these highly-trained memory men need to issue a ticket.

James White was in his usual champagne mood at a Victoria Club dinner, boasting of the time when he won £50,000 on a single bet. In the end, of course, the bookmakers had a handsome revenge. Nothing pleased him more than to leave his office in the Strand and stroll into the Savoy Grill with a patronizing hand on Donoghue's shoulder. He was once overheard to say in a stage whisper, "Ride me three winners tomorrow, Steve, and I'll give you a thousand quid." Donoghue duly obliged.

In his thick Rochdale accent White called everyone by their Christian names, talked incessantly of having won 'a bundle' and invited all and sundry to his palatial home at Foxhill. On many mornings after an evening's dissipation he would enter the American Bar with bloodshot eyes and shaky hands and growl, "By gum, I could do wi' some beer, cheese and pickles." It always seemed to revive him. Within an hour he would be in the grill-room ordering oysters, caviare and magnums of champagne.

Donoghue always loved to celebrate at the Savoy during his heady years of triumph. After winning the Derby on Humorist in 1921 he went on to win that same Classic three times more in the next four years. He maddened his friends by being unpunctual but the waiters adored him when he marked their cards on his many lucky days. He was sitting in the Grill one day grandly signing autographs, when Tom Webster paused at his table. "I'm thinking of writing my life story," he said loftily. "What with, your whip?" asked Tom. Not for months did Donoghue forgive the remark.

Webster was at that time probably the highest-paid sports cartoonist in the world. His name will always be associated with

79

Sir Abe Bailey's Tishy, the ill-fated filly who was regarded as an unbeatable favourite for the Cesarewitch and backed to win enormous sums. She finished last. Webster's immortal cartoons showed her running with legs crossed, a figure of fun which made even her unlucky backers smile.

Tom liked to savour the rich bohemian atmosphere of the grill-room after his long years of struggle. One evening he and his employer, Lord Northcliffe, were driving along by the river in a huge Rolls-Royce when Tom remarked casually, "That used to be my hotel."

"I didn't know you lived at the Savoy," said Northcliffe in surprise.

"No, Chief, I slept on one of those Embankment benches for three nights when I was broke."

"Well it probably did you good," commented Northcliffe, unsympathetically.

Inseparable from his long cigarette-holder and drinking an enormous quantity of strong tea, Edgar Wallace had more time for jockeys and trainers than the literary celebrities who liked to stop for a word at his table. Although never a punter on White's lavish scale, he also had a fatal urge to bankrupt the bookmakers. Too late in the day he found that he could only make racing pay by becoming a tipster on one of the popular newspapers. Although a sombre and outwardly rather forbidding figure, Wallace had a very soft heart. He would enjoy racing talk with the staff and always listened to their troubles. His regular waiter, Coleman, once discovered a cheque for £250 beside the plate instead of his usual pound note. Wallace had somehow learned that the waiter's mother was in danger of losing her little house because she had fallen behind with payments on the mortgage. Later, Coleman's wife became the author's cook and stayed with him for many years.

Almost like a plot for a Wallace racing thriller was the series of conferences which took place behind closed doors at the Savoy in the autumn of 1923. Ben Irish, a farmer from Sawtry, had bought a yearling colt at the Doncaster sales for 3,500 guineas.

With Basil Jarvis as trainer and Donoghue on his back, Papyrus went on to win the Derby and was regarded as a wonder horse, perhaps the best in the world, a view not shared by August Belmont, the wealthy head of the Westchester Racing Association. Anxious to make racing more popular in the United States, he offered a prize of £20,000 for a race to be run on the Belmont Park track between Papyrus and Zev, the American champion.

To arrange the Match he sent over his representative, C. J. Fitzgerald, who installed himself in a vast suite at the Savoy and started the delicate negotiations needed to transport Papyrus, Donoghue and their entourage across the Atlantic. Mr. Irish was at last won over but could not travel himself because his doctor thought the excitement might prove too much for a weak heart. Instead he was represented by his lawyer who sat in on all the conferences.

Donoghue finally agreed to ride for a fee of £3,000. In addition to Basil Jarvis, a leading veterinary surgeon was engaged and Fitzgerald even agreed to ship over special tanks of Newmarket water and native fodder so that Papyrus would feel completely at home in America. Since the Match clearly involved national prestige, the promoters had to hammer out the smallest details about the conditions for the race and, above all, transport.

While Fitzgerald and the British contingent discussed details, often late into the night, excitement had become feverish on both sides of the Atlantic. Despite the failure of Papyrus to follow up his Epsom victory by winning the St. Leger, he was being backed for thousands of pounds and slowly emerged an odds-on favourite. It took nearly six weeks before Papyrus and his working stablemate, Bar of Gold, trotted on to the *Aquitania* and settled into their magnificent padded boxes, attended by several stable lads. Donoghue went over on another liner. Papyrus had a good crossing and landed only a few days before the race. He had some fast work-outs but did not seem to take too kindly either to the American dirt track or the almost certain soft going. Last-minute rains had made the ground like treacle. The blinkered and bandaged Zev, with the great Earl Sande on top, was now a strong favourite and his owner, the oil magnate H. F. Sinclair, was backing him on a mammoth scale. He was right. Zev simply ran the Derby winner into the ground.

There was almost as much ballyhoo surrounding the arrival in London of Tony, the endearing hero of a hundred Westerns. National hysteria marked the visit of the cowboy idol, Tom Mix, who was given a civic reception at the Mansion House and presented London's Lord Mayor with a stetson. On his return to the hotel he rode Tony, hooves thoughtfully padded, up the steps and into the ballroom.

The Savoy management has acquired vast and at times painful experience in handling celebrities—and nonentities—who are usually fanatically opposed to publicity or avid for it. Among the most retiring of all guests was ex-King Ferdinand of Bulgaria who would go to extraordinary lengths to avoid people. Armed with camera and sketch-book, he liked to make excursions to study birds and always went out by the unobtrusive Parcels Office. By contrast Arnold Bennett recorded in his diary for 20 October 1924, "Dined at the Savoy grill-room. Four photographs of me had been circulated among the staff so that there could be no mistake about recognizing me." In later years it was almost impossible to miss the famous quiff, pleated evening shirts, bulky fobs and white waistcoats.

The unexpected is always routine in a cosmopolitan hotel. Often, however, it can be anticipated with the help of a card-index of guests' likes and dislikes which are transmitted from the Reception to housekeepers and others likely to be concerned. Housekeepers come to know which guests like sleeping with their heads to the north or south, facing the window or not, and any other special tastes, from colour schemes to the angle of a favourite armchair. In a matter of minutes beds can be levered up to the required height and covers changed for chairs, settees and bedspreads.

When motherly Kate Butler first came to the hotel as Lady

Superintendent she was horrified that coverlets made from satin and brocade, costing even at that time thirty shillings a yard wholesale, were often left spattered with ink or used as table-cloths for pet dogs. Many thousands of pounds' worth of the finest carpets have been ruined by overflowing baths. Since the hotel pumps its own water, the rate of filling and emptying baths is at least four times faster than the normal, an amenity for most guests but a hazard with the careless. Cigarette burns have left grievous scars; the hotel welcomed Lionel Barrymore but knew that he was a chronic fire risk due to his habit of reading in bed while he chain-smoked. Neat burns in sheets and eiderdowns always marked his visits. He was finally issued without his knowledge with an almost fireproof eiderdown.

Mrs. Patrick Campbell could be charm personified but had a violent temper. In a rage she once broke up her bed and clawed down all the curtains. During lesser crises of temperament she would merely smash all the vases in her room.

Dorothy Paget's arrival meant an immediate signal from the Reception to the night manager and restaurant kitchens. On the stroke of 3 a.m. she would often demand a full-course dinner. There was also the Spanish lady who abhorred yellow roses, while another liked only unscented flowers. An American, strange to relate, had such a horror of the telephone that the instruments and extensions had not only to be cut off but removed before he would set foot in his suite. One visitor had very firm views about lighting; before his arrival the chandelier had to be dismantled in his sitting-room and every electric light bulb replaced by frosted ones. A fastidious woman insisted on having all the dress-hangers in her wardrobe bound in pale blue silk as they were, apparently, in her own home. Another was emphatic that the colour scheme in her suite clashed with the shade of the frock she was planning to wear for a dinner party that evening. The transformation was made in good time. Strangest of all was the daughter of an American banker who, during the whole of her six weeks' stay, never once let the sunlight into her suite after having firmly demanded a river view.

The superstitious and sentimental are always considered. Just before leaving for South Africa early in 1898, Woolf Joel, the brother of Solly and Jack, gave a dinner party at the hotel. One guest had to cancel at the last minute and thirteen sat down to table. The host laughed at the old superstition that the earliest to leave the table would be destined to die first. A few weeks later Woolf was shot dead in his office in Johannesburg.

Since then, if there happened to be thirteen guests at a party, a member of the hotel staff would be recruited to sit down to table, but this proved unhelpful when the company wished to relax or discuss private matters. In the mid-'twenties, Basil Ionides was commissioned to design a three-foot-high cat which he carved from a single piece of plane tree. Christened Kaspar, he now lives on a high shelf in the Pinafore Room with his back to a wall mirror. At a party of thirteen he always takes the thirteenth chair with a napkin tied round his neck, and is served the whole meal, dish after dish, complete with the full complement of china, glass and cutlery. Not since 1927 has he missed a single dinner of The Other Club in accordance with the strict wishes of 'the pious founder', Sir Winston Churchill.

A visitor from New York, John Parham, always spent the whole of each thirteenth day of the month in bed, having once been nearly blinded in an accident on that date. By contrast The Thirteen Club used to meet for lunch when Friday happened to fall on the 13th. They sat under opened umbrellas, gaily spilled salt and walked under ladders. The secretary, Mr. Randall, insisted on a skull and crossbones for the main table decoration. One of the staunchest members was C. B. Cochran who liked to defy superstition by opening new plays on a Friday.

Elderly Lord Lambourne was never seen in the hotel without a green flower in his lapel. When someone once asked if it was a rare orchid, he explained that it was a sprig of myrtle from his wife's wedding bouquet over half a century ago. He had worn it since the day of her death.

Alex Angus, a businessman from New Jersey, first stayed at the hotel in 1919, when his wife was recovering from a serious operation. She loved to sit by the window looking over the river. Often the pigeons and sparrows used to fly up to their balcony for titbits and became such favourites that they would settle on Mrs. Angus' bed, when she was ill, or feed from her hand if she happened to be sitting in the Embankment Gardens near the Arthur Sullivan memorial. The couple used to return every year and stayed several weeks. When Mrs. Angus died in 1933, her husband set up a small trust fund to reward two Savoy waiters for feeding the birds in the Embankment Gardens, punctually at 2.30 every afternoon from June to the end of August, from napkins laden with bread and cake crumbs.

Superstition or sentiment may explain an odd discovery made in the mid-'twenties while workmen were renovating statuary in the Winter Garden. In the mouth of an alabaster snake at the base of the fountain they found a gold ring of Russian design, set with a single topaz. It was never claimed.

One guest, George Galli, appeared to have no idiosyncrasies but provided the management with one of its strangest mysteries. Galli, a handsome star of the silent screen and at one time a serious rival to Valentino, had starred in successes like *Red Roses* and *The Man with the Hispano-Suiza*. A three-year contract for Hollywood was in his pocket when he rang the Reception and arranged to leave next day, 20 October 1925. That same night he walked through the swing-doors and was not heard of again for thirty-three years. He had paid his bill, and his shirts, ties, suits and many pairs of shoes were left tidily in the wardrobe and later forwarded to his parents, who alone knew the secret. At the hotel a search was made from boiler rooms to roof, but with no trace of the missing man. Before the affair was tucked away and forgotten, there were wild rumours that in a moment of melancholia he had turned his back on the twinkling lights and leapt into the Thames.

A few years ago in a small sunlit church in the village of Sanary, near Toulon, a girl from Marseilles was married to a bullfighter. One of the guests looked twice at the still handsome priest who was addressing the couple: "My children, keep all your

85

thoughts on the gravity of the pledge you are going to give each other. Forget the spotlight and all the rest, for all the rest is vanity." He was Father Galli, who had given himself to the welfare of a peasant flock, completely ignorant of his past. His large fortune had gone on the building of a model settlement, 'the City of Youth'. On that far-off day in 1925, he had suddenly decided to tear up a contract that would have brought him only years of vanity in the spotlight and entered a Belgian monastery.

The nine-hour sensation of Galli's disappearance was quickly forgotten in the splendour of the most brilliant Season since the war. London received Royal visitors like the King and Queen of the Belgians, King Alfonso and Queen Ena, and the Queens of Yugoslavia, Rumania and Norway. The Savoy's house-list included guests of eighteen different nationalities. Under its roof at the same time were four Maharajahs, a tribute to the reputation of the hotel but also a heavy responsibility. This was the heyday of princely India, and the Maharajahs often demanded entire floors for themselves and their retinues, apart from the press-button service which only a great smooth-running hotel can guarantee round the clock. Their residence usually stretched over several weeks and might include calls at Buckingham Palace, Windsor and important Imperial Conferences, with invariably lavish shopping expeditions to tailors, jewellers, gunsmiths and breeders of polo ponies.

For one of his visits the former Maharajah of Patiala, who had a personal income of £640,000 a year and a territory larger than Yorkshire, took the whole of the fifth floor, the 35 suites being decorated daily with 3,000 fresh roses. His fifty-strong retinue included five private secretaries, a bodyguard of lithe dusky men who curled up at night outside their master's bedroom, and a team of chauffeurs to drive the party's twenty limousines.

At home the Maharajah would shoot tiger from the roof of his Rolls-Royce but in England he was more interested in the gentler joys of bat and ball. His first visitor at the Savoy was Prince Ranjitsinhji, otherwise the legendary cricketer, 'Ranji', with whom he soon left for Lord's. It was His Highness's proud boast that, at his palace in the mountains, he owned the highest cricket ground in the world.

On the fifth floor, a special kitchen was built and the Maharajah and his lady dined from their own solid silver dishes. Among numerous little 'extras', a silver bath was installed and also a private lift in scarlet and gold lacquer. The prince's cooks prepared curries and many native delicacies but the hotel kitchen had still to be on cue for sudden demands. When the Maharajah expressed a desire for quail—it was late in the season—telegrams were flashed round Europe. The final haul was only six from Egypt. As a soothing gesture, grouse was soon despatched from Scotland and the restaurant chef was also inspired to offer an elephant carved in ice on which the choicest pineapples reposed. From the Reception he had discovered that the Maharajah's crest was a pennanted elephant which adorned his two hundred pieces of luggage and the numerous jewel cases, each an interlocking miniature steel safe.

A bulky man with a curly black beard and waxed moustaches, he usually wore an apricot turban over most stylishly-cut Western clothes. With half-crown-sized pearl ear-rings and a thick jewelled bracelet, he was a more dazzling figure than his graceful, demure Maharanee who always followed him at a respectful distance. He was capable of unexpected gestures. After lunching privately with King George V at Buckingham Palace, he insisted suddenly on a conducted tour of a typical Salvation Army hostel and left a handsome cash gift to be shared among the inmates. On this particular visit to London, which the Maharajah had stressed was 'semi-private and *informal*', the party departed in a long procession of Rolls-Royces, followed by five truckloads of cricket gear, sporting guns and a hundred new suits from Savile Row. Six polo ponies and other heavy shopping went home under separate cover.

When General Smuts was in London trying to cool De Valera down on the Ulster question, his sleep was disturbed by sounds of revelry from a suite below. The gay Maharajah of Kapurthala was short and plump but fond of dancing. He had conscripted the Savoy Havana Band for a private party and Smuts decided reluctantly to send a secretary downstairs and request a little quiet. Kapurthala's A.D.C. shrugged. "My master is a king," he said loftily. "And mine the adviser of kings," replied the secretary.

As peace negotiations were in danger of breaking down, Smuts descended in his dressing-gown and presented his compliments. "I love music, particularly jazz," he said soothingly. "Dancing is a bond of Empire but drums and cymbals—whether of peace or war—always create discord." The Maharajah stroked his moustaches and declined to stop the party. However, for the rest of the night the South African Premier slept peacefully to a muted symphony of violins and tenor saxophones.

Kapurthala was a camera enthusiast and always had extra lighting installed in his suite with special tanks for developing his films. He would spend hours 'shooting' the Strand from his window, leaning out at angles which terrified his servants, but none of his photographs could have been as dramatic as the scene which took place not long afterwards in one of the suites he had recently occupied.

While luncheon was being served in the restaurant, the orchestra leader politely asked a pretty and petite French lady if she would care to hear any special piece of music. "Thank you very much," she said in a low voice. "My husband is going to kill me in twenty-four hours and I am not in the mood for music." The man forced a smile and murmured, "I hope you will still be here tomorrow, madame." A few yards away at his usual table sat Sir Edward Marshall Hall, K.C., unaware that this lady was soon to become his client.

That night a violent thunderstorm rocked London after a torrid, breathless day. Just after 2 a.m. a porter named Beattie was trundling some luggage along the fourth floor when he heard three pistol shots. He called the Night Manager, Marini, who found the frightened lady from the grill-room bending over a man's body. The victim was dressed in pyjamas, and blood was oozing from his mouth. Beside him lay a Browning automatic

88

and three spent cartridges. The woman was hysterical and kept moaning in French, "What have I done? What will they do to me? I have been married six months and have suffered terribly."

There was little doubt of that. A pretty and sophisticated Parisienne, she had fallen in love with Fahmy Bey, then employed on light duties at the Egyptian Legation, a post which gave him ample leisure and the social contacts he enjoyed.

The wastrel heir to a great industrialist, he had no need to work at anything but pleasure. At twenty-three he had an income of £100,000 a year, a palace on the Nile, yachts, a racing car and four Rolls-Royces. He became infatuated with the fascinating French-woman who had been married before and had a daughter at a London school.

She was dazed and delighted by the gifts Fahmy lavished upon her and accepted an invitation to visit him in Cairo. "I see your head encircled by a crown which I reserve for you here," he wrote lyrically. It became a crown of thorns for poor Madame Fahmy whose husband's idea of marriage was that of a medieval Oriental potentate. She had willingly agreed to become a Moslem (otherwise her husband would have lost his inheritance), but her friends in Paris became uneasy when Fahmy insisted on including a clause in the marriage contract by which he had the right to divorce her at will, although denying it to her.

The first few days of the marriage soon proved that she was at the mercy of a pervert and sadist insanely jealous and possessive of his new chattel. On the honeymoon yacht six coloured servants watched and reported her every movement to their master. When Fahmy went ashore, his wife and her maid were locked in a cabin with a huge Negro standing guard outside. He was a sinister and terrifying man whose life Fahmy had once saved.

In a few weeks this gay young woman, once so popular in Parisian society, had become a pitiful nervous wreck. The husband, brutally sensual, inflicted the worst indignities upon her. At other times he would humiliate her by making her travel by tram while his chauffeur followed in one of the Rolls-Royces. She had bought a revolver to protect her jewels and possibly herself. It appeared that Fahmy liked to amuse himself by firing a gun over her head and more than once had threatened to kill her if she attempted to leave him. A few weeks before the final tragedy at the Savoy she left a letter with her lawyer. It was to be opened on her death or disappearance and accused her husband of having sworn on the Koran that he would 'avenge' himself by killing her.

Fahmy died soon after reaching Charing Cross Hospital. His wife, still with bloodstains on her white evening gown, kept repeating to the doctors, "I have pulled the trigger three times." A murder charge was inevitable, and her position looked very grave indeed. The killing had taken place not in Paris, where a Frenchwoman so shamefully treated might expect sympathy and acquittal, but in the heart of London. She would stand trial at the Old Bailey under the cold figure of Justice whose scales were at that time rarely weighted in favour of crimes of passion.

Madame Fahmy was fortunate in her counsel, Sir Edward Marshall Hall, whose full-blooded style was always at its best in a case that touched his quick sympathies. He made every effort for a client who could speak no English and seemed quite broken by her ordeal. Slowly and very gently, he extracted more facts and, thanks to Madame Fahmy's many friends in Paris who spared neither money nor trouble to make the fullest inquiries about her disastrous marriage, he was able to piece together a defence that not even a stolid British jury could lightly dismiss.

For the jury which included three women, Sir Edward quietly sketched the background to the tragedy. He proved that the accused had come to London, sick in mind and body, and needing a serious internal operation. She had wanted desperately to see her daughter but Fahmy made this difficult. Without money or friends in England, she was at the mercy of a sadist who had amused himself by dangling his wallet in front of her but refused to pay for her operation. When she threatened to leave, he had half-strangled her. Again and again he played his favourite trick of pointing a pistol at her.

Madame Fahmy was in the witness-box for seven long hours.

She told defending counsel that on the night of the tragedy her nerves were shattered by the violent thunderstorm and her husband's attempt to strangle her. To frighten him, she had picked up the gun and fired out of the window, quite unaware that it was loaded. As Fahmy leapt towards her, the gun went off and he had slumped to the floor.

In a most dramatic scene Sir Edward reconstructed those terrible moments. He ended by dropping the pistol in that hushed courtroom. The impact was electrifying, although counsel always maintained that it was an accident due to his own excitement and strain, and not a planned stage effect.

The jury's verdict of 'not guilty' was greeted with such applause that Mr. Justice Swift could not make himself heard above the clapping and stamping. He took the very rare course of having the court cleared before discharging the prisoner. Marshall Hall celebrated at the Savoy that evening. More important to him than his triumph in Court was the satisfaction of relieving his client of her appalling suspense. They became close friends, and some years later his family found many affectionate letters from Madame Fahmy among his papers.

A few months after this, the future Maharajah of Kashmir became involved in a scandal which ended in an attempt to swindle him out of £125,000. His wealth and ostentation, accompanied by a weakness for women, made him attractive game for confidence men. At the Savoy he sometimes invited a few favoured guests to inspect his collection of pearls, some as big as plovers' eggs, his tiaras set with brilliants, and ear-rings of an Arabian Nights splendour. But his unpleasant experience in the sensational blackmail case (during which he was referred to as 'Mr. A.') had made him wary of over-generosity. One night, after dinner in the restaurant, he offered a guest a cigarette from a solid gold case with his initials set in rubies. She thanked him and, to his astonishment, promptly slipped the case into her vanity bag, thinking it was a gift. By a coincidence her initials were the same as the host's. Sir Hari bit his lips and stalked out. A few minutes later, and before the lady's departure, an A.D.C. explained very firmly that she had been the victim of a misunderstanding. The case would have to be returned at once.

Poor Gertrude Lawrence also had an unfortunate experience. A young prince from Hyderabad had asked her to a supper party in the grill-room after her dazzling performance in *Oh, Kay*, with Gershwin's wonderful score. Beside each lady's napkin was a gold kidskin bag, a gift from the host. 'Gee' picked up hers and felt several small hard objects inside. All through supper she was in a flurry of impatience to explore further but had to wait for a suitable moment to go to the ladies' room. Inside the bag, alas, was no fortune in rubies but betel nuts used in India for chewing and no favourite with our Miss Lawrence, who prided herself on her dazzling white teeth.

Another prince created a certain anxiety at the hotel when he announced his forthcoming visit. He had such a vast harem that his enemies referred to him behind his massive back as His Exhausted Highness. Happily, he was travelling light on this occasion and behaved as decorously as if he were at the Viceroy's Garden Party.

A more romantic figure was young Prince Abassi, son of the Nawab of Bahawalpur. He was breakfasting in his suite when his eye fell upon a newspaper picture of a new beauty queen, Katherine Scott, who had won a screen test with Ray Milland. She was the sixteen-year-old daughter of a railway porter. The prince rang down to the flower shop and ordered a huge bouquet of roses which blossomed into a meeting, and later marriage. Soon afterwards the couple left together for India.

The ruler of Darbhanga had a less happy stay. While entertaining some friends to supper after the theatre, a cat burglar broke into his suite and robbed him of all his jewels. Nevertheless he was back the following year and gave a dinner for two hundred friends to celebrate his birthday. Before the party broke up, he placed round the neck of each guest a garland of gold fashioned by his native craftsmen. A man of most hospitable character, he himself ate practically nothing and appeared to subsist on a diet of fifteen cigars a day.

The great wealth of such princes was an obvious temptation to burglars, and the hotel security staff always took special precautions. However, danger once came from an unexpected quarter. It was noticed that a certain prince was almost inseparable from an Englishman of the sporting ex-Regular Army type. The hotel detective's instinct made him so uncomfortable that he started a few private inquiries. It appeared that the two men had first met on the voyage from India and the shipboard acquaintance matured rapidly through a common interest in the Turf. The prince was so taken with his new friend that he had invited him to stay as his guest at the hotel. A little further investigation disclosed that the charming and dapper "officer" had a prison record for burglary and known talents as a confidence trickster. At this point the detective took the racing man aside and warned him off. The prince was tactfully not told of his narrow escape or why his guest had suddenly decided to cut short his stay.

Cardsharps, confidence men anxious to impress the staff by ostentatiously depositing valuables, and gamblers who used to take suites for illegal roulette parties were quickly spotted by O'Donnell, whom Reeves-Smith had engaged as security officer at the Savoy when he retired from Scotland Yard. Affectionately known to the staff as 'Bubbles', this gentle Irishman had a bald head crowned by a gingerish halo. He was in every sense a 'character' and quite unlike the nondescript hotel detective of fiction. His bulky figure was encased in severely respectable clothes of Edwardian cut, never worn without a stock and pearl pin. A most delightful man with a fascinating brogue, his very firm sense of propriety emerged in all his long daily reports to the management. Written in elegant longhand, they are minor masterpieces of police 'officialese'. Each opens with a phrase like, "I kept quiet observation in the front hall and was surprised to notice that ... *Most unfortunate.*" The slightest deviation in conduct which might bring the Savoy into disrepute caused him to pounce swiftly, but always with impeccable courtesy. Suspicious of a certain young woman's social standing, he tried to conceal himself behind a marble pillar. His report next day to the Night Manager told all. "I kept observation for some time. I noticed that the gentleman was fingering her neckwear. I informed them of the hotel's regulations. She left the hotel. *Most unfortunate.*" These 'regulations' were a mystery, even to the management, but O'Donnell used them as sword and buckler against the indecorous. His greatest trial was to keep out young ladies of the town who, in the old days, used to drive up in carriages and leave their visiting cards for guests at the hotel.

As security officer he had other serious problems. He had to be on his guard against the familiar hotel pest who stays a night or so merely to make an impression of his room key or to study the layout of the floor. At a later date he breaks in, usually posing as a waiter or porter. O'Donnell had a remarkable memory for faces and an instinct which made him suspicious of guests likely to issue bad cheques or depart without paying their bills, and those liberal-seeming spenders whose expensive luggage is often found later to be stuffed with old newspapers.

One of his first cases, however, was a puzzle which seriously affected staff morale. The waiters always dropped their tips, wrapped in tissue paper and with a note of their names and the amount, into the *tronc*. It was kept locked and only opened in the presence of two or three head waiters who counted and then divided the money among the staff, according to rank and grade. Although the box showed no signs of having been forced, money was steadily disappearing. At the same time several of the directors' offices were broken into and rifled.

O'Donnell soon discovered how the petty thieving was being done. A twisted wire was inserted into the *tronc* and the slips dexterously fished out by someone who obviously had the time and opportunity to work at leisure, probably in the small hours. Suspicion fell on one individual but, without catching him in the act, little could be done. Nevertheless, a series of pointed questions was enough to stop the pilfering and remove the suspected cause.

The hotel's security staff had all had some previous experience of C.I.D. or Special Branch work. They knew how to be

94

unobtrusive but close at hand if there were any danger from fanatics or political opponents. Most of these potentates were amiable and co-operative, and the staff came to understand their little eccentricities. There was one oil-rich Sheikh from Saudi Arabia who dictated a 20-page cable to his fifteenth mate describing exactly what dress she was to wear to greet him on his return. Less communicative was the Pasha of Marrakesch who liked to be incognito. He would slip into a quiet corner table wearing an unobtrusive blue suit, and at once bolt for the door if strangers stared at him. He paced up and down, restlessly counting the hours until he could get to Coombe Hill for his golfing lesson from Archie Compston.

The staff had always to be on its toes for strange demands from guests so fabulously wealthy and autocratic. Aware of discontent at home, one potentate had decided to invest in a bullet-proof vest. He then asked Hansen, the Head Porter, to send one of his linkmen up to his suite. "Please put this on," he ordered. The man did so, somewhat mystified. "Now, come with me to the Embankment Gardens and we will test it." The porter hurriedly took off the vest and departed, mumbling an excuse. It was later tactfully explained to His Highness that floor service, even at the Savoy, did not include being fired at with a revolver at close range. Another prince wanted to take some playing cards home with him and was recommended to a certain shop where he spent several hours inspecting the exquisite patterns. Quite unable to make up his mind, he bought the whole stock for £1,000.

The Maharajah of Rajpipla disliked the enormous retinues of some of his fellow-princes and contented himself with a secretary and valet. A wireless enthusiast, he was never without a brown leather case containing a portable radio. His other passion was the Turf. One afternoon he went off to see his horse Windsor Lad run in the Derby, but before leaving for Epsom booked a table for twelve in the restaurant. As soon as Smirke passed the winning post, the delighted owner rushed off to send a telegram to the Savoy requesting a hundred covers for dinner.

Derby Night dinners were already very popular, a vogue which started when Lord Derby first entertained his friends in the restaurant after winning the great Classic. Thereafter, Derby Night has always been celebrated at the hotel, and a special cake iced at the last minute with the winning owner's name and racing colours.

When Santarelli received the Maharajah of Rajpipla's wire the restaurant was already heavily booked, but he managed to shoehorn space for the huge party by calling for smaller chairs and making other improvisations. The cake was soon created and Craddock quickly devised a cocktail with the Maharajah's colours as the motif. The florists worked at high speed to decorate the table. Eager for novelty, Santarelli telephoned a zoo and arranged for a baby elephant to be brought to the Embankment entrance. Garlanded in purple and cream, he was to make his bow to the prince and his guests. After some hurried conferences behind the scenes, the General Manager, Gilles, decided not to risk his famous carpet.

The dinner party was a success but the Maharajah remained completely unaware of the surprise originally planned for him. Although his plan had misfired, Santarelli was consoled next morning by yet another addition to his collection of cigar and cigarette cases, cuff-links, tiepins and other handsome gifts from appreciative guests. His Highness presented him with a solid gold cigarette case with the princely crest set in rubies.

The graceful doe-eyed Maharanees were rarely seen in the public rooms of the hotel. They would only emerge, fey-like in a rustle of saris, for brief shopping expeditions and always accompanied by a page from the hotel. A certain princess was difficult to please and one page after another earned her disfavour, usually over trifles. In the end she would invariably demand the boy originally assigned to her.

More fortunate was a page who had been born in India where his father was serving in the Army. Having some knowledge of Hindustani, he was in considerable demand when the Indian princes were in residence. His special task was to escort the Nizam of Hyderabad's young son on sightseeing tours around London. He was always handsomely rewarded, if not on the scale of a certain floor-waiter who attended one prince year after year and anticipated his every wish. At the end of one visit, the prince dispensed with the customary liberal tip and instead invited the waiter to spend six months as a guest in his palace. The management granted leave of absence.

The princes were not alone in demanding space and individual service. Almost from its opening months, the Savoy has offered sanctuary and unique advantages to the stars of the operatic and concert worlds. Accessible to Covent Garden and other great theatres and halls, it is equally suited to lavish celebration suppers after excitable *premières* and the usual private meetings with impresarios, arrangers and agents. Doctors are at hand for first-night nerves or the many crises that may affect voice and throat. A practised staff is geared to deal with fan mail, telephone calls, cables and all the many complications of living in the limelight, not forgetting the hysterical cranks who will try and climb drainpipes or even hide in wardrobes to be near their beloved—or hated—victims.

For those desiring privacy, the incognito can be wrapped in cottonwool; others, anxious to make an entrance, are offered an almost stagelike setting. For numerous operatic stars, from the earliest days of Melba and Caruso, the Savoy has always been a second home where caprices can be indulged by veteran chefs, while chambermaids and waiters become like family servants, ready to listen to tales of triumph or offer condolence when the critics or audiences prove less than kind.

No guest was more loved or lovable than Tetrazzini who would sweep regally into her suite, No. 412 overlooking the Embankment, fling off her ermine cloak and promptly start to cook a meal for her friends and herself. Her suite was almost a self-contained service flat with its own kitchen where she often prepared a huge breakfast, always with spaghetti.

Her rooms were decorated in advance in duck-egg blue which

she found soothing, and a favourite thickly-padded mattress was reserved for her bed. Two grand pianos were specially tuned for wet or dry days, and she would spend many hours practising her scales, much to Melba's annoyance. It was a dislike warmly reciprocated. One evening Tetrazzini passed Melba's suite and winced at the famous voice in full throttle. Turning to Mrs. Kate Butler she asked sweetly, "Have you *many* cats in your lovely hotel?"

This gay petite brunette was never without her own private menagerie of pekingese, a tame crocodile and several parrots including one who sang 'E' in alto. When a reporter once asked if she had really made £75,000 on her recent American tour, this parrot made the piercing sceptical comment, "Oh, la, la." During this particular tour Tetrazzini had visited 'dry' California whose mayor, quite hypnotized by her charm, invited her to sit in his official chair. "Can I now be mayor for the day?" she asked coquettishly. He nodded. "Very well," laughed the *diva*. "Everyone is to have a drink who wants one."

She arrived late one night at the hotel, wrapped in layers of chinchilla, her tiny red nose peeping through a thick knitted scarf. A suite was somehow found for her—an admirer at once insisted on moving out—and the devoted staff fussed over her with hot drinks. She had left her large house in Milan to do a single charity concert in the United States but could not resist disembarking at Southampton for a night in her beloved London. Latry at once began to prepare some of her favourite Italian dishes. Before dawn she had spent a couple of hours wandering about Covent Garden market which always fascinated her. Every porter stopped work to shake her by the hand.

One Christmas night she enchanted the other diners in the Restaurant by standing on a chair and singing *Home, Sweet Home* in a strong Italian accent. When the guests had all departed, she promptly gave an impromptu concert for the waiters, singing everything they requested, from Grand Opera to *The Last Rose of Summer*. Although running to fat she never looked anything but a star. Once she espied Anita Loos waiting for the lift in tweed slacks. Her stony look of disapproval would have embarrassed anyone but the author of Gentlemen Prefer Blondes who gave an impish smile. Soon afterwards Tetrazzini arranged to join some friends on the roof after apéritifs in her suite. She begged a few minutes to change her clothes. Her 'casual' roof-top outfit turned out to be a green velvet coat trimmed with sable and worn with long emerald-studded ear-rings.

Very amorous and sentimental, she always spoke with emotion of her first meeting with Caruso in Petrograd when he advised her to go to England and be recognized as 'the soprano of the world'. At the Savoy three days before he died, she received a postcard in which he wrote, "I am waiting for you with open arms, waiting every moment to salute you with a golden note." Shaken and distraught she completed her engagement in London and hurried off to Naples, arriving a few hours too late. On her return she stayed alone for days in her suite, weeping over a framed portrait on a piano covered with lilies.

When Gracie Fields was appearing at the Lyceum in *The Show's the Thing*, one of the scenes called for her to burlesque popular arias in the manner of famous *prima donnas*. One night she was horrified to learn that Tetrazzini herself was in a box and watching the show through lorgnettes. Gracie became even more distressed when a message arrived during the interval requesting an aria from *La Traviata*. Somehow she struggled through the number and managed to hit all the right notes without guying the song. As she came off, little Tetrazzini was patiently waiting outside her dressing-room. She kissed Gracie with affection and sobbed, "My darling, my darling, you must sing in *real* opera and leave all *thees*."

Her voice is said to have earned her more than £1,000,000, but she could be casual over accountancy. After a three months' tour of Britain her fees brought a tax claim for £1,500. She took a light-hearted view of the matter until the authorities became rather less than gallant. Finally she asked an inspector to call on her in Suite 412. It was Christmas Eve. Perhaps, he thought uncharitably, she would try to soothe him with song and promises. He arrived to find the room sparkling with decorations, a magnum of Bollinger bobbing merrily in its bucket. On the table stood bundles of one-pound notes—1,500 of them, neatly tied with red ribbon, which the rather dazed official transferred to his briefcase. But Tetrazzini had not quite completed the transaction. That morning she had baked a magnificent Christmas cake. With a gay smile and seasonable kiss she handed a large slice to the man from the Inland Revenue.

Often staying on the same floor was Chaliapin who rightly considered himself one of the Savoy's family. Even Reeves-Smith would have hesitated to invade the maître-chef's holy of holies without reasonable warning, but the big blue-eyed giant used to lumber downstairs and advise the grinning cooks exactly how he wanted his spicy *bortsch* prepared. He would then slip into Latry's office, tell him some funny tales and usually stay to share any luscious 'scraps' from the kitchen. He never seemed to stop nibbling cheese which he swore was good for the throat. No doubt he would have stayed to peel potatoes or help clean the knives if they had given him the chance.

A lesser man would have taken offence when Gilles tactfully suggested that he might move up to a suite on the top floor as his booming arias in the bath were disturbing some unmusical neighbour. 'Charlie Pine', as Lady Diana Cooper used to call him, simply roared with laughter and meekly packed his bags.

He particularly enjoyed lunching with Heifetz and Marconi. The violinist, usually so mandarin-like and impassive on the concert platform, seemed to become almost like a schoolboy at the hotel. Once he dragged Chaliapin up to the roof where he was taking lessons on the bagpipes from Sir Harry Lauder until other guests implored him to return to the violin. To conceal his disappointment, Lauder wanted to teach Chaliapin English but the offer was declined.

At meals, the six foot four basso had an endearing habit of jumping suddenly to his feet whenever he saw a friend in the distance. He would clasp both hands above his head in a boxer's greeting, quite oblivious of frigid lorgnettes and monocles. In the grill-room he once hurled himself at the Duncan Sisters who were looking glum after their disappointing first night in *Topsy and Eva*. Hugging them to his bosom he gave each a stout kiss of consolation and propelled them to his own table.

One afternoon he was wandering round the hotel like some shaggy bear bent on mischief when he overheard the Orpheans at rehearsal. He went in at once and promised to listen quietly but, like Heifetz, he was far too fond of syncopated dance music to keep still. Beating time with his feet, he then started to hum until Debroy Somers finally resigned the baton and let him carry on. The band adored him.

Sitting one evening in his dressing-room at the Paris Opéra, he was handed a telegram from Somers and the boys welcoming him back from a triumphant tour of the United States. Very moved, he jotted down the opening bars of a new foxtrot on the back of the telegraph form and mailed it back to the Savoy. Somers promptly arranged the number, called it *Chaliapinata* and played it for dancing on Derby Night in the composer's presence. Chaliapin was so delighted that he insisted on giving the Orpheans and the waiters a free concert before they went home.

He always wore three large rings, claiming that each was useful as a code signal to his three girl friends. Very solemnly he would turn a ring on his finger, if Madame Chaliapin were anywhere in the neighbourhood. He liked to make this joke in the presence of his wife who used to return his wink with rather less enthusiasm.

Everyone at the Savoy spoiled Chaliapin and his pet monkey, Boris, who died from eating too much chocolate in the Winter Garden. But he would be irritable before a concert, often through stage fright, and particularly temperamental during his many terms of dieting. While thinning for *Don Quixote*, he sulked in his suite, looking like a dehydrated buddha until he could once again call on Latry with the old careless rapture.

Between courses in the Grill he would often draw caricatures, mainly of himself. Another brilliant cartoonist was his close friend, the bearded American sculptor Jo Davidson, who once signed the hotel register with a self-caricature. The receptionist stuck to protocol and insisted politely on a more formal registration. If Davidson were offended, he was mollified when commissioned later to do a bust of Reeves-Smith. He grew so attached to the Savoy that it became his working base in London. Here he did a series of busts of leading writers, among them Shaw and Arnold Bennett, which George Doran commissioned at £1,000 each. During one long and gay meal together in the grill-room, Davidson made seventeen lightning sketches of Chaliapin on the pink tablecloth which an enterprising waiter whisked off as a souvenir. Unhappily for him, someone in the kitchen promptly sent it off to the laundry.

In his room Chaliapin liked to try on each of his thirty suits, nearly all checks tailored in Savile Row. His boots were made to measure in Jermyn Street but he was only the dandy in public. He usually received visitors, from Royalty downwards, in trousers and an open-necked shirt or, more often, wearing only a vast flowered silk kimono.

One of his gayest parties was a farewell celebration with his cronies, Gigli and Tauber, after a gala performance of *Boris Godounov*. Latry rose to the occasion by serving a delightful supper which included caviare in honour of Chaliapin, *jambon de Parme* as a gesture to Gigli, and chicken in the pot to which Tauber was devoted. Afterwards they staggered up to Chaliapin's suite, arm in arm, settling down to a night of entertainment which included opera from the host and *lieder* from the others. The Italian cartoonist, Autori, was enrolled to play the guitar. A hilarious jam session soon started when Tauber stuck a fish knife into a bread roll and played the accompaniment on glasses, vases and the window pane.

This exuberant trio had many sentimental points of contact. With tears rolling down his cheeks, Tauber often recalled that his first agreement to sing in England was signed on the back of a restaurant menu and witnessed by Franz Lehár and Chaliapin.

Tauber's chief link with Gigli was food, particularly a love of rice which they used to consume in prodigious quantities while they talked music. Tauber's widow, Diana Napier, says that the word 'rice' finally became almost a password between them. One New Year's Eve, Gigli sent his friend a greetings telegram which read, "Thanks Fuer Guten Wuenschen Risotto Today Aufwiedersehn." With tears in his eyes, Gigli recalled his first performance at the Metropolitan Opera House in New York when he was told to sing, standing behind Chaliapin. Gigli turned to the gigantic bass. "How could I stand behind *you* without a chair?" he laughed.

Gigli had trouble with his weight and used to arrange for cases of lemons to be sent over from Sicily. He would only drink Italian mineral water. His countrymen all adored him, of course, and made quite a ceremony of serving his starchless *pasta* which had to be specially prepared by the kitchen. His little vanities included wearing high heels on his pearl-buttoned boots and insisting on being addressed as *Cavaliere*, a title Mussolini had bestowed on him. He loved jewellery and always wore a huge diamond scarf-pin and ruby and onyx cuff-links. He had beautifully manicured hands but assured everyone that he could have become a champion boxer had he wished.

Like Chaliapin he suffered torments before a concert and drank pints of tea and tomato juice while nervously playing patience. When he had 'flu and was running an alarming temperature, he once defied the hotel doctor and went to the Albert Hall with wads of paper under his boiled shirt to soak up the sweat. The taxi-driver began to whistle an aria from *Tosca* in which Gigli joined, suddenly relaxed. "Would you like to hear me tonight?" he asked gaily. The cabby nodded with delight but, alas, there was not a seat to be had. For ten minutes Gigli argued with the manager until his new friend was given a box to himself with liberal refreshment in the interval.

The morning after a concert he was usually boisterous and would give a saucy and highly personal rendering of *Mr. Gallagher and Mr. Sheen* with his valet. Nothing could stop him singing. In his bath he sang Verdi and emerged to throw open the window and sing loud and clear across the Thames. To greet early visitors he would fling his bathrobe over one shoulder like a toga and sing, "Yes, we have no pyjamas." He liked to round up Chaliapin, Maria Caniglia and any other singer in residence and lead them into the restaurant chanting the Quartette from *Rigoletto*.

Tito Schipa, another favourite with the staff, had always to be carefully handled because of his volatile temperament. Like Tetrazzini, he was fond of animals and had a pet marmoset which was quarantined when he landed. He was so gloomy about the loss of his mascot that his manager feared disaster for the forthcoming concert at the Albert Hall. Luckily, a friendly waiter happened to mention the tragedy to an admirer. Within a few hours a two-year-old monkey named Mickey was sent up to the suite, dressed in a scarlet coat almost identical with that worn by the cherished marmoset. While Tito practised, Mickey sat attentively on the grand piano and even joined in the applause. The concert was a success.

Another crisis occurred at Covent Garden when plump Lotte Lehmann walked off the stage in the middle of Act One of *Der Rosenkavalier*. Suffering from a heavy cold and the effects of a rough Channel crossing, she missed her husband who was ill in Switzerland and usually supported her at all her concerts. She was hysterical when she arrived back at the Savoy, with Lady Cunard and the Taubers trying to comfort her. During the next two hours her suite was filled with incoming bouquets from sympathetic admirers, including one from the always tactful manager, Gilles. Two nights later she was back on stage at the Garden giving one of her finest performances.

In pincenez and looking like a nervous heron, Stravinsky used to lend an ear to a torrent of Russian and quaint English from Diaghilev who always made an impressive entrance in his fur-collared coat with an Edwardian homburg tilted over hooded eyes. A massive tiepin and the many rings on his fingers almost lit up the table where he ate a considerable meal while he talked feelingly of his imaginary illnesses. Even on the hottest day in

July he would huddle into his big coat, fearful of catching cold.

Not far away, Beecham would usually be addressing Lady Cunard whose eyes grew misty with mascara and adoration. A double-breasted imp with that splendid head perched on a high starched collar, his very cigar smoke curling in disdain, Beecham would pepper the many conductors, musicians and composers who had earned his displeasure.

Tiny snow-capped Toscanini, whom Beecham had once dismissed as 'a glorified Italian bandmaster', was also a lion at concerts but only a nervous lamb blinking tired, weak eyes in the vastness of a luxury hotel. He ate a little fruit, sipped a glass or two of wine and usually crept away to sleep the clock round, while the Grill served gay suppers into the small hours for admirers who had come on from the Albert Hall. At one table after a triumphant Elgar concert, Arnold Bennett was entertaining Harriet Cohen and Arnold Bax who were joined later by William Walton. Nobody seemed too unhappy when Elgar departed. Congratulated politely on the performance of the Variations, he declared sourly that he never went to hear his own music.

Kreisler also disliked the limelight but could be a more agreeable host. After one concert he gave a supper party for big, jovial Melchior, Backhaus and Gerhardt. None of them guessed that he had played for two hours in the most crippling pain from neuritis.

Richard Strauss revelled in the high-pitched atmosphere of the grill-room and would rarely permit the long business talks over his operas to interfere with his enjoyment of the food and wines. To Savoy gastronomes, however, his name will always be associated with the classic heresy of demanding raspberry jam with his mutton chop.

Most of the musical celebrities seemed to enjoy the relaxation of dance music, among them Stokowski and gay Harriet Cohen, who was so popular at the hotel that Latry created *poires Harriet* in her honour. There were exceptions like Sir Hamilton Harty, who attacked the leprosy of jazz with the enthusiasm of a Schweitzer, and Puccini who pleaded for a suite high above 'the noise'.

The Savoy bands were meanwhile tickling toes far beyond the Strand.

THE AMERICAN thread in the history of the Savoy Hotel also runs through its ballroom. Of the first two resident band-leaders one was American and the other hailed from Dublin, although the hands across the sea motif was quite accidental in origin. After the First World War people were more eager than ever to kick up their heels. There was wild enthusiasm for American musical comedies, and the Original Dixieland Jazz Band made a sensation when they played at the Savoy's Victory Ball to celebrate the signing of the Versailles Treaty. More and more visitors crossed the Atlantic with stories of the lavish George White and Ziegfeld shows; others rhapsodized over Paul Whiteman's Band.

Himself fond of ballroom dancing, one of his favourite forms of relaxation, Reeves-Smith listened to the distant drumbeats. Bert Ralton and his Havana Band were invited over from California and registered an immediate success. Almost every star from the musical comedy stage would come on from the theatre to dance to Ralton's saxophone and Billy Mayerl's tinkling piano.

Dancing at the hotel become so popular that Reeves-Smith readily agreed to enlist another band which was to become world-famous as the Savoy Orpheans. They were headed by 'Bill' Debroy Somers, first of the personality band-leaders who in pre-war years topped music hall bills wherever they performed. Today it is difficult to visualize the extraordinary personal following enjoyed by men like Debroy Somers, Carroll Gibbons, Jack Hylton and Ambrose. They were paid vast salaries; their records sold in hundreds of thousands and few film or stage stars commanded more admirers. At the hotel, a little to the surprise of the management, guests followed some of the band-leaders with the devotion usually accorded to favourite head waiters. The musicians had their own sitting-room, a masseur and a valet, but even more of an attraction to them was the Savoy's prestige which often became a passport to richer billets.

Somers was born in Dublin, the son of an Army bandmaster, and received his early musical training at Kneller Hall. One of his first jobs was as John McCormack's accompanist for which he was paid a guinea, half the singer's fee. He was a thoroughly likeable man with a ripe brogue, flashing smile and a Ronald Colman moustache. Reminded by Reeves-Smith that entertainment had to be as worthy of the hotel's tradition as its cuisine and service, Somers took the hint and for six months drilled his band with almost military discipline before allowing them to play in public.

The final dress rehearsal was an elaborate affair. A dinner was arranged by Richmond Temple, the publicity director, for a number of newspaper editors headed by R. D. Blumenfeld and a few selected patrons like Sir Philip Sassoon and Arnold Bennett. The Orpheans, twelve in number, went through their paces and earned Bennett's rather grudging tribute, "They play bad music well."

The American saxophonist had a bird-cage under his chair, complete with canary. When this musician sailed for England he had to leave his pet behind. It fretted and so did its master who finally cabled in despair to New York. The canary was shipped over and harmony once more prevailed. A few weeks later, a rather festive diner insisted on entering the restaurant with *his* canary who also wanted to listen to the Orpheans. He was only dissuaded after some argument.

The band cost the hotel £450 a week, an outlay quickly justified by publicity alone. Soon all England was dancing to *Missouri Waltz, Three o'clock in the morning, Margie* and *Valencia*. Among the many guests who danced to their music were a future

King and Queen of England, then the Duke of York and Lady Elizabeth Bowes-Lyon, who were married soon after the Orpheans came to the hotel. They loved Scottish reels and old-time polkas. The gay young Prince of Wales also enjoyed their music and was among the first to wear midnight-blue evening dress and a white waistcoat under his dinner jacket. His brother, Prince George, was easily the most graceful of the Royal dancers, and he and the lovely Greek Princess Marina who became his wife always made a strikingly handsome couple on the floor.

The two Savoy bands were the first to broadcast regularly from any hotel. It began in October 1923, following a daring experiment some months previously when a 2LO combination of nine members of the Wireless Orchestra, 'with a saxophone added', gave a performance on the air before the opening of Savoy Hill. The hotel's subsidiary, the Strand Power Co., supplied energy not only to the Savoy but to the B.B.C. in its early days.

'Dance Music from the Savoy Hotel in London' quickly pulled up rugs all over the world. Millions tickled their crystal sets six nights a week to listen to the Orpheans and the Havana Band. Their music was relayed to places like Cowes where couples danced by moonlight on their yachts, and ham operators picked up the syncopated beat as far away as Long Island. Marconi reported that a French force in North Africa, while besieged by the Riffs, had tuned in to the Savoy and those not on duty danced together to kill the *cafard*. Soon afterwards, half an hour's truce was called every night so that both armies could enjoy the dance music in peace.

Towards the end of 1923, radio history was made by an exchange of messages between the B.B.C. and the United States. Marconi delivered a personal greeting of goodwill with only a kilowatt or so impact to the transmitters. He was followed at the chattering box by John Reith, Georges Carpentier and Capt. Peter Eckersley, the B.B.C.'s Chief Engineer. They cut into the Savoy Orpheans, then on the air, and listeners on their crystal sets were able to hear the voice of America for the first time. Marconi and his friends celebrated later at dinner in the Restaurant.

The inventor liked to have his meals at the Savoy which was only a few minutes from Marconi House. He would eat sparingly of broiled chicken followed by a glass of wine and blistered any waiter who attempted to heap his plate. He wore a monocle over the eye that he had lost in a car accident, but even more distressing to a man of his Latin blood and temperament was the English cold. At the Savoy he felt warmer and a little more relaxed before dashing headlong into the Strand, buried in an immense fur-collared coat with his hat pulled well over ears and nose.

He could never resist the dance music. Often he would take the floor with a pretty young débutante and become quite animated, particularly if she were one of the Cowes Set. He and Sir Thomas Lipton were on the most friendly terms, and it was Marconi's supreme delight to drive down with him to the Royal Yacht Squadron Club and proudly hoist both the White Ensign and the pennant of the crown of Savoy on his luxury yacht *Elettra*.

Other men of distinction also honoured the hotel bands. When Stokowski, always a keen dancer, was entertained in the Pinafore Room by the Young Poets of England, he abstained from a highbrow speech and paid tribute instead to the pleasure given him by the Orpheans. William Walton went one better and wrote a Concerto specially for them.

The single microphone which dangled precariously over the platform in those early days was primitive by modern technical standards but there was nothing amateurish about the orchestras who regularly delighted over two million listeners until midnight. Ten grand pianos were in use, each played for only two hours daily and meticulously tuned every morning.

Debroy Somers received a prodigious fan mail. From Teignmouth one admirer sent barrels of Devonshire cream so that his late-night musicians would be kept happy and well-fed. Above all he prized a sixpenny postal order sent by an old lady who asked him to share it among the Savoy 'orphans' she had heard so much about. At this time his band included three M.C.s and a D.S.O., apart from his brother who had lost a leg in the war. He had a soft spot in his heart for all ex-Servicemen and rarely refused an invitation to play at one of their shows, in which he was always supported by the Managing Director. Not for many years did it come to light that Reeves-Smith was the guiding spirit behind the fund of £300,000 raised to buy Preston Hall, near Maidstone, for the treatment and care of war veterans suffering from tuberculosis, and later given to the British Legion.

Among the highlights of those early days in the Savoy ballroom was the memorable visit of George Gershwin, a composer with one foot in Tin Pan Alley and the other in Carnegie Hall. He was mobbed every time he walked into the Savoy, with the orchestra standing to play *Swanee* in his honour. On arrival, he at once asked the management to send a grand piano up to his suite. One night the specially augmented Orpheans, inspiringly led by Debroy Somers and with the composer playing the solo at the piano, gave London its first hearing of *Rhapsody in Blue*, a performance which most experts considered superior to that of Paul Whiteman himself.

Tall and bronzed but a secret hypochondriac who devoured pills at all hours and demanded patent foods of every kind at breakfast, Gershwin was the lion of Mayfair Society. He was sponsored by his close friend and admirer, Prince George, and taken everywhere by the Mountbattens. On shopping sprees to Savile Row and Bond Street he was usually accompanied by Gertrude Lawrence who offered guidance on his suits and ties. They would return to the grill-room for lunch, Gershwin with bowler hat and furled umbrella looking anything but a graduate of New York's Lower East Side. At the Savoy there was genuine sadness among the staff when news arrived that he had died of a brain tumour, at the age of 38.

Over-stimulated perhaps by his popularity, Somers decided to leave the hotel and tour with his own band but was never again to enjoy the same success. In the end he found himself in serious difficulties, partly due to his open-handedness. He died from a stroke, leaving only £170. Among the numerous wreaths at his funeral was a huge cluster of tulips and roses sent by the old Sultan of Johore who had not only enjoyed dancing to the Orpheans but used to love talking cricket with Somers. Bert Ralton also died in tragic circumstances. While touring in Rhodesia with his band he went out on safari and was shot by accident. As he waited for the ambulance, he picked up a ukelele and sang *I'll be lovin' you always*.

Meanwhile, a successor to Debroy Somers had come to the Savoy. Carroll Gibbons, whose famous white piano was to dominate the hotel ballroom for nearly thirty years, was born in Clinton, Massachusetts, studied music at the Boston Conservatoire and toured the United States as a concert pianist before he was sixteen. During his college days he kept alive for a time by playing the organ in local cinemas.

After a brief spell as a composer in Hollywood, he decided to try his luck in England and crossed the Atlantic with Rudy Vallee who joined the Savoy Havana Band, put sex into the sax and later became celebrated as both band-leader and crooner. Gibbons first went to the Berkeley as a pianist with the Boston Orchestra but, in 1926, he was engaged by De Mornys, the entertainments manager, to play under Debroy Somers, with Billy Thorburn on the other piano. Soon he formed his own little band, the Savoy Sylvians, before taking over the Orpheans.

His familiar warm greeting, "Hallo, *everybuddy*," delivered in a husky New England drawl, became almost a signature tune for dancers. He had a lazy relaxed talent for making the millions who listened to his broadcasts feel as if they were at a private party. In the hotel the staff had soon nicknamed him 'Little Kim' or everybody's pal, and he was as polite and tactful to some silly deb. as to the Royal Family with whom he became a warm favourite.

He had an enormous repertoire of syncopated music. Each year he liked to go home to see his parents, always returning with dozens of new tunes which he arranged and streamlined into his own individual style of quiet rhythm and melody. At one time he became so homesick that he decided to return to Hollywood and compose for the films. Musicals were, however, out of vogue and soon he had departed for New York to write some of the hit tunes for the Broadway show *Sweet and Low*.

He was being missed at the Savoy; in 1931 the Board invited him back to re-form the Orpheans which had been disbanded. With Howard Jacobs as co-leader, he set to work. When Jacobs went over to the Berkeley, Gibbons formed an orchestra which later included Rudy Starita on the xylophone, Maurice Elwin as the vocalist, and Geraldo's twin brother, Sid Bright, at the other piano. In a relaxed moment to amuse a friend he wrote *On the Air* which was to become his signature tune right to the end.

Throughout the 'twenties it was rare to see fewer than seven or eight hundred people, in full evening dress, dining and dancing every night at the Savoy. Early one morning in 1925, a squad of seventy men quietly laid the world's largest carpet in the foyer and restaurant before breakfast. It covered an area of half an acre and weighed over 21 tons. Experts were specially brought over from Samarkand to wed the sixty oriental rugs into one piece.

Against a backcloth of tailcoats and gardenias, and with Lanvin and Lelong sending hemlines and waistlines dizzily up and down, the Turkey Trot yielded to the fox trot and, before long, the Eton crops and cummerbunds were jigging to the livelier Charleston and the Black Bottom. However, nobody at the hotel regretted the end of the vogue for flapper frocks each of which shed an average of twenty beads during an evening. The dance floor had to be ironed smooth every morning after the splintered glass was cleared. The havoc from stiletto heels was yet to come.

There was a clamour for still hotter music which was supplied by visitors like Gus Arnheim and his Californian Cocoanut Grove Orchestra and Fred Elizalde, a charming young man who had made a sensation at Cambridge with his undergraduate band, the Quinquaginta Ramblers. The son of a Spanish sugar magnate, Elizalde had studied under Ravel, composed a symphony at the age of eleven and performed before the King of Spain a year later. His family would have preferred him to follow a commercial career but, after an unsatisfying session studying Law at Stanford, he made his way to the night club pianos off Broadway where he was discovered by Paul Whiteman. This cost him an allowance of £150 a week from his father.

He stayed eighteen months at the Savoy, bringing with him Chelsea Quealy, the trumpeter, and other famous jazz musicians who had played with leading bands like the Californian Ramblers. Among his vocalists was the very popular South African, Al Bowlly, later to be killed in London's blitz. They served fresh and very lively music with some highly polished solos by Elizalde whose piano was tuned half a tone lower than the two others. No expense was spared to present this orchestra as a symbol of super-sophisticated entertainment. The musicians used to sit on a platform turreted like a medieval castle and painted in red, gold and silver. Elizalde himself was soon the darling of London Society and brought huge nightly bookings to the restaurant. For his opening appearance, Mrs. Louis Oppenheimer gave a dinner party for 120 guests and presented him with laurel wreaths, but Elizalde began to grow weary of the glitter and ultimately returned to his first love. Some years later he was back at the hotel, this time as a guest in one of the best river suites. For many hours every day he practised for an Albert Hall recital at which he performed his own Piano Concerto.

Geraldo came to the Savoy in 1930 as a companion band to the more sedate but very popular Orpheans. During the 'twenties there had already been various flirtations with tango music which the Prince of Wales particularly liked. At one time the dance became such a rage that tango teas started at the hotel and some hostesses in search of novelty even gave tango breakfasts, with sleek-haired professionals gliding between the kidneys and savoury omelettes for 100-guinea fees. A special orchestra came over from Deauville and a handsome young dancer, M. Max, was engaged at an enormous fee to demonstrate intricate steps like the Scissor, long and short. He used to ride in Rotten Row and then drive his Rolls-Royce back to the Savoy where his luggage included 120 pairs of shoes.

Although popular, nobody had eyes for him when another young man took the floor. This was the film idol, Rudolph Valentino, whose sinuous grace and almost perfect profile caused equal havoc among matrons and their daughters. In his case, however, silence was indeed golden since his voice proved unpleasantly reedy and emasculate. Instead of hissing languorous sweet-nothings, he would talk endlessly about his collection of swords, guns and 17th century plaques of which he was fanatically proud.

Geraldo played not only tangos but an exciting variety of other Latin-American rhythms suited to the new longer dresses and the craze for Spanish fans. His music, absolutely authentic in style, pioneered the rumba in Europe. Seeing the handsome olive-skinned leader in his gaily-coloured *gaucho* costume, diplomats from the Argentine and Brazil used to greet him warmly as a fellow-countryman. They were surprised by his understandable reluctance to speak their language, as was the Prince of Wales on one hilarious occasion.

The London-born son of a master tailor, Gerald Bright had studied music as a boy and played the piano for a time in an Old Kent Road cinema. After several jobs in drapery and insurance he became restless and decided to go out to Brazil and take up coffee planting. Instead, he became fascinated by the local dance rhythms. On his return to England he formed his own band and played at the Majestic Hotel, St. Anne's, where he made several broadcasts. In those days his singer had to go to the centre of the lounge, climb a step-ladder and croon into the solitary microphone.

With some audacity he applied to the Savoy for an engagement and was given a month's trial. He was determined to introduce the Latin-American style but there was then such a shortage of musicians who could play it that he scoured Soho and Archer Street before at last scraping an orchestra together. Many of them could play only by ear but Geraldo, like Carroll Gibbons, was a gifted arranger and managed to drill them into a programme that passed the audition.

The month's probation hardened into an engagement lasting ten years. Geraldo made some two thousand broadcasts which brought an avalanche of fan mail. One elderly admirer liked the lilting romantic music so much that she used to send him and his men a hundred carnations every week.

While the Savoy was establishing its reputation for lively contemporary music, others were not inactive. From Richard Collet, the director who divided his time between the D'Oyly Carte Opera Company and arranging bands and entertainment for the hotel, Reeves-Smith heard frank and slightly disconcerting reports of competition from the May Fair and the Cecil who were also providing dance music. Inevitably, the glamour and radio monopoly enjoyed by the Savoy was being challenged by the very polished orchestras of Jack Hylton, Roy Fox, Jack Payne and several others; while from the United States came high-prestige touring combinations led by Whiteman and Vincent Lopez.

Preoccupied with maintaining the Savoy's prestige and service, Reeves-Smith was not at first sensitive to this challenge but became concerned when his restaurant and grill-room managers confirmed that regular supper-time visitors were finding certain clubs a rival attraction. Luigi Naintre, himself a Savoy graduate, had first taken over Romano's and then moved to the Criterion before finally opening the Embassy in Bond Street where he ruled Society with a rod of velvet. His club, gay and luxurious, was becoming like an annexe of the Royal Enclosure, with the Prince of Wales and his brother, George, almost nightly patrons, while London's sophisticates spread ecstatic reports about the cuisine and Ambrose's music.

Luigi enjoyed only a few years of his deserved success, and died suddenly one night on his way home from the club. His working schedule was phenomenal even by the exacting standards of a profession notorious for its tradition of hard labour. He would leave the Embassy at 2 a.m. and be in the market four hours later, selecting luxury foods. By noon he used to be back in Bond Street, looking fresher and more debonair than most of his members.

Into the lively Kit Kat in Haymarket eager guests crowded to see American stars like Ted Lewis, Sophie Tucker and the glittering orchidaceous Dolly Sisters, who soon enslaved and helped to bankrupt Gordon Selfridge. Already there was riverside and chic entertainment at the Château Madrid and the Hungaria Club at Maidenhead. All these places were beginning to provide expensive and exciting cabaret acts between dances, an innovation first introduced to London by Sir Francis Towle at his Hotel Metropole where the Midnight Follies included 'Whispering' Jack Smith.

The Savoy, however, pioneered this type of entertainment on a scale never before seen in Europe. To a man of Reeves-Smith's fastidious and civilized taste, revue acts between courses seemed almost a blasphemy, but he had swiftly appreciated the appeal of cabaret. As always he showed a remarkable anticipation of public taste and nobody moved faster once he had decided on policy. Without hesitation he authorized Collet to find the most gifted acts in the world at whatever the cost. The first to be engaged were the Two Black Crows, followed by many other international stars, including the dazzling Can Can dancers from the Bal Tabarin. At thé dansants Victor Silvester and partner demonstrated the newest dance steps to Carroll Gibbons's music, with Christopher Stone as compère.

For an hotel with the Savoy's reputation it was not enough to engage stars with cosmopolitan appeal; they had to twinkle in a setting with which no other hotel or club could compete. Walking into the restaurant one morning on his way from the General Manager's office to his own, Reeves-Smith pointed with his cane to the new £25,000 ballroom and said briskly, "That floor should go up." He explained what he had in mind and the astonished engineers set about preparing plans. It was decided to raise the floor 2 ft. 3 ins. above the ordinary level so that hundreds of diners, wherever they sat, would have a clear and undisturbed view of the cabaret. Suspended on springs and bolts, the 16-ton floor could be operated hydraulically from the basement. It was made from 9,200 pieces of long-seasoned Balkan oak, reinforced by Oregon pine and baked for several days in special ovens to make it unsplinterable and resistant to temperature changes. 400 sq. yds. in area, it would support 250 tons of dancers. The new floor took over six months to make, the actual installation being completed in six nights after the diners and dancers had gone. It was achieved by a series of 'dress rehearsals' on a vacant plot near the Savoy so that, when the moment arrived for the final installation, not a single unnecessary screw needed to be turned.

Meanwhile, apart from reputable places like the Embassy and the Kit Kat, there was a rash of dubious clubs and later bottle-parties which particularly attracted the younger set despite their exorbitant prices for liquor and 'cover-charges'. Mrs. Kate Meyrick, always dressed in demure black—"I'm the mother-in-law of two peers, dear"—was driven time and again in her limousine from her notorious 43 Club in Gerrard Street to the dock at Marlborough Street.

The usually equable Reeves-Smith was angered by licensing laws which invited such scandalous evasion. In America he had seen the social havoc caused by speakeasies and bootleg liquor but remained tactful when a reporter demanded his views on Prohibition. "I think you have the best water in the world," he joked. He was nonetheless aware that American tourists were not taking kindly to our rigid drinking hours after their own irritations at home. On his many trips to the Continent during which he constantly added to the Savoy's priceless stocks of wines housed under the Thames in the crypts of the old Palace, he could not but envy the freedom which foreign hotels and restaurants all seemed to enjoy. In his own hotel he felt humiliated by restrictions which resulted in an undignified scramble, almost like closing-time in a gin palace, while the bottle-parties or 'pirates', as he called them, could flout the laws in dimly-lit cellars between 10 p.m. and 5 next morning, charging £4 10s. for a bottle of doubtful Scotch and 4s. for a glass of ginger ale. Simply by filling in a form, 'members' ordered their drinks in advance and played ring o' roses round the licensing laws. To redress this grotesque situation, he began almost a one-man crusade. As Chairman of the Hotels and Restaurants Association of Great Britain, he had already impressed the Royal Commission on Licensing with the need for reform. Now he was exposing yet another weakness in the law, the bottle-party. Year after year, he put the case for hoteliers and restaurant-owners constantly harassed by cranks.

"The hotel de luxe is still classed for licensing purposes as a public house," he reminded the Government tartly. When a member of the Royal Commission had sarcastically asked him to define a bona fide meal, he replied, "One which is not taken as an excuse for getting drunk."

At this time, on the eve of the 'thirties, other and more pressing problems had to be faced. On the surface all seemed well. A sense of euphoria lingered over the hotel like a chic and discreet perfume. The restless party-giving, party-taking Jazz Age was roaring to its close, leaving scarcely a mark on the Savoy's patina of elegance. The limousines still curved gracefully round the courtyard which, in 1929, was completely reconstructed to the designs of Sir Howard Robertson, R.A. The pavements leading to the hotel from the Strand were now sheltered by awnings of steel and glass, protecting visitors from the hazards of London weather. The old flying arch spanning the roadway was replaced by a beam of polished steel over which the gilt statue of Count Peter was preserved. Seven plaques round the courtyard would henceforth commemorate the ancient Palace and its historic site. At the same time, the adjoining theatre and the façade of Savoy Court were refaced to harmonize with the marquise of the hotel entrance. Aptly enough, Lord Dewar was present at the reopening ceremony and proudly recalled being the first tenant of Savoy Court.

The Grill was extended to take in a comfortable foyer, while the cedar walls of the Pinafore Room, studded with silver buttons, were reflected in a new floor of cherry, myrtle and ebony. Thousands of tons of paint were used in the redecoration of the hotel, apart from a vast mass of equipment which was again pre-assembled nearby and installed at incredible speed. Each with its own colour scheme, fifty new bathrooms were built through which artificial sunshine could be flooded by pressing a button.

The hotel's balance sheet was satisfactory. Shareholders, unaware of the depression soon to come, seemed at peace with a dividend which had climbed steadily. If some grumbled that too much was being ploughed back into Reserve or drained by never-ceasing improvements, they were silenced by Reeves-Smith who had the backing of his Board and could produce convincing arguments. He had no difficulty in persuading his fellow-directors that profits would only be maintained if the Savoy kept ahead and made itself as self-supporting as possible.

That policy has been confirmed and reinforced through the years. With a luxury palace of several hundred rooms, catering to the tastes and whims of a critical international clientèle, the possibilities of disruption are obvious. Even the finest limousine comes to a standstill when petrol pumps are sealed or spare parts not readily to hand. The Savoy's answer was a perfectly-geared mechanism operated from the centre, ranging from a private press for printing the hotel's menus to a roasting plant which today not only supplies coffee to guests but ships three-quarters of a ton of the special blend each month to customers all over the world.

The Savoy became the first hotel in Europe to be air-conditioned and to Vita-glaze its windows to admit ultra-violet rays. Equipped with its own 2-megawatt power station, and oil-fuelled since 1930 to avoid too heavy a reliance on precarious coal supplies, it now produces 200 million pounds of steam per year, apart from serving a refrigeration plant which supplies up to six tons of ice daily. Deep wells had long been sunk to produce half a million gallons of London's softest water on a peak day.

Since 1921, the hotel's laundry at Clapham has handled a vast quantity of sheets, pink table-cloths and napkins, apart from the guests' frilled shirts, silks and lace. With an army of upholsterers, painters, decorators, plumbers, carpet-layers, carpenters and bricklayers swiftly recruited from the hotel's own resources,

Piping in the haggis has become a Savoy tradition on St. Andrew's night

The raised stage. Operated hydraulically from the basement, the four hundred square yard dance floor can be lifted twenty seven inches from floor level to give diners a perfect view of the cabaret

A triumphant Suzy Volterra drinks champagne to celebrate Phil Drake's victory at Epsom. Derby Night parties are usually given by winning owners and cakes and floral arrangements made in their racing colours

Above, for one of the Maharajah of Patiala's dinner-parties, elephants and camels carved from ice were laden with pineapples and other fruits
Below, the Nawab of Bahawalpur and his party arrive on Coronation Night for 'The Ball of the Century'

Elaborate table decorations and the finest crystal and silver in Europe adorn the tables for a private banquet in the Mirror Room (now the Abraham Lincoln Room). For Edwardian gastronomes, a ten-course menu with the rarest delicacies was customary

the décor of a suite or reception room can be smoothly re-planned, and any upholstery or furniture repaired, by expert craftsmen on the premises. The Savoy soon decided to make its own mattresses, and some of the clients have found the beds so comfortable that often they ask to have them shipped over to the United States or India. The management has usually shown reluctance to export such an obvious attraction.

Reeves-Smith's ideal, in which he was fully supported by the Board, was to make the hotel a centre of relaxed elegance, unexcelled for food and service. From foyer to roof, each of its thirty and more departments had therefore to become a smooth-running unit. The smallest items of maintenance would henceforth be speedily handled, from oiling a lock to rewiring an entire electrical system. All the Irish linen was to be woven to specification, with the finest china and glass made specially for the hotel and ordered direct from carefully selected manufacturers, prepared for hundreds of replacements every month. From the early days of Ritz and Escoffier, it had quickly become clear that requirements in the luxury field could not best be guaranteed on a day-to-day competitive basis. Wines have long since been bought direct from the growers, while comestibles and scores of other quality goods are ordered from firms who have served the hotel for generations.

Every floor is now self-contained and staffed by a housekeeper with a squad of waiters, valets, chambermaids and cleaners. Bedrooms lead into a marble bathroom, complete with telephone, with half a dozen fine linen face towels changed daily, and a variety of hard and soft bath towels. The sitting-rooms are furnished with Louis Seize escritoires and gold-nibbed pens, and the most stylishly ornamental mirrors blend into a décor adaptable to a guest's personal taste.

It has long been routine to switch furniture at a moment's notice, to supply a perfectly-tuned piano for a composer or a lectern for an author who suffered from sciatica. When one artist wished to have his sitting-room made into a temporary studio, the conversion was done while he was at lunch. Dust covers were neatly laid over the carpet and the Works Department at once supplied trestles, easels and improved lighting.

As soon as a suite is vacated, the housekeeper carries out a meticulous inspection for the smallest damage to carpets, sheets or furniture by burns and stains. It is now almost ritual to close a whole floor of the Savoy once a year for redecoration and cleaning, an operation completed in ten days.

All this unremitting attention to detail has had to be achieved with unobtrusive efficiency. One can understand the astonishment of an American visitor, H. Ridgeley Bullock, Jr., who once arrived at breakfast time, unshaven and bleary-eyed after a rough night flight. In the foyer with its blazing log fire, ormolu clocks, easy chairs and thick beige carpet, waiters in tails and reception clerks in morning dress were moving about with a smiling unflurried calm. There was no evidence of the showcases and arcades which confront visitors at almost all luxury hotels. "I walked into the lobby and there were all these elegant-looking guys standing around," he recalls. "I thought, someone's had a helluva party here last night. Why don't the guests go home?"

The house-party effect was subtly created even before the guests registered. Convoys of trunks and pigskin cases purred majestically to and from the boat trains. Before air travel became popular, guests never arrived without evening dress and an extensive wardrobe for every social emergency. Some brought fifteen or more trunks, and few who disembarked from their Cunard staterooms had baggage standing less than four feet high on the quay. At Plymouth and Southampton the hotel's representatives were at hand to meet guests and help them through routine formalities, a service which often began on board the liners at Cherbourg. From the earliest days of air travel, the Savoy was the first hotel to have its own reception and couriers at the London airports, today a large organization.

On a business trip to the United States in 1927, Reeves-Smith was invited to make his headquarters at the Ambassador Hotel where he was an honoured guest. On his initiative a Savoy office had already been established in New York to maintain profitable contact with American travel bureaux, hotels and steamship companies. Its success inspired others to follow, if not on the same scale.

At this time Wall Street was still in a gay spiral, as many as two hundred hotel guests often decanting from a single liner. Long-stemmed roses, camellias and orchids glowed in the florist's boutique at the Savoy. Behind the scenes, girls wired countless bouquets and fashioned table decorations in the shape of ships, speedboats, airliners and regimental badges; a kangaroo of roses and carnations was even created for one Australian dinner.

An exquisite and most romantic request came from a young man on his honeymoon. For the double-bed in his suite he asked for a cover to be made entirely from the bride's favourite flowers; roses and lilies of the valley. The couple's initials were florally entwined, with their wedding date delicately picked out in tiny blossoms.

In the hairdressing salon celebrities were shaved, shorn and anointed. Clients would have costly pomades sent to their homes in faraway Texas and even Tokyo. One Indian prince used to order a dozen bottles of hair lotion at a time, assuring the manager that his servants found it truly excellent for riding boots. A £5 tip was commonplace for the manicurists who included a pretty French girl later to achieve literary fame as Mrs. Robert Henrey. Sometimes the staff received excellent Stock Exchange tips; in charge of number two chair, John Rose once made £250 from a whisper about a textile company passed on by a friendly client.

Sir Charles Higham, the publicity genius who first made Americans drink tea, was among many grateful guests who have remembered favourite waiters in their wills. He always had the same table in the Grill where the staff could set their watches by his appearances every day for lunch at one, with dinner sharp at 7.30. Invariably he left the choice of food and wine to his waiter. For him the Savoy was a second home and the management once found a unique occasion to serve him. His son was taken ill suddenly and the hotel doctor advised an immediate operation. As every moment counted, Sir Charles would not risk having the boy taken to a nursing home. The manager was summoned and at once arranged to have a large room converted into an operating theatre. A distinguished surgeon arrived with an entourage of nurses and an anaesthetist. The operation was performed in the soundproof, air-conditioned room and proved a complete success.

Between the wars the daily house-list was always rich, varied and cosmopolitan. Sandwiched between *Debrett*, *Who's Who* and New York's *Social Register*, it offered a remarkable cross-section of the most celebrated statesmen, lawyers, bankers, men of letters and theatrical stars under one roof. Sinclair Lewis started work on *Dodsworth* while awaiting the arrival of his bride, Dorothy Thompson, whom he married in the Savoy Chapel following a Register Office ceremony. After a gay wedding luncheon with Rebecca West, Hugh Walpole and Anita Loos among the guests, the couple left on their honeymoon in one of the largest and most luxurious caravans ever seen in these islands. Often so many French delegations were staying at the hotel that the staff referred to the best river suites as 'the Quai d'Orsay'. Daladier always asked for turbot braised in Burgundy and was one of many countrymen who used to send for Latry and congratulate him. The great maître-chef was later rewarded with the Legion of Honour for his devotion to *la grande cuisine*.

Night after night the private banqueting room were engaged by every kind of Club, solemn or frivolous. Zavattoni and the restaurant chefs took endless pains. At one reunion dinner for twelve naval officers, the centre of the oval table was dressed to represent a miniature sea on which floated models of cruisers, torpedo boats and destroyers surrounded by icebergs. Sea water was brought up from the coast and dyed extra blue. For this occasion Latry devised a salad made from chrysanthemum petals, sprinkled with spiced oil and served with the quails.

Latry always spent his holidays at home in France where his

mother, herself a *cordon bleu*, kept the Hotel Bellevue at Gex near Lake Geneva, only three miles from the birthplace of Brillat-Savarin. He rarely came back without some of her well-tried recipes which he would adapt to the Savoy menus. Like Escoffier he always enjoyed a challenge. To celebrate the centenary of Carême, Talleyrand's pastry-cook and later *chef des cuisines* to the Prince Regent and the Baronne de Rothschild, the Food and Wine Society in London arranged a commemorative dinner. As this fell on Shrove Tuesday, Latry created *crêpes du Mardi Gras*, pancakes thin as sixpenny-pieces, stuffed with butter sauce and flavoured with Kirsch. His friendly genius also initiated a pleasant tradition that still persists at the Savoy. On Shrove Tuesday the Restaurant's master-chef personally cooks a pancake and serves it to his youngest *commis* who in turn makes them for all the other chefs. A glass of good wine from the hotel's cellars is the ritual accompaniment.

When two of Latry's French friends arrived in London with their new-born baby, they were welcomed with the largest Easter egg ever made at the Savoy. For many days the pastrycooks had prepared a huge chocolate sphere inside which rested a full-sized baby's cradle. Latry was meanwhile at work on the order of a wealthy German industrialist who had demanded sixteen Easter eggs of identical size and appearance. Fifteen of them were for his dinner guests, the other reserved for his wife. Inside its chocolate shell were tiny hooks and pulleys so that, when she pulled a small tab, the egg fell open and a jewel casket slid out. The 'yolk' was a magnificent diamond pendant surrounded by a fortune in uncut gems.

At a dinner party attended by King Alfonso, Latry offered strawberries prepared in the Spanish fashion with quartered oranges. The liqueur was in the royalist colours. Guests arriving for supper after first nights at the Ballet were served *blinis*, *bortsch* and other Russian native dishes. The first Scotch salmon of the season was sent down to the Savoy with special canisters of Tay water to bring out its flavour, and the season's earliest spring mushrooms were always flown in from the French Alps.

In those lavish days it was commonplace to serve a portion of three woodcocks of which two were used for the magnificent sauce alone. Examining his bill after one princely dinner, a guest grumbled, "Everything at the Savoy is French except the prices; they are tropical and grow to a great height."

The remark was reported back to Reeves-Smith who commented urbanely, "The Savoy is expensive, but not *dear*."

6   The Savoy Grill

PEOPLE IN Show Business, whatever their standing, always have
a strong addiction to 'shop' talk and sentiment. They laugh, cry
and kiss very easily. With its bitter-sweet intimacies, its gaiety
and intrigues, the milieu seems to demand a semi-public Green
Room. Restaurants like Sardi's and Delmonico's in New York
and the Ivy and Caprice in London have become fashionable in
turn, but from the end of the 1914 war the Savoy Grill has
remained unchallenged as the almost official rendezvous of all the
leading stars, impresarios and critics. When that genial cynic,
Alan Melville, was once asked how you could tell whether or not
your new play was a success, he quipped, "It's simple; when the
management invites the author during the *second* interval to
supper at the Savoy."

Apart from veterans like A. P. Herbert and Noël Coward,
the faces and names have changed but the atmosphere surprisingly
little. It remains flippant, chic, professional and sentimental. The
air is nostalgic with reminiscence or charged with the adrenalin
of a new hit. Through the years one sees the same phalanx of
fast-talking and heavy-lidded agents, all looking surprisingly like
Oscar Levant; the massaged cheeks of the big producers permanently tanned by sun or lamp; wispy new authors, composers
and dress designers nervously trying to catch the right eye;
starlets perched on a spindly talent and wearing sables from the
studio wardrobe; bullet-proof blondes with eyes that have
covered much mileage; and always the current gods and goddesses
of the theatre and cinema backing gracefully into the limelight.

127

There are minor and superficial changes in style; dark glasses are in and out of favour; the hatted and unhatted fight their battles; proteins and vitamins enjoy their season while régimes, ranging from yoga to yoghourt, claim disciples. The emphasis has usually been on slimming, although this was carried rather far in the 'twenties when busts were strapped and even adhesively taped to ensure the flat and modish 'débutante slouch'. A sudden change came when C. B. Cochran was preparing his *1929 Revue*. With his instinct for publicity, he announced dramatically that some of his lovely Young Ladies were fainting during rehearsal as a result of over-slimming. Sir William Arbuthnot Lane drew up special food charts, rich in calories, and for weeks Virlogeux and his staff were sending up rich puddings and pastries. Curves and chocolates were back. When the fad passed, the theatrical world returned to its traditional oysters, pink champagne and almost anything *flambé*. Above all, its unchanging meat and drink is gossip of salaries, agents, tours, rehearsals and run-of-the-play contracts, while notes and kisses flit between the tables like butterflies. Here nobody knows everybody, but everybody knows somebody.

Between the two wars the Savoy grill-room had a plethora of gay after-theatre suppers and first nights. Pinter, Wesker and Osborne were as yet unborn; it was caviare, not chips, with everything for playwrights like Ivor Novello and Noël Coward. Every new film or play was launched like a battleship, with champagne crashing against the side and orchids as plentiful as *canapés*. The Widow Clicquot bobbed in every other ice bucket.

On first nights the Grill seemed almost an annexe of the star's dressing-room. The gentle softly-spoken Manetta never forgot an actress's favourite flowers, while the inspired, but publicity-shy, Virlogeux always conspired with his pastry-cooks to create a special cake or some lavish dessert with the new play or film as its motif. This gifted maître-chef could also be a terrifying figure, huge and burly, with heavy bags under sharp eyes that became almost steely if his staff seemed to fail him. He had been at the Grill since 1923 after previous service at the Metropole in Monte

Carlo, the Crillon in Paris and the Metropole in Moscow, before the Revolution. Many, including his *sous-chef* and successor Alban, owed much to his gastronomic mastery.

Waiters had always to be more than tactful and attentive after first nights, when nerves rose and fell like a soufflé. They would follow the fortunes of new plays and films with all the devotion of racing punters. Often they were invited to dress-rehearsals or given seats for second nights and matinées.

While corks popped and telegrams were ripped open, a play's author, stars, producer and 'angels' would be at peak voltage. Behind the smiles and kisses lay a smouldering anxiety about the Critics, and always the eternal wait until a spry little page entered with the early morning papers in his newly-starched gloves. They would pass from hand to hand in ecstasy or despair. Not for many hours would the liturgy of praise, complaint and might-have-beens end over the coffee, curly rashers and grilled kidneys.

Nobody was more feared than Hannen Swaffer who stalked the grill-room, day and night, wearing a high collar, Victorian cravat and the eternal cigarette-end on his lower lip. As London's most influential dramatic critic, he had a captive audience at every table, clamped by his nasal monologue. None escaped his flow of advice, criticism and often encouragement. Even a non-stop talker like A. E. Matthews would be stricken dumb. Typical of Swaffer was his much-quoted remark, "Oh yes, I knew the old King was beginning to break up, you know. He failed to recognize me at his last Garden Party." He delighted in twitting the mighty, not excluding his newspaper bosses. This was his public way of asserting independence, particularly when he had accepted too many drinks. (In later years, he would become a complete teetotaller.) One night he was making his usual round of foyer, American Bar, grill-room and restaurant when he saw Lord Beaverbrook, Lloyd George and the first Lord Rothermere supping together and obviously in serious conference. "Look," he muttered to an American fellow-journalist, "there's Beaverbrook pretending to listen to Ll.G. but hatching a political plot. Rothermere is wondering how much his investments will be affected by what Ll.G. is saying. Now, my old chief, Northcliffe, wouldn't have been seen dead with Ll.G. in public." He plucked at his cravat, lit another cigarette and waved off-handedly to Frederick Lonsdale in one circular motion. "If Ll.G. had wanted to see him he'd have had to call at *The Times* office and been kept waiting twenty minutes to cool off."

The next evening he was dining as the guest of Lord Beaverbrook whom he privately admired, more especially after they parted company. The host turned to Valentine Castlerosse and asked him for a shilling to tip the cloakroom attendant. "Just like Northcliffe," commented Swaffer in a stage-whisper. "He never had any money on him, either. Only a millionaire can go around without a bob in his pocket." Not that Lord Beaverbrook could ever be fairly accused of stinginess, particularly towards friends like Castlerosse who loved to tease him with preposterous bills and, on a celebrated occasion during a water shortage at Cannes, ordered eight hundred bottles of Vichy to fill his bath.

One night Swaffer stopped to harangue Somerset Maugham who was trying to eat a quiet chop. Swaffer remarked that he had just met a woman upstairs who was wearing three wedding rings. She had confided to him that she never travelled without her three bridal dresses and photographs of each wedding group.

"I'll make a play about that one day," stammered Maugham.

"No you won't, Willy," rejoined Swaffer. "I've just 'phoned it through as a paragraph to my paper."

Some of his victims suffered in silence, but not all. When he announced one day that he was on his way to have his hair cut, a very brave actor murmured, "Don't forget to have your heels shaved." An American actress, Lilian Foster, took more direct reprisals. With all his faults, 'Swaff' always considered it his public duty to speak out honestly about plays and leave faint praise to more cautious scribes. Miss Foster opened in *Conscience* at the Little with a performance which had apparently tempted him to rush out of the theatre. He wrote, "In the play the man murdered his wife to save her from a life of shame. I prefer to think it was her affected baby voice which reminded me of a ventriloquist's doll."

He was lunching in the grill-room when his victim walked in, made straight for his table and slapped his face. He called for the head waiter but, before he arrived, Miss Foster had administered another resounding slap as an encore. This famous incident ended in farce. Swaffer relished the publicity and promptly invited Carnera to join him as his bodyguard at first nights. Very soon every gossip-hungry or unemployed actress took to the slapping habit. While Tallulah Bankhead was enjoying her lunch, a woman rushed over, slapped her and tore off her hat. Tallulah lit a cigarette and murmured huskily to her companion Sir Gerald du Maurier, "What were you sayin', dahlin'?"

Swaffer had a kindlier side to his nature. Among those who had wilted under his pen was Ivor Novello, not yet a matinée idol and anxious to make his way to Hollywood. He found himself sitting one day at the next table to D. W. Griffith, a director he much admired, then in London for the première of *Orphans of the Storm*. Puffing nervously at cigarettes after his usual large helpings of ice-cream, Novello was too shy to introduce himself.

He was walking out of the grill-room past Swaffer's usual corner table when the critic beckoned him back with the inseparable cigarette butt. Apparently he had dropped a friendly word in Griffith's ear and now urged Novello to follow up without delay. It was sound advice. The actor telephoned Griffith at the Savoy and duly called on him. Griffith walked up and down the room studying Novello's cameo features, and later confided to his friends that the young Welshman could be a rival to Richard Barthelmess and even Valentino. He promised enthusiastically to cable if a suitable part offered itself.

Months passed before word came inviting Novello to leave at once to star in *The White Rose* opposite Mae Marsh. The picture, directed by Griffith, helped to make him a box-office sensation in America where he was acclaimed as a Greek god with the most

131

sensational profile since Francis X. Bushman. His one embarrassment was the film company's publicity campaign to invent a violent romance between Gladys Cooper and himself.

Swaffer was not the only London critic whose pen could make or break a play between the wars. James Agate made an enemy of Olivier among others by his churlish habit of always returning, late and unsteady from the bar, after the first act. In the Grill, supping off turtle soup, Gruyère and a pint of Bollinger, he became more relaxed and often entertaining, with a stream of gossip that was either derisive or adulatory. Even more feared was St. John Ervine whose many scalps included that of Sir Patrick Hastings. The great advocate was a busy part-time playwright and became one of the Grill's regular patrons. In his early days he had known hardship and never forgot the time when he had to stuff his boots with newspapers to keep out the wet. Often he had trudged past the Savoy on his way to peddle articles and stories in Fleet Street, and the hotel became a glittering success symbol in his mind. "I hankered most of all for a dinner at the Savoy," he once recalled. "That feeling has never entirely left me." As one of the most highly-paid K.C.s at the Bar, he could easily indulge that taste and his big mahogany Hispano-Suiza became a familiar sight in the Savoy forecourt.

He was always happiest and most relaxed in theatrical company. One day he was walking back from lunch in the hotel with Tallulah Bankhead, wearing her usual uniform of mink and slacks. In Seven Dials they were accosted by an urchin who offered to stand on his head for sixpence. Tallulah promptly volunteered to do it at half-price. Sir Patrick handed her a threepenny bit, and she then advanced into the middle of the road and performed to perfection. The small boy gladly accepted sixpence and fled.

Alec Rea had put on Sir Patrick's play *Scotch Mist* at the St. Martin's. After the opening performance, the author supped gaily in the Grill with his leading man, Godfrey Tearle, and later joined a party which Lord Beaverbrook was giving for the other star, Tallulah. But the champagne seemed very flat next morning when St. John Ervine dismissed *Scotch Mist* as "the worst play

I have ever seen". Despite this the House Full boards soon went up, thanks to a violent pulpit attack by the Bishop of London.

The play was only one of Tallulah's many triumphs during her tumultuous eight years in the West End, when she was idolized by gallery girls who would queue in the street for thirty hours before opening nights. Once again the Savoy Grill had played a part in theatrical history. Cochran first met Tallulah at a New York party where she did her devastating impersonation of Ethel Barrymore. Back in London, he lunched with Sir Gerald du Maurier at the Savoy and sang her praises. Rather apathetically, the actor-manager agreed to try her out in a new play. Shortly afterwards he changed his plans and Cochran at once sent a cable, urging her to stay at home. Tallulah characteristically ignored the advice, borrowed a letter of credit for $1,000 from an old family friend, General Coleman du Pont, and sailed grandly for England.

Sir Gerald, charmingly apologetic, explained that he was already rehearsing another girl, but his 'pumice stone voice', in Cecil Beaton's apt phrase, left her in no doubt that she had wasted the general's dollars on a one-way ticket. That evening, in deep-dyed gloom which no number of Martinis could dissolve, she dined with Cochran and his wife who tried to console her. Out of the blue, Evelyn Cochran asked if Du Maurier had seen her without a hat.

The following evening she was back in his dressing-room, displaying her spectacularly blonde hair. Du Maurier stared admiringly while his daughter, Daphne, breathed an aside, "Daddy, that's the most beautiful girl I ever saw in my life." Tallulah was promptly engaged to play in the melodrama *The Dancers* at thirty pounds a week. It ran for nearly a year during which the actress she had replaced was paid her contract salary of £50 a week and even had time to have a baby!

Scarcely a day passed when Tallulah's husky alto-sax was not heard in the Savoy Grill at luncheon or supper, often both. Her inseparable companion was 'Bea' Lillie, as slim and vital as an

133

exclamation mark under her skull-cap. They insulted each other, drank together and commuted gaily between parties at Tallulah's house in Farm Street and Lady Peel's suite at the hotel.

At this time only two people in England were instantly identified by their Christian names: Tallulah and the champion jockey, Steve. Her diamonds flashed at every party in London; her private life, often distorted by gossip, was never off the lurid front pages. Most of all she enjoyed the parties given by Lord Beaverbrook who would waggishly decline to confirm or deny frequent reports that they were engaged. "When the occasion called for an outsized rout," she recalls in her brilliant auto-biography, "Max would hire a couple of private rooms at the Savoy, bring in an orchestra and such headliners as Sophie Tucker and Rudolph Valentino."

Ethel Barrymore was only one of her many victims. At fancy dress balls she liked to masquerade as Borotra and bounced about in lifelike imitation of his style. Tennis-mad, she would fly to Paris merely to see a single Davis Cup match. After lunching with Bea Lillie in the Grill, they drove off together to Wimbledon. By the time Bea had parked her car and entered the Centre Court, the umpire had given up his seat and Tallulah was expertly croaking the score into the microphone. That night they were back as usual at the Savoy and dancing to Elizalde's inspired jazz, partnered by Tilden, Lacoste and Frank Hunter.

Every evening the stars of the theatre and cinema twinkled in the grill-room. Often the management had to stop the flow of requests for autographs of Noël Coward, Gertrude Lawrence, Gladys Cooper and many more. 'Gee' and 'Bea' were supping together before setting forth for Broadway when a sad admirer sent over a menu on which he had written, "England is losing her Gainsboroughs, her Reynolds and her Lawrences. Alas! Gertrude! Alas! Beatrice!"

While fashionable actors and actresses attracted all the sighs and stares, the true centrepieces were the tables presided over by producers and impresarios like C. B. Cochran. He presented dozens of stars, from Duse to Delysia, hired Chaliapin at £1,250 a performance and, less happily, the temperamental Suzanne Lenglen. Between the pink champagne corks were sundry writs and petitions in bankruptcy, and towards the end he became a pathetic figure, crippled by arthritis in the hip and in professional decline. When he put on his ill-fated *Lights Up* at the Savoy Theatre, the kindly Reeves-Smith presented him with a suite in the hotel for the run of the show.

For over twenty vintage years his table had been a gay and glittering carousel of London's most brilliant talents. Warm in his friendships under the flippant veneer, Noël Coward would always stop for a glass of wine or a bowl of his favourite bouillabaisse, laced with garlic, and talk 'shop' with Cockie. They liked to fondle old triumphs, from *On With the Dance* to the great days of *Bitter Sweet, Private Lives* and the unforgettable *Cavalcade*.

For *This Year of Grace* at the London Pavilion, Coward had written the entire words and music including *Dance, Dance, Little Lady*. Jessie Matthews sang *A Room With a View* with Sonnie Hale whom she afterwards married. Another of Cochran's favourite stars, Evelyn Laye, had divorced Hale, and Manetta was always careful to keep the two ladies as far apart as possible when they chanced to arrive for supper on the same night.

Oliver Messel was another who would never pass the impresario's table without paying his respects. Cochran was telling Arnold Bennett over lunch one day that he had commissioned Gordon Craig to stage a play for him. Bennett shook his head and said bluntly, "Why bother about Craig when you have a real genius in Messel?" Cochran took the hint and engaged the young man for *This Year of Grace*. The result was a brilliant masked number which stopped the show.

Looking around, Cochran returned the greetings of many other gifted young men who had served their apprenticeship with him as composers, writers or designers. They included Beaton, A. P. Herbert, Hartnell, Vivian Ellis and Beverley Nichols.

No supper in the Grill had its true accolade without Noël Coward or Gertie Lawrence. Coward's *bon mots*, always astringent and often self-mocking, were passed round the room like peppermint creams. The first-night party for *Cavalcade* will not soon be forgotten. The play had opened during a period of depression, slump and the 'dole', when national morale was low. It brought a lump into the country's throat, particularly Coward's line, "After all, it's still a pretty exciting thing to be an Englishman." That night there was little need to sit gloomily awaiting the critics. The hardest-boiled of them had stood and cheered through a dozen curtain calls. At the hotel, obviously delighted but still managing to wear his mask of nonchalance, the playwright was swaddled by adoring friends. 'Darlings' fell like confetti, and incense rose high to the ceiling.

Sara Allgood of the Abbey Theatre was one of many who struggled to reach the Master's side. To his surprise, politely concealed as always, she began to chatter about the weather, her health, unemployment, and the state of the box-office in Dublin; indeed, everything but *Cavalcade*. Coward finally wrinkled his eyebrows and asked her what she had thought of the show. "Well, Noël," she replied sweetly, "everyone can say it's tripe if they want to, but I liked it."

Looking back on the period between Versailles and Munich, the grill-room has the luminous quality and glamour of a photograph in soft focus. The spectacular glitter of the theatre was perfectly reflected off-stage by stars like Gertrude Lawrence. Although no beauty, she had a grace of carriage and a magnetism which made every other woman seem a trifle dowdy. She would walk through the Grill, trailing glamour like a cloak. It was always the same, whether she wore a tiara and sables or the simplest frock unredeemed by a single jewel. The Savoy staff loved her. At Christmas she would lead a crocodile of pages, staggering under armfuls of presents for waiters, porters and chambermaids, including their families, whose names and ages she always kept up-to-date in her diary.

Another idol was Alice Delysia whose sequins, sheathed gowns and *panache* decorated some of Cochran's most glittering musicals. Temperamental and the very embodiment of Parisian chic on stage, Delysia lived quietly at the Savoy. From Biarritz her mother wrote practically every other day, reminding her to go to bed early and not forget her hot milk at night.

On one occasion she returned from a tour of Egypt, arriving as usual with over a dozen suitcases and a cabin trunk. Among various pieces of baggage, a wicker basket was taken up to her suite. Before the porter could close the door, the lid lifted slowly. Two large snakes slid out and began to slither along the corridor, flicking very unfriendly tongues. A chambermaid fainted, a waiter called the Reception and suggested an S.O.S. to the Zoo, while a resourceful page applied his sketchy knowledge of hypnotism. Meantime, the porter who had formerly served as valet to a peer and used to accompany him on safaris, rushed to the service room and armed himself with a pair of fire tongs. With considerable delicacy he popped the unpleasant guests back into their baskets, and peace reigned once more on the sixth floor.

Delysia was among many of her compatriots at the Savoy. She chatted with plump volatile Yvonne Arnaud and kissed handsome Carpentier who was passing through on his way to New York to appear in cabaret at £600 a week.

In his river suite Sacha Guitry strutted in a long silk dressing-gown with a gold dragon running down the back, received visitors in the manner of Louis XIV and plied them with champagne and caviare. With his wife Yvonne Printemps, he was then appearing in *Mariette* at His Majesty's, and his skill in edging her into the background while they posed for photographs was a superb piece of theatre in itself.

Mistinguette was another who always gave the Savoy's patrons a star performance. Flashing the famous legs, she would gesticulate violently to show off immense bracelets of emeralds and pearls. One evening, however, she stared open-mouthed when Lady Londonderry swept in, wearing the magnificent amethyst and diamond parure given to Lord Castlereagh by the Tsar Alexander I.

Maurice Chevalier was mobbed whenever he made an appearance. At dinner parties with the French Ambassador or old friends like Adèle Astaire and Jack Buchanan, he laughed and joked but drank only ginger ale, ate little and always plain English food, much to the chagrin of Virlogeux who expected a Frenchman to keep the gastronomic tricolour flying. Chevalier was almost fanatically concerned with physical fitness and his waistline. At the window of his river suite he performed his physical jerks and a deep-breathing régime but struggled to overcome an addiction to fifty cigarettes a day. After smoking one or two after breakfast, he used to fling the tin out of his window. Until he was cured, the happy porters always waited below to share the spoils.

On an earlier visit and before Hollywood had made him an international star, he was flattered when the Grill's head waiter greeted him with a lavish attention which became distinctly cooler when Chevalier was not joined by his more celebrated partner, Mistinguette. She had stayed behind in Paris.

Emlyn Williams would quickly become a regular patron of the grill-room, fêted by managers and actors, but he never forgot his first visit to the hotel when, a very nervous undergraduate down from Oxford for the day, he arrived for a meeting with a most important man of the theatre. "I took the Tube to the Strand and walked to the Savoy . . . watching the people endlessly crossing the Babylonian foyer, velvet with success." After waiting two hours, he had departed, hungry and disconsolate, to eat two buns at an A.B.C. café.

Dietrich, cool and remote as a mannequin, made regal entrances yet disillusioned Manetta and the chefs by occasionally following her caviare and pheasant with a request for suet pudding. Managers and publicity agents loved to see her at *premières* but the cast was far less happy. When she walked in, always a sensational figure, any first scene used to lapse into anti-climax.

Among other beauties who adorned the silk-covered *banquettes* one saw ash-blonde Claire Luce, dining with 'Bunch' Keys; Evelyn Laye, celebrating with Alan Herbert and Max Reinhardt after the opening of *Helen!*; and Jenny Dolly, looking like a Selfridge Christmas tree in sequins and ostrich feathers, often wearing a £50,000 pearl choker with bracelets manacled up to the elbow. Elfin Elisabeth Bergner was in almost permanent conference with J. M. Barrie over *The Boy David* which would prove such an expensive failure for poor Cochran.

None of the professional actresses was lovelier than Lady Diana Cooper who had an experience at the Savoy more familiar to Hollywood extras than the star of Reinhardt's *The Miracle*. After lunching with Morris Gest, the showman responsible for the American production, she took the lift up to his suite and listened to some bubbling advocacy. He was on his way to see Reinhardt in Salzburg and determined to sign this arum-lily beauty for the name part. Mercifully hidden from her were plans which included dressing even the Broadway programme-sellers as nuns. In *The Rainbow Comes and Goes* Lady Diana describes the interview with delightfully wry humour: "He told me to take off my hat and gloves and hold up my skirts. I signed something provisional that I did not read and got a two-dollar bill thrust into my breast for luck."

More accustomed to the rough vigour of show business was Mrs. Patrick Campbell, resembling a cottage loaf draped in black velvet. After a heavy rôle in Ibsen she once sailed into the grill-room under her feathered hat and put away a formidable supper of partridges cooked on charcoal, following it with a huge dish of belladonna pears. Between mouthfuls, she informed an admiring circle of her imminent departure for Hollywood to teach the talkie stars how to speak English.

One catches nostalgic glimpses of many others; shy Flora Robson, reading a new play in her room where she had all her meals alone and shut herself off from letters, telephone calls and even newspapers; Gwen Ffrangcon-Davies, studying the script of *Tess of the D'Urbervilles* while the orchestra played *Tea for Two*; Marie Dressler, slipping into the Savoy Theatre and confiding to the manager that, as a girl back home, she once sang contralto parts in Gilbert and Sullivan and had remained a lifelong admirer of the operas . . . And blonde, much-married Peggy Hopkins Joyce, down to seven stone after a nervous breakdown, knitting a woollen scarf in bed and dosing herself massively with vitamins.

More exuberant and every inch the star was Marion Davies, the snub-nosed and freckled 'flapper' of the films, who was greeted shrilly by scores of friends and hangers-on who had either visited Hearst's baronial San Simeon or hoped to do so. Looking rather like a strawberry ice, she laughed, pouted and made wisecracks in her fetching stammer while downing champagne from a beer tankard. Nobody doubted her affection for William Randolph Hearst but she was obviously enjoying a holiday from that forbidding dictator who never permitted his guests more than one cocktail before dinner and always had paper napkins on the table. Throughout her stay she was pelted with kisses, autograph albums and begging letters.

In the Pinafore Room at a gay farewell supper with turbaned Ethel Levey and Binnie Barnes, Sophie Tucker presided in a beaded frock with four huge mauve orchids on the shoulder after her triumph at the Palladium. At a corner table in the grill-room Michael Arlen argued, as usual, with Frederick Lonsdale. John McCormack would be roaring with laughter while he discussed his records with Louis Sterling, the cigar-smoking gramophone magnate who had once sold newspapers in New York and came to England in a cattle-boat with twenty dollars in his pocket. Both men were generous and hospitable and it became almost a music-hall act when each insisted on paying the bill, always a heavy one. The Irish Caruso had a prodigious thirst. On being asked by someone what he was drinking, he put a finger to his lips and said dreamily, "Mumm's the word." He would keep the wine waiters on the move as he emptied bottle after bottle before walking out, still amazingly erect and steady, to the waiting Rolls-Royce which he changed every year. There was no possibility of mistaking his car among the many others in the forecourt. Attached to the luggage rack was his lucky mascot, a humpbacked black cat in shiny velvet. McCormack would blow kisses or send rude notes over to his friends, the Taubers, Chaliapin or Grace Moore, whom one often saw with her new film partner, Tullio Carminati, eating Latry's *rognons*.

There seemed no end to the parties for first nights, birthdays and long-running play anniversaries. Marie Tempest celebrated her jubilee in a swathe of velvet and, even without a tiara, made all the duchesses look like seaside landladies in the off-season. After the opening of *Excelsior*, Gladys Cooper supped with Ernest Thesiger and emerged to an astonishing scene. Five hundred of her admirers were waiting outside the hotel and the police had to clear a path for her two-seater Rolls. When Maugham gave a cocktail party to the company of *For Services Rendered* his guests included Noël Coward, Gerald du Maurier and H. G. Wells. He could not reach them, however, being pinioned to the wall by Lady Oxford who was explaining in the grisliest detail precisely what was wrong with his play.

The wedding breakfasts and luncheons are too numerous to list but one, in particular, had an amusing and unexpected sequel. When Florence Desmond married the pilot and insurance broker, Charles Hughesdon, it became an all-star occasion. Clive Brook gave the bride away, Elizabeth Allan was maid of honour and her husband, Bill O'Bryen, the best man. After a gay reception at the Savoy, the newly-weds went off to honeymoon at the Eden Roc Hotel, having warned the management in advance that there was to be no publicity of any kind. Alas, Carroll Gibbons and his orchestra happened to be there on a holiday engagement and promptly struck up *The Wedding March* as the couple slipped into the dining-room.

Rivalling Cochran's entourage was the table over which Alexander Korda presided with such wistful charm. There was no more generous or fascinating host. From making quota 'quickies' he had graduated to a suite at Claridge's, a Rolls-Royce, a knighthood and a yacht at Antibes, although often on a financial see-saw in between. During the 'thirties, his London Films dominated the industry. He teamed up Dietrich with Donat, and helped Charles Laughton and Leslie Howard, among many more, to become international stars. Looking around the grill-room with the casual majesty of a sleepy lion, he greeted many of his beautiful discoveries whom he had affectionately nicknamed 'Korda's Follies'. They included Binnie Barnes, Joan

Gardner (Zoltan's wife), Diana Napier and Wendy Barrie. In a softly-accented, almost hypnotic voice he would outline plans involving millions of pounds while he caressed his *ballon* of brandy. He generated charm even when, under doctor's orders, he was on one of his frequent spartan régimes and had to give up spicy foods.

It was fascinating to glimpse him with Winston Churchill through a rich cloud of Havana while they discussed the film rights of *The Life of Marlborough* or a scenario to be based on the reign of King George V. Like so many of Korda's grandiose projects, neither of these properties ever reached the screen but Churchill always warmed to this civilized and cultured dreamer without ever suspending judgment.

"Korda would make a wonderful Prime Minister of Hungary," he once chuckled, adding thoughtfully, "if he had Rockefeller for his Chancellor of the Exchequer."

Korda had a continental weakness for matchmaking, in his case allied to a flair for casting. He always claimed to have played Cupid to Vivien Leigh and Laurence Olivier. The Savoy Grill was in fact the first setting for the romance which opened almost like a film script. One morning in May 1935, the manager-critic Sydney Carroll telephoned Korda urging him not to miss a lovely young actress who was opening that night at the Ambassadors in a new play, *The Mask of Virtue*. Her name was Vivien Leigh, married at that time to a barrister.

Korda was dining in the Grill with Joe Schenck, Murray Silverstone of United Artists and Montague Marks, 'The Man from the Prudential', which was later to back London Films, not with the happiest results. Suddenly Korda remembered both Carroll's invitation and the first-night tickets in his pocket. He asked the others to accompany him to the theatre where they arrived for the last act but still in time to acclaim a dazzling new star.

Breathing heavily, they forced a way into the young actress's dressing-room. Korda and the Americans were old friends and experienced enough in the ways of show business to read each other's minds. Korda being the host, there was a gentleman's agreement that he should have first bite. Schenck was obviously ready with Hollywood bait but not too hopeful of his chances against Korda's charm and magnetism. In a matter of minutes the Hungarian magician had waved the silken wand of a long-term contract, rising from £1,300 a year. Characteristically, he then became so absorbed with films and his very complicated finances that he promptly forgot his new discovery. A little disillusioned, Vivien Leigh continued with her stage career.

Supping one night in the Grill with Gladys Cooper's son, John Buckmaster, she noticed Olivier with a party of friends at the next table. She had admired him in *Theatre Royal* and could not stop talking about his bravura and style but had never seen him off-stage before that evening.

"What an odd little thing Larry looks without his moustache," commented Buckmaster. His companion disagreed. "I think he's easily the most handsome man in the room," she said dreamily. By chance the two parties collided in the foyer while waiting for taxis. There was a brief introduction and a little pleasant chatter.

They met again a month later at Denham on the set of *Fire Over England* in which Flora Robson enjoyed a triumph. Korda had at long last found a part for his young star and was too wise and sentimental not to observe how she and Olivier always managed to meet in the corridors.

One day Vivien Leigh told Olivier how very much she had enjoyed playing in the same company with him.

"We shall probably end up by fighting," he laughed.

NO HOTEL, however well-equipped and impressive, can function to perfection for twenty-four hours a day, year after year, without an enormous variety of gifted experts. They, and only they, can breathe life into the rosy waxen cheeks of the boar's head in the shop window. Perhaps the most remarkable feature of the Savoy's administration in three-quarters of a century of changing social history has been the unvarying composition of its staff. With rare breaks due to war it has always been overwhelmingly British, with Italians, French, Swiss and other nationalities forming the rest of the nucleus.

"During my forty years as Managing Director of the three hotels in the Savoy Group, I have engaged for the Company thirty-two chefs, all French except one—and they were all excellent," Reeves-Smith recalled when he was presented by the French Ambassador with his Insignia as Chevalier of the Legion of Honour. From its earliest days the management has usually been French, Italian or Swiss, under an all-British Board.

George Reeves-Smith never lost sight of the importance of staff training. During his many visits abroad he was impressed by the well-trained personnel who lent character and distinction even to the smaller hotels on the Continent. Back in London, he worked assiduously to train young people for the hotel trade which he was among the first to recognize as the real key to tourist expansion. He was particularly pleased on hearing of a little incident which to him personified inspired service. An author staying for the first time at the hotel gave his breakfast order to the floor waiter and was astonished when asked if he still took his customary grapefruit and coffee. "How do you know that is what I have for breakfast?" he asked. The waiter smiled. "In 1921 [several years previously] I used to bring you your coffee and grapefruit in the Royal Hotel in Guernsey."

Every leading hotel in the world, from New York to Hong Kong, owes much to the Savoy in London. Reeves-Smith could proudly claim a long list of noted hoteliers who had worked under him in their salad days, but he was more concerned with encouraging his staff to regard their work as a lifelong career, with promotion open in priority to those at the Savoy and its sister hotels in the Group.

Key personnel have always had their heirs apparent, trained to take over unobtrusively when the top man retires or dies. Under shrewd surveillance and awaiting their own day of fame, were men like the Swiss-born Hofflin who was to become an outstanding General Manager; dark-haired Amanda would glide into the Restaurant after the celebrated Santarelli and his successor, Gandolfo; Manetta would eventually depart from the Grill, leaving his crown to the princely Luigi; and even in the two vast kitchens where Latry and Virlogeux had officiated so long that they seemed as permanent as Reeves-Smith himself, the genius of Escoffier's colleague, Alban, and the future Restaurant maître-chef, Laplanche, was mellowing with bland certainty. Mercifully hidden was the tragic fate which would overtake Zavattoni.

It has long been the Savoy's special quality to create managers and maîtres d'hôtel who will inspire and retain the affection of clients but whose passing, while regretted, would leave no scar. Smooth succession, rather than carbon copying, is the tradition. Every new holder of office is expected and encouraged to make a contribution from his own stock of talent and taste. Change for its own sake or dictated by the conventional yardstick of age has never been the hotel's practice.

Continuity of service and tradition is equally important to hotel and club. When Frank Chauncey Weaver once handed in his hat and stick he was delighted to be greeted by the dignified cloakroom manager with a "Good morning, Mr. Weaver." He was even more impressed when Townsend recalled that exactly fifty years ago he had received the banker and his wife at the Savoy on their honeymoon visit. He remembered not only the guest's name but his amazing cane with its ivory fox-handle and two ruby eyes. Mr. Weaver's visit had in fact coincided with Townsend's first day as a page at the Savoy in 1891.

Many others had grown up in the hotel, men like Walter Hore, the Secretary, who had started as a junior clerk before the end of the century and devised the Savoy's ingenious audit, checking and book-keeping system which remains in operation to this day; Peter Fordyce, who left Aberdeen in 1901, paid his own fare to London to apply for a job in the Savoy bakery and completed half a century's service; Frederick Spilling, a discovery of Rupert D'Oyly Carte, became Comptroller of Supplies and during his sixty years with the Company received goods valued at over £20 million; and numerous other veterans like James Donnelly, the Head Storeman, whose favourite party trick in his seventies was to carry twenty sherry glasses and ten large brandy *ballons*.

It was fitting perhaps that Arnold Bennett's admirable documentary novel, *Imperial Palace*, should have rung down the curtain on the 1920s when the Savoy enjoyed such prosperity before a troubled decade. Bennett, who once confessed that his early ambition had been to manage a grand hotel, spent many months of congenial research at the Savoy, cross-examining Richmond Temple and touring every department with Rupert D'Oyly Carte and the Managing Director as his guides. He dedicated his novel to George Reeves-Smith, "from one of the warmest of his admirers". Later, when Bennett's papers came up for auction, Reeves-Smith paid £200 for the original MS., now the property of Bridget D'Oyly Carte and deposited with the hotel's private treasures.

Bennett was impressed by the Savoy's intricately meshed cogs, gears and springs with his friend, George Reeves-Smith, as the balance wheel. Under thinly-veiled pseudonyms he has left a vivid picture of the men who surrounded the Managing Director at this time. The heads of departments met every morning in the office of Gilles, the General Manager, following which Reeves-Smith would call on him with unfailing regularity to discuss the business of yesterday and today. Just after ten o'clock he would hang up his silk top hat in his own office and summon his private secretary, Reginald Bentley, a jovial man with almost as profound a knowledge of wines as his chief.

Reeves-Smith would cut and light his first Havana after breakfast with deft surgical precision. There was much of the man in the operation. Match reverently caressed tip until the perfect glow was achieved. At his desk, after visiting the managers of Claridge's, the Berkeley and the Savoy, the starched cuffs shot from the sleeves of his frock-coat as he reached for pencil and pad. His correspondence, like the many queries which confronted him, was answered with short clear sentences in his neat, upward-sloping handwriting.

In the General Manager's office Albert Gilles was always the first to speak. A well-built man, with a thoughtful face but a most decisive manner, he had his unerring finger on all the buttons and responded intuitively to the prod of crisis. The son of an hotelier in France, he had started his career peeling potatoes in a kitchen *auberge*, trained in Germany, Italy and Switzerland and won the Croix de Guerre with the Chasseurs Alpins during the 1914 war. He came to the Savoy in 1927 from its namesake near Fontainebleau.

He knew every branch of the business and had a firm but courteous way of handling a temperamental staff and all the day-to-day rubs of hotel administration. He and the Night Manager once had to restrain a Canadian soldier who was practising for Bisley by shooting at every vase and lamp in his bedroom. He was equally assured when greeting either Royal guests or flamboyant celebrities but always gave a little extra attention to Wimbledon stars. Himself a first-class tennis player, he invariably captained the Savoy's team in their occasional matches with the Berkeley and Claridge's.

Perhaps the only time his mask ever slipped was soon after his

147

arrival at the hotel when the Talmadge sisters sailed in with Joe Schenck, Norma's husband, and Ali Mackintosh who later married the beautiful Constance. Gilles ushered the quartette to a brand-new lift, the latest and fastest model in Europe, with even its own telephone. The attendant moved the lever and nothing happened. He tried again and still without effect. Not since the day when Charles Frohman had stuck between the third and fourth floors were there so many red faces in the Chief Engineer's department.

Every morning Gilles would acquaint Reeves-Smith with the unfolding picture of the hotel's problems, details of equipment and the inexorable graph of income and expenditure. There would be the list of expected arrivals for that day and one for departures. The typed night report would be studied and a careful note made of some unruly or perhaps suspect guest.

There might be a discreetly worded memo. from the hotel's security officer who needed the photographic memory of a casino inspector in spotting international cardsharpers, confidence men or guests with a temptation to issue bad cheques. Always he had to be alert for the notorious pests who suffer mysterious attacks of ptomaine poisoning or falsely complain that furs or jewels have been stolen from their rooms. Apart from the nightmarish problems of V.I.P. security which demanded the maximum discretion, he would be occupied with a dozen routine irritations, from the loss of a key to the pilferings of souvenir-hunters who could not resist silver cruets and other mementoes. Even more ambitious were one respectable-looking couple who paid their substantial bill with a cheque on a non-existent account. Before departing, they had efficiently stripped their suite of all curtains and covers.

More facts and figures would be supplied by the neat, ascetic-looking Night Manager, Arthur Marini. Before joining the Savoy, which he would serve for thirty-six years, he had appeared in *Madame X* with Arthur Wontner whose son was to become the hotel's Managing Director. But nothing he had acted would ever efface from Marini's memory that terrible night when he had

148

been summoned to Madame Fahmy's suite on the fourth floor.

Victor, the small, plump and dynamic Reception Manager, reported on incoming and outgoing guests and any special problems of accommodation. When Scullin, Menzies or other Prime Ministers arrived for Imperial Conferences, he would seal off whole floors for their private use and smoothly arrange direct telephone lines to Australia House, the House of Commons and other focal points. His task was to create at all times a sense of relaxed order and ease, to arrange advance bookings and exclude undesirables with tactful but firm diplomacy. He had to have an almost electronic memory of every suite in the hotel, apart from the foibles and spending ratings of guests who might not have stayed at the hotel for years but expected to be remembered like near relatives. His team of clerks all spoke half a dozen languages with easy fluency and could handle smoothly grandiose and often vague reservations or querulous complaints. Their next-door neighbours in the Front Hall were the equally unruffled staff of the Enquiry Office. They were ready with answers to questions which might range over the trading hours in the Caledonian Market, the services of a Korean interpreter or a stenographer fluent in Esperanto, temporary membership of a golf club or even the current price of the best hotel room in Amsterdam or Rio. This department also controlled the white-gloved squadron of pages, ready to take off smartly at the tinkle of a bell.

By no means untypical, though difficult, was the sudden S.O.S. for some genuine bagpipes which an American family wished to take home as souvenirs. They were flying back that very night. This would have been a simple task had it not been a Sunday with all shops closed. The Enquiry Office groped for inspiration until someone thought of Petticoat Lane. The visitors were taken in tow by a porter who escorted them to the famous East End market. They were soon back at the Savoy, clutching their bagpipes in addition to a considerable amount of excess baggage which a sharp salesman had sold them. And only a perfectly-trained enquiry clerk could have kept a straight face on being asked for 'the Petticoat Suite' by an Italian visitor. With unblinking courtesy he was conducted to the Pinafore Room.

Like all the other heads of departments, Victor worked long erratic hours and often had to neglect the prize roses which he grew in his garden at Ealing. At these morning conferences he would remain bland and amiable until someone put forward a suggestion for publicity which he regarded as out of keeping with the dignity of the hotel. Only then would he become indignant and appeal, usually with success, to the General Manager's sense of decorum.

Each department was jealous of its own prestige, and vigilant for the smallest threat to its independence. From experts with so many different backgrounds, often nourishing rivalries of almost Mafia-like ferocity, it seemed impossible that a pattern of quiet perfection could emerge. Yet, behind the exasperations, a common dedicated loyalty to the hotel and its image always won the last battle.

Zavattoni, bull-necked and formidable, would throw out a staccato comment to make it clear that *his* department was the true cornerstone of the Savoy. He could speak from the experience of handling over ten thousand banquets during a career started in the humble apron of a *commis*-waiter. He might talk fiercely in the manner of Mussolini, whom he much admired, but had no rival in Europe for spicing a function with the showman's dash of Latin *bravura*. At a State Dinner given by the British Government to the delegates of the London Naval Conference of 1930, he had presented the five hundred guests with a menu worthy of the Ritz-Escoffier tradition. Still not satisfied he consulted the Managing Director on the wine list, hinting that the occasion demanded something memorable. Reeves-Smith agreed, went down to the cellars and selected the almost legendary Château Lafite of 1865. Six hours before the banquet, twelve jeroboams of this nectar were reverently decanted. As a compliment to the delegates with a rare vintage, Reeves-Smith himself drew off the corks with red-hot tongs to avoid the slightest crumbling or stirring of sediment.

Zavattoni's only relaxation seemed to be professional boxing and he would rarely miss an important fight. Carnera, briefly champion of the world, was his idol and the hotel valets were warned to pay special attention to his clothes and the most enormous shoes ever left outside a hotel bedroom. After his countryman's thrashing by Max Baer, Zavattoni went into sullen mourning during which head waiters trembled and even the mighty Latry chose his words. But the hotel would inevitably claim his deepest love. Once he snatched an evening to see the Carnera-Stribling fiasco at the Albert Hall. As that bout was quickly over, Zavattoni dashed back to the Savoy, tumbled into full evening dress, which always seemed about to burst at the waist but somehow did not, and was soon bustling about to see that his earlier instructions for a banquet had been carried out to the letter.

Unlike his managerial colleagues in the restaurant and grill-room, he rarely wasted time on courtliness. On one occasion, almost incoherent with outraged pride, he stormed up to the Managing Director's office bearing a tray of two dozen oysters which he condemned as below standard, whatever Latry might say. Reeves-Smith agreed soothingly without, however, giving offence to the maître-chef, and peace was once more restored.

The accolade for a client was a wave from Zavattoni's menu which he carried about like a field-marshal's baton. When Royalty or ambassadors were present he spared no pains in supervising the smallest detail, from the kitchen to the table. If the Prince of Wales chanced to be a guest, he would personally ensure that his favourite dishes were on the menu; caviare, lamb cutlets, and inevitably savouries like scotch woodcock, mushrooms on toast or welsh rarebit.

Zavattoni might grumble and the Works Department mutter threats about resigning but they liked nothing so much as a challenge, backed preferably by a handsome budget and a free hand. When Claude Leigh, the property magnate, drew the Derby winner, Blenheim, in the H.B. Club's sweepstake, he celebrated by asking sixty of his friends to dinner. To make them feel at home, he asked Zavattoni to provide a racing setting. "Make it a bit original," he ordered. That night the party sat down to dine at a horseshoe-shaped table in a private room transformed into a corner of the paddock at Epsom, with flower-beds and a special background painting of the Derby Day scene. Among incidental items was £60 for artificial grass.

Nobody knew better than the Banqueting Manager that split-second timing for cooking and serving was of the essence. At one typical banquet for three hundred diners the supplies included 80 dozen oysters, 10 lbs. of caviare, 140 lbs. of salmon, 65 pints of turtle soup, 30 saddles of lamb and 300 quails with *paté de foie gras* stuffing. At half past seven Zavattoni telephoned down to the kitchen to announce that the diners were at table. Working on a basis of ten minutes a course, Latry deployed his chefs, *sous-chefs* and servers with the precision of toy soldiers. While the guests in the Lancaster Room ate their salmon, a hundred bunches of asparagus were being plunged into boiling water. Hooked on the board near Latry's desk were the pink slips stamped with the time of each order and its destination.

Soon all the flimsy slips would find their way into the glass-partitioned Accounts Department where Hore's assistants swiftly funnelled them through red-bound ledgers and into the graphs of income and expenditure. Catering demands wise, selective buying and the ability to 'cost' a banquet for five or five hundred which must satisfy the guests and still show a profit to the hotel.

As soon as Zavattoni had given his explosive account of the previous night's functions and his frustrations with the kitchen or the temporary banqueting waiters who could never measure up to his ideal, it would be the turn of his quieter but no less gifted countrymen, Santarelli and Manetta, to make their reports.

Each had a distinctive clientèle and, almost traditionally, one manager showed respectful, if slightly aloof, condescension towards the other, rather in the fashion of Monarchs and Presidents of Republics. In the Restaurant, Santarelli graciously fed delicacies to his cage of peacocks and shrugged at the screeching macaws who flew from table to table in 'the other dining-room'. The Grill was less formal and basked in the limelight of stars who did not care for music while they ate and chatted, more than happy to provide their own 'cabaret'.

Tall elegant Santarelli had a gentle courtesy which was proof against guests who recklessly practised One-upmanship over vintages and gastronomy. In his youth he had trained for the priesthood and something of a cardinal's presence still clung to him as he took his stately constitutional in the Embankment gardens. His regular patrons knew better than to tip him but if, as sometimes happened, a guest gave him an appreciative five-pound note, he would thank him graciously and later ask the head waiter to share it among his staff.

His opposite number in the Grill, Manetta, was younger, perhaps even more suave and endowed with such charm that, during his holidays at St. Moritz, the débutantes and their mammas would often desert all the skiing instructors. They would scarcely have identified him with the family man, an apron round his waist, cooking Sunday dinner at his home in Hammersmith.

Their empires might differ but both men were formed in the same smooth mould, rounded off by an accented English of almost flawless perfection. Politely they listened to complaints, often imaginary, purred sympathetically over allergies and achieved the twice-daily miracle of making each guest feel that he or she was the most important and attractive person there. Both men were adept, however, with the invisible velvet rope which kept the best tables for regular patrons and celebrities.

Manetta constantly refreshed his memory from a file of several thousand entries which he kept locked in his office. Faces, names and fads—almost everything except fingerprints—were registered. He knew, among many other secrets, that the vegetarian George Arliss was safest at a corner table. His stare of disapproval, hardened by the monocle, could be anything but pleasant for diners enjoying the first of the season's grouse. Others had less rigid tastes. Traditionally, on the first day of grouse-shooting

153

many banquets are held at the hotel. When one sporting peer asked for something special as a table decoration, the florists created a miniature shoot, complete with floral guns.

Apart from the appraisal of guests, both socially and financially, and the confident allocation of tables, the manager has also to be an authority on food and wines. He is not only the arbiter on all staff disputes in his kingdom, but a father confessor tactfully neutral when a guest's confidences become too free or loyalties conflict. He develops a built-in calendar of birthdays, wedding anniversaries and divorces; above all, the graceful art of complimenting a lady on a becoming new hat or a 'silk' on his elevation to the Bench. He must always appear natural, whatever the circumstances. Luigi Pellosi, second in command to Manetta and later manager of La Banquette at the Berkeley, once ushered to his table a magistrate who had that morning given him a very stiff fine for a minor motoring offence. They discussed the menu most amiably without either, of course, referring to their previous meeting that day.

Restaurant and Grill have long had separate staffs and kitchens. Each maintains its own corps of waiters but with an identical approach to service. The head waiter ushers the guest to his table; a waiter slides his chair, another places the pink napkin on his knee, a third unveils the menu, a fourth makes ready to serve the meal while the wine waiter gives his benediction to the guest's choice or, very discreetly, offers sage advice. The whole overture is brief and played with fingertip delicacy, the product of hard training and discipline. The Savoy's managers and head waiters might not have gone quite so far in their pursuit of perfection, but each would have understood and sympathized with the Fratellini sire who broke the legs of one of his sons to make him walk more convincingly like a clown.

Protocol is traditionally the same in both dining-rooms. The hierarchy is topped by three head waiters; the station head waiters, each an overlord of six tables, are supported by the *chef de rang* who actually serves at table and a *commis* who brings the food from the kitchens, assisted by a *commis débarrasseur* when working under pressure. The wine butlers and wine waiters, the first buffet chef in charge of the trolley and carving, and the demi-buffet chef who is responsible for the sweet and cheese trolleys, complete the ensemble. All are under the eye of the Manager or his First Head Waiter (the Maître d'hôtel), both unobtrusively watchful for any lack of courtesy or dislocation of service.

Staff upsets are seldom a major problem to either the Restaurant or the Grill Manager who pick their men carefully and submit them to a long period of probation. Almost without exception, every waiter and *chef de rang* has started as a long-aproned *commis* in a short black jacket.

More important to Santarelli and Manetta was the smooth liaison between kitchen and tables, the focal point of service and efficiency. Heading specialists like the sauce, roast and fish chefs, the pastry chefs dedicated to sweet mysteries of life like petits fours and soufflés, the chef in control of the larder, the *hors d'œuvriers*, and the artists who had composed nothing but omelettes for a quarter of a century, was the mighty Chef des Cuisines who needed the most tactful handling when guests became unreasonable or his authority was challenged in the smallest way. The manager had to discuss the day's menus with this dictator of the kitchen and persuade him that the impossible was routine.

Brooding in his tiny office, microphone in hand and watching his noisy acolytes bustling around the red-tiled kitchen floor, the head chef might often think wistfully of owning a restaurant somewhere in France where a few chosen habitués would do honour to his *specialités de la maison*. It is a traditional if self-deceptive pipe-dream, since every dedicated cook knows in his heart that the true gastronome needs the post-prandial relaxation and leisure which very few small restaurants can offer.

Between them these maître-chefs, Latry and Virlogeux, controlled two hundred cooks over 60 per cent of whom worked in the Restaurant kitchen which was also responsible for banqueting. Both started the day by carefully examining all the market supplies ordered the night before or, in the case of meat, poultry and fish, chosen by the hotel buyers at four that morning. A small squad of clerks kept a check on the flurry of slips and order forms but it was the head chef's responsibility to watch costs without sacrificing quality, a daily challenge with an average of some four thousand meals to be served.

When the Restaurant and Grill managers spoke at the morning conference it was not to raise routine matters like the megalomania of chefs or a guest's temporary insanity. Reeves-Smith and Gilles were receptive to suggestions for improving décor or making good the constant wear and tear but much more concerned with *trends*. Had the clientèle changed significantly in their tastes in food and drink? Was there a sudden rise or falling-off in spending power? If so, was there some good reason? Had a certain celebrity transferred his patronage to a rival hotel, and was there an explanation? What special arrangements were being made for Derby Night or New Year's Eve?

Soon came the turn of Mrs. Kate Butler, the Lady Superintendent since the eve of the Great War, to give her views. A diminutive white-haired widow, exquisitely turned out, she reigned supreme over the squads of housekeepers, valets and chambermaids on each floor of the hotel. She offered her ideas with vigour, sparing neither the Reception Office nor the Works Department. Having looked after such diverse celebrities as Smuts (who used to read sections of his books to her and invite her views), Einstein, Kreisler and Bernhardt, she could claim a respectful hearing if she insisted that furnishings and upholstery needed closer attention. As usual she was ready with facts, figures, estimates. Suddenly her face would lose its sternness and she became wholly feminine about her trials. Mr. X had made a booking and that meant more cigar burns. Another American eccentric had just demanded that all the furniture except the bed be removed from his room and replaced by rows and rows of luggage stools! This would give Gilles the opportunity to make one of his usual jokes. He enquired solicitously about the welfare of his favourite non-paying guest, Harry, a snail who occupied a window-box in the American Bar where, apart from his vegetables, he had thrived for years on a daily sip of Crême de Menthe.

The atmosphere would relax a little until the Audit Manager, the Works Manager and the Chief Stocktaker began to produce their unyielding statistics. Even Zavattoni then became quiet and thoughtful and Santarelli's swallow-tails drooped a little as the hard facts of estimates and expenditure spluttered around them like bullets. With relief they would depart for their own little kingdoms and a day's work which might not end until the early hours, often too late for the journey home. From the Managing Director downwards, they had all known what it was to be recalled in the middle of a family vacation. When he retired, Gilles would confess seriously that he looked forward to his first real holiday in thirty-eight years.

After a conference, Reeves-Smith would slip quietly through the hotel, an unknown figure to all but a few clients, but with a gentle smile for some old member of the staff who had served the hotel since the days of Ritz. His own age was a secret but, almost in his eighties, he still walked like a guardsman and his eyes were sharp and expert.

In a way isolated by his own power, he stood between the hotel staff and the Board. It was no light burden but he was fortunate in his directors, and they in him. The Chairman, Rupert D'Oyly Carte, a shy retiring man, was formal in manner but gentle and considerate. He disliked publicity for himself and others, so much so that he would not permit the stars of his Opera Company to make curtain speeches even on sentimental last nights. He started a school for talented singers but insisted that everyone should begin in the chorus. Like Reeves-Smith whom he resembled in character, he was kindly of heart and found it notoriously hard to resist an appeal to his generosity. Many small amateur companies were excused payment of fees and royalties for performing Gilbert and Sullivan.

His manner was diffident and remote, and nobody had seemed less likely to assume the romantic, dangerous rôle of a Secret Service courier. More than once in the 1914 war, while ostensibly

157

visiting an opera company, he would be on some delicate mission for Naval Intelligence. Although in later years he occupied a suite at the Savoy, he was happiest of all in his adjoining theatre or in the home he built in Devon where he could swim from his own private beach or wander among the rare shrubs he cultivated with such knowledge and affection. When living in Mayfair, his white pony would be brought to the door every morning, and he would often wave a greeting in Rotten Row to Reeves-Smith cantering homeward before the serious day's work had begun.

From his father the Chairman had inherited a remarkable instinct for décor which he would in turn bequeath to his daughter, Bridget. He was always a powerful ally whenever Reeves-Smith pressed for costly alterations, extensions and improved furnishings, and they made a shrewd and sympathetic partnership, conscious of tradition yet sensitive to the undertones of a changing world. Both pondered deeply on a future which must inevitably shape their complicated budget. The Cecil was being pulled down to make way for Shell-Mex House but a new hotel, the Dorchester, would rise in Park Lane. Already there was talk of building the Cumberland, while from America, a country both men knew and understood so well, came reports of new blocks of luxury service apartments which might prove a threat to the whole hotel business.

There were others, largely recruited from the City, who could also give practical guidance. The Savoy Company has always favoured working directors rather than guinea-pigs. For many years until his death in 1929, Colonel 'Freddie' Browning, chairman of the wine shippers, Twiss, Browning and Hallowes, had been on the Board. Famous as soldier and athlete, he possessed a fine business brain and an immense circle of influential friends. The family tradition was continued when, some years later, his son Lt.-General Sir Frederick Browning, Daphne du Maurier's husband, was elected to the Board. Another director, R. S. L. Boulter, died within a few months of Colonel Browning. His wife was the widow of Richard D'Oyly Carte. He, too, was a

City man and the financial links he forged with the Savoy are maintained to this day.

Miles Thornewill, now Vice-Chairman, joined the Company in May 1919 and became a director five years later. A man of great personal elegance and a product of Winchester like Rupert D'Oyly Carte, he successfully applied a legal training to the complexities of hotel administration. For many years he was at Reeves-Smith's right hand and his staunch aide in fostering the hotel training schemes to which both were devoted. Blessed with the constitution of an athlete—he won his Blue for boxing at Oxford—perfectly dressed at all times, punctilious and never willing to accept the second-rate, he was marked out for success.

Another asset in the Savoy's policy of creative and practical direction was Claude Serocold who served on the Board for over thirty years. An Oxford rowing Blue, with a fine war record as one of Admiral Hall's closest associates in Naval Intelligence, he was to become a most successful stockbroker with a magic flair for business and widespread influence and prestige in and beyond the City.

New blood was introduced in 1929 by Major Frank Goldsmith, a barrister and former M.P., who once defeated Bernard Shaw in an L.C.C. election. He was the head of several famous hotels in France, from Paris to the Riviera. There was also Richmond Temple, who was to prove invaluable in handling Press and entertainment problems and developing the vital tourist traffic from the United States.

The Board was soon confronted with Wall Street's dramatic collapse. Industries crumbled; sterling teetered; and unemployment was spreading like a malignant cancer. With rising costs and the continuing effects of a world economic depression, the Savoy shareholders had to swallow some bitter medicine. From £99,000 in 1930, the net profits slumped to a bare £10,000 in two years. The glittering post-war era seemed to be over, although Arnold Bennett would have thought it wildly ridiculous that his magnificent Imperial Palace could be truly threatened or his friend saddled with an exhausted Reserve.

A few months after his novel was published and shortly after attending the wedding reception at the Savoy of his publisher's son, Desmond Flower, Bennett died of typhoid fever, the result of drinking infected water during a visit to Fontainebleau. He narrowly missed a drama which would have appealed to him. For a Fancy Dress Ball at the hotel Johann Strauss, the composer's nephew, had been specially engaged to bring over his Viennese orchestra. A thousand guests, among them four Maharajahs and half the peerage, sat down to supper. It was a gay and glittering occasion, the ladies in bustles, period curls and dazzling jewellery, and many of their partners wearing picturesque Magyar costume of the Imperial days.

Only a few members of the Charity Ball Committee and a hotel staff, pledged to silence, knew what had taken place the night before in that very ballroom. Some of the guests, including Thelma, Lady Furness, had decided to rehearse quadrilles, minuets and other dances. While waltzing too energetically, Admiral Sir Charles Royds, the Deputy Commissioner at Scotland Yard, collapsed from a heart attack. He was taken by ambulance to Charing Cross Hospital where he died soon afterwards.

This was the last big ball before the world depression. It was quickly noticed that less wine was being drunk and much more lager beer. To keep clients from losing the habit, Reeves-Smith agreed reluctantly to reduce the price of his superb wines to a level which hardly showed a profit. Even rich men had begun to count their change and although the restaurant and grill-room had not greatly suffered, room bookings were sparse and for shorter periods. The management became tactful over unpaid or outstanding bills, confident of an appreciative clientèle with tradition and tastes passing from father to son.

The vast reconstruction programme had been completed in 1929, otherwise the trade slump might have made it more difficult and much costlier, and the coming of war would have shelved it indefinitely. Fortunately the Chairman's zeal for modernization never flagged. Like Reeves-Smith, he was determined that the

Blitz Hotel'. *Right*, Red Cross nurses, all staff volunteers, were on twenty-four hour duty. In charge was the Manager's wife, Mrs Greta Hofflin. *Below*, flanked by Allied flags, Count Peter stands guard under protective barrage balloons

Miles Thornewill's office after a landmine exploded outside the Embankment entrance

Carroll Gibbons plays for wartime dancers at his famous white piano in the reinforced River Room

Savoy should be 'always up-to-date and if possible a little ahead.' With shareholders eager for dividends and proud of the hotel's loyal clientèle, it would have been tempting to defer more expenditure, but that was not the Chairman's way. Having agreed that improvements were necessary, he had quickly approved the estimates and set the wheels in motion.

The fall in profits was a shock but the Board remained confident that the recession would not last. At the height of the depression while the cassandras were wringing their hands, a small party of men dined privately together at Claridge's. The host was the American railway magnate and philanthropist, Edward Stephen Harkness, and his guests Lord Macmillan, Sir James Irvine and John Buchan. With few formalities The Pilgrim Trust was created to help and encourage national and other worthy projects and promote the ties of affection between the two countries. In opening the Trust with a gift of £2 million, Harkness said it was "a thank you for the heritage and tradition which America owed to Britain." Devoted to 'anything but politics', the Trust lost no time in relieving the worst-hit depressed areas.

Slowly but steadily the flow of American visitors started. Charles M. Schwab crossed the Atlantic yet again, quickly followed by confident magnates like Ralph Pulitzer, James Speyer and Harrison Williams and his elegant wife, who headed the world's best-dressed women list year after year. The first consignment of American-brewed beer was unloaded at Waterloo and rushed to the Savoy. With the repeal of Prohibition imminent, Augustus Nolle of the Waldorf-Astoria arrived to restock his wine cellars. He spent many hours consulting Reeves-Smith and inspected the Group's bottled treasure drowsing under the Thames before going wistfully on his way to Epernay and Bordeaux.

Business began to pick up, at first nervously and then in a crescendo. Otto Kahn and other millionaires rented grouse moors; flocks of American débutantes practised their curtsies in the cabins of the Cunard Line; the familiar carousel of Ascot, Henley, Goodwood and Cowes accelerated, and the Season had its brilliant peak in the wedding of Prince George and the lovely Princess Marina. At a luncheon in the hotel the Marquis de Polignac was happy to report that 720,000 bottles of champagne had been drunk in England during the first three months of that year. Parties, balls and banquets became so popular that for a time London had a famine of toastmasters. The Shikar Club met again on Oaks Night, with Lord Lonsdale in the Chair, its members displaying an exuberance that offered poor life insurance for big game in Africa and Asia.

Gossip writers snuffled the rich pastures of restaurant and grill-room. Douglas Fairbanks was bunkered by autograph albums as he fought his way to lunch with Glenda Collett and the American women golfers. His son was easily the best-dressed man in the room and made an electrifying entrance with his bride, Joan Crawford. Ben Lyon and Bebe Daniels, on their first visit to England, were the centre of a crowd of friends, including the Duke and Duchess of Sutherland and Adèle Astaire, Lady Charles Cavendish. Hollywood and Broadway were back in force. In his suite Stan Laurel entertained his father and mother at a riotous party with his partner, Oliver Hardy, acting as the least Jeeves-like butler in town. It was also a sentimental home-coming for big Victor McLaglen, reunited with his four brothers whom he bear-hugged and wrestled with in his luxurious suite until four in the morning.

Rod la Rocque and his dazzling blonde wife, Vilma Banky, were mobbed; Cary Grant played hide-and-seek as usual with Society hostesses; and Josephine Baker was inconsolable at having to leave her menagerie at home in Paris. Jerome Kern and his wife occupied the adjoining suite to the Oscar Hammersteins and moved back and forth for conferences on their Drury Lane musical *Three Sisters* which they hoped would be another *Show Boat*. It ran for only two months. In the Restaurant where eight hundred people in full evening dress danced every night, the Prince of Wales kept Geraldo busy with encores for the tango while Lady Astor applauded him between glasses of ginger beer. Across the room Hedda Hopper, the Hollywood columnist, had to acknowledge one of her very rare defeats at the hands of a maître d'hôtel. She had sailed into dinner wearing one of her famous hats, a charming confection which would have delighted the Grill but, alas, could not be tolerated in the Restaurant. To her credit she made a perfect exit rather than submit.

All the old clubs emerged from austerity, and a Derby Club Dinner, now an annual event, was held for the first time, replacing the banquet of the H.B. Club which had met for many years to discuss racing and breeding. It took its name from the members, known as 'Honey's Boys' after their genial secretary, Tom Honey.

Every night, as in the heady days of the 'twenties, there was a banquet of some kind graced by the best after-dinner speakers of the day, often Sir Patrick Hastings and his fellow-barrister, jovial Sir Henry Curtis Bennett. The waiters always enjoyed the appearances of J. H. Thomas, a caricaturist's delight with his cigar and bulging dress-shirt, but suffered torments when Ramsay MacDonald rose to speak, the chandeliers sparkling on his wavy white hair. Toastmasters would age almost visibly under that waterfall of sonorous platitudes. Almost equally pompous was Sir Hugh Walpole whose earnest lectures used to send strong men screaming into the night. When Francis Brett Young was being fêted by his publishers before leaving on an American tour, J. B. Priestley made a witty speech and John Squire, enjoying his whisky, was making his neighbours—Sybil Colefax and Rose Macaulay—weep with laughter. Then came Walpole's turn to pontificate on 'The English Novel'. However, poor Brett Young's troubles were not yet over. In the Main Hall, he was reportedly accosted by an attractive young woman who assured him breathlessly that she adored *all* his novels, her favourite being, *The Luck of Roaring Camp*.

At one dinner in his honour, Einstein was naïvely asked if he believed his Theory of Relativity to be correct. "There is no knowing until I am dead," he replied solemnly. "If I am right, the Germans will say I am a German, and the French that I am a Jew. If I am wrong, the French will say that I am a German, and the Germans that I am a Jew." He was hurt but concealed his feelings when Bernard Shaw indulged in some tasteless baiting. At one literary party after reproving the others for drinking cocktails, he said cheerfully, "Hitler is perfectly right. Right up to the hilt," and vanished like a genie as soon as the photographers had taken his picture.

Adolf Hitler was only one of many irritations during the see-saw 'thirties which marked the birth of Nazi Germany, a militant Mussolini, the nightmare of the Spanish Civil War, three million unemployed in Britain, Mosley's Fascists, and the coming upheaval of Edward VIII's Abdication. George Orwell and Aldous Huxley were etching with acid but Novello's Ruritania and Coward's cigarette-holder still pointed to the brave old world. While hunger-marchers paraded, Society women took enthusiastically to the new craze for face-lifting and diets. The Eton crops had gone, with the solitary exception of Bea Lillie's, and with them, somehow, the gaiety of a feverish decade.

With its ear close to the City and sensitive to international suspense, the Savoy Board had to prepare shareholders for a long period of uncertainty. True, the striped awnings were out again in Grosvenor Square but even dukes complained of rising death duties, and blocks of flats were creeping steadily towards Belgravia. Trusting his instincts, Reeves-Smith decided with Thornewill that this mood of restlessness might be countered, not with retrenchment but by making the Savoy more attractive and contemporary. One step was to change the staff uniforms from the old Oxford and Cambridge blues to an elegant grey whipcord. While severe economies were made in various ways, they were not obvious to guests.

To offset the new taste for flat-dwelling, the hotel had to offer superior service, food and accommodation. With the closing of so many town houses through heavy taxation and a servant shortage, there was now more restaurant and private party entertainment, particularly for weddings and anniversaries. The Banqueting Department was flourishing but remained alert for competition from hotels like the May Fair and the new Dorchester.

In the mid-'thirties, scores of bedrooms, sitting-rooms and bathrooms were modernized and every window replaced by soundproof casements. Fresh-washed air streamed through the hotel and no American critic could fault the air-conditioning, the lifts or the lighting. The grill-room was relit and redecorated. The Silver Rooms with their tureens, candelabra and cutlery were minutely inspected for the smallest flaws and the latest machinery installed, including an apparatus which applied a fine burnish to cutlery after it had been washed in a lathery dish full of ball-bearings.

All this could not be achieved cheaply, either by the hotel or its patrons. Sir Charles Higham, cynical but shrewd, gave a young man this practical advice: "Eat at the Savoy Grill, then people will think you are a success because you can afford to eat there." More important, however, was the hotel's fame as a social and business rendezvous.

In restaurant and grill-room there was a diminishing sense of crisis, although some Americans prophesied doom if Roosevelt remained in the White House. King George V's celebration of his Silver Jubilee on a sparkling day in May seemed an augury for a carefree Summer Season. At memorable dinner-parties the hosts included King George of Greece, the Duke of Westminster and the Wernhers. On Derby Nights the Maharajah of Rajpipla and other owners spared no expense in celebrating victory or consoling each other in defeat. Sir Henry Lytton's monocle flashed amiably as he strolled in from the theatre next door for 'a bite and a bottle', and there was always a spasm of excitement when corpulent Lord Castlerosse appeared in his sable-lined overcoat, the waiters making bets on which of his three dozen fancy waistcoats he would favour that day.

Dom Pérignon mated equably with the perfumes of Havana, Worth and Chanel in an ambience with less anxiety about tomorrow. One visitor sent out a page to collect a shaving brush which Asprey's were offering for only £100, while some

American art collectors, feverish to become a new Knoedler or Duveen, rang joybells up and down Bond Street.

In the autumn of 1935, the nation rejoiced in the marriage of the Duke of Gloucester to Lady Alice Montagu-Douglas-Scott, daughter of the Duke of Buccleuch and Queensberry. Again the Savoy foyer was crowded and table reservations reached another peak. In the swing doors Big Bill Tilden and his tennis rackets were locked with the Nizam of Hyderabad's polo sticks, reverently carried in by his retainers. An unexpected guest, a tramp of over seventy, was found fast asleep behind majestic Count Peter. He had spent the night there, having somehow climbed twenty feet, unseen by four doormen and hundreds of people hurrying in and out of the hotel.

Louis Lumière, still a distinguished figure with the looks of a stage diplomat, was ushered to his table in the Grill, unrecognized by flushed young Hollywood stars busily dropping excited asides about their new pictures. Only his old forgotten 'flickers' could have registered those quick-moving times. High above the sparkling Thames, André Maurois sat correcting proofs of his Dickens biography. Count Grandi, handsome and arrogant, received guests at the Italian Ball. The Japanese magnate, Baron Okura, lunched with the equally silent Sir Philip Sassoon, looking remarkably like a Velasquez portrait modernized by Savile Row; Shaw, for once in white tie and tails, celebrated H. G. Wells's seventieth birthday with Maugham, Julian Huxley, E. V. Lucas and J. B. Priestley; and The Two Club was inaugurated with the worthy object of improving the status and payment of golf caddies.

Some occasions were less social. Negley Farson, then London correspondent for the *Chicago Daily News*, recalls being summoned to the Savoy by his boss, Colonel Frank Knox, later U.S. Secretary of the Navy. Knox was over for the World Economic Conference and apparently thought that Farson's reports were too uncritically pro-British. He began a long lecture which must have been unconsciously funny since he was simultaneously doing violent physical jerks in his underwear. Farson tried to listen but failed. He threw up his job, rushed off to Yugoslavia and wrote his best-selling autobiography, *The Way of a Transgressor*. Years later, whenever he stayed at the Savoy or perched in the American Bar, he would suddenly burst into roars of laughter. The Colonel's ghost in B.V.D.s was always too much for him.

Within a few weeks of the Gloucester wedding, King George V died, after establishing at the end of his life a new intimacy with the British people through his Christmas message on the radio. Six months' Court mourning automatically cancelled a long list of dinners, banquets and celebrations of all kinds. Soon London was buzzing with American newspaper reports of the Prince of Wales's association with a Mrs. Ernest Simpson. The British Press kept a discreet silence but the new King's closest friends, Winston Churchill, Duff Cooper and Walter Monckton, looked significantly grave and declined to add to the swarm of rumours. Over at Claridge's, Lord Rothermere asked Mrs. Simpson to lunch and tried helpfully to explore the expedient of a morganatic marriage, while at Fort Belvedere, Lord Beaverbrook was closeted with the Prince of Wales.

The shock of the Abdication was gradually absorbed by preparations for the Coronation of King George VI. Soon the Savoy Restaurant was transformed into a huge tent, and guests parted draperies of blue and gold silk to see a representation of the Thames, with the Royal Barge gliding past historic landmarks, under magnificent paintings of monarchs like William the Conqueror and Queen Elizabeth.

Heavy bookings were expected but the flood of visitors was so large and not only in luxury hotels like the Savoy, that housing them became a problem. Foreign Royalties, Presidents, Prime Ministers and others could stay at the leading hotels or in embassies and private houses but the pressure grew incessant from the Foreign Office, shipping lines and tourist agencies. Hotels, moreover, wished naturally to satisfy their own faithful clientèle. Reeves-Smith was consulted and under his leadership a Coronation Accommodation Committee was set up to avoid the inevitable chaos and ill-feeling.

It was to play an important part in the history of the Savoy. Reeves-Smith had quietly noted the skill of a young man who successfully took over the direction of the Committee's work. After leaving Oundle, Hugh Wontner went abroad to study languages, returning to join the secretarial staff of the London Chamber of Commerce. At the age of 25 he was appointed General Secretary of The Hotels and Restaurants Association of Great Britain which he represented at many international conferences. Reeves-Smith, who had been Chairman since it was founded in 1910, was now brought into regular contact with him.

Hotel history has a way of repeating itself. Just as Richard D'Oyly Carte had first noticed Reeves-Smith at the opening of the new Claridge's forty years ago, the veteran Managing Director was now impressed by the rather reserved Association Secretary who always mastered his brief and spoke clearly, and to the point, at meetings. His father was Arthur Wontner, the distinguished actor and manager, and he too was keenly interested in the theatre, in itself a recommendation to a hotel with the Savoy's background. Apart from the D'Oyly Cartes, Reeves-Smith's own brother, Harry, was a fine actor of most impressive appearance who had starred in successes like *The Great Waltz* at the Rockefeller Center Theater.

The Wontners had a long City tradition dating back to the days of the first Elizabeth, and for centuries past several among them had been Masters of the Company of Feltmakers. Hugh Wontner added cosmopolitan taste and travel to an instinct for commerce. Apart from the theatre he had cultivated a nice palate for wines which Reeves-Smith, an old pupil of Calvet's, could appreciate and value. He had also spent some time at the Meurice in Paris, learning the business, from answering correspondence to counting the linen. His guide and mentor was that great hotelier, Schwenter, who had served at the Savoy as Assistant Manager to Pruger in the early years of the century.

Reeves-Smith still held himself proudly and could work eight hours a day, but he had served the Savoy for forty years, apart from supervising Claridge's, the Berkeley and numerous other interests. For over half a century he had been happily married to his wife, Maud, also a native of Yorkshire. She alone knew the strain he often concealed, morning after morning, as he put on his swallow-tail coat and silk hat to begin a working day.

It was a proud moment for the Company when the new King conferred a knighthood on this most distinguished of hoteliers. The staff marked the occasion by presenting him with a bronze bust of himself by Jo Davidson. An illuminated address and an album with over two thousand signatures were handed to him by Spilling, the veteran Comptroller of Supplies, who had come to the Savoy almost on the same day and would later receive the award of the British Empire Medal.

Within a few years Sir George invited Wontner to join the Company as his assistant. In normal times a leisurely and congenial 'indoctrination' would have followed. The Savoy, with its variety of departments and a highly individual staff of experts, called for months of patient tactful research before its intricacies could be mastered; but these were not normal times. Although everyone made jokes about the Siegfried Line and Goering's medals, workmen were busily fortifying the Abraham Lincoln Room in the Savoy with thousands of feet of steel tubing and timber beams, reinforced with concrete. The adjoining Pink and Green rooms now had steel girders and were stacked with thousands of sandbags. Air Raid Wardens and Red Cross nurses, all staff volunteers, were being briefed by Miles Thornewill who also made orderly arrangements for an A.R.P. control room, linked by telephone with complete observation posts and a round-the-clock alarm system.

Nobody doubted that the hotel's position on the river near Shell-Mex House would make it an inviting target. From his window Governor Moore of New Jersey saw men grimly digging pathetic slit-trenches. Hundreds of Americans and clients from the Continent had already cancelled their bookings.

Suddenly the nightmare seemed to be over. On the evening of 28 September 1938, an excited man jumped to his feet in the grill-room, waving a magnum of champagne, and proposed a toast to Mr. Chamberlain. Everyone stood up on chairs, cheering wildly. The Stock Exchange and Wall Street did a fandango, and the Savoy's Reception Manager was soon using his shoehorn to fit in bookings for the most expensive suites. Briefly, miraculously, it was 'business as usual' again. Cables showered from nostalgic and valued clients in bullish mood. In a matter of hours the first grouse were being flown out via Imperial Airways to clients in Durban, as well as to The Brown Derby in Hollywood.

With his gentle courteous smile, Manetta greeted Bea Lillie and Leslie Henson who were soon joined by Douglas Fairbanks and his pretty wife, Sylvia. In high spirits at the prospect of playing more golf at Sunningdale, Fairbanks kept them laughing with his conjuring until he used one of his favourite 'props', a trick knife, which gave Henson a violent electric shock. Someone retaliated by referring to Sylvia Fairbanks, perhaps by accident, as Lady Ashley which always infuriated her husband. They were soon greeted by a previous Mrs. Fairbanks, the now very plump Mary Pickford who came over with Korda and the Goldwyns. Sam dutifully delivered himself of his latest Goldwynism: "I'm looking for girls to make into stars," he declared, "but they must be more than beautiful. They must be *effeminate.*"

Night after night the Grill was solidly booked by a gay and glamorous crowd of celebrities. Hitchcock, the Lunts and Olivia de Havilland . . . Robert Sherwood, accepting congratulations on *Idiot's Delight* . . . Adolph Menjou, twirling his moustache and wearing the quizzical look from a hundred films . . . Max Kriendler of New York's 21 Club, in town to buy vintage wines and proudly sporting his honorary sheriff's badge from back home . . . Wheatley and Peter Cheyney, looking at Arlen's photographs of his Riviera villa and teasing him about his magnificent new overcoat. "Hard-earned, my friends," the novelist assured them. *"Per ardua ad astrakhan."*

Adolph Zukor, the head of Paramount, greeted Reeves-Smith and demonstrated his astonishing memory by recalling not only exactly where he had sat at a luncheon in 1912 but every detail of the menu including even the vintages served. Robert Donat, the new film idol, looked unbelievably young and robust for one already under a cruel sentence, while Leslie Howard, so soon to be shot down by the Luftwaffe, dined alone at a side-table playing an elusive Pimpernel with casual acquaintances.

Lady Diana Cooper, still miraculously preserving her beauty, sent all the ladies into a flurry of imitation with her new 'granny' cap of gold filigree and flowers. Among many refugees from Europe was Emil Ludwig whose suitcase bulged with the manuscript of his new biography of Bolivar. He assured reporters jokingly that he was grateful to Hitler for burning his books; his sales had shot up at once. As soon as he walked into his room, Ludwig carefully placed two strange paperweights on the desk. One was a huge iron nail and the other a block of pure aquamarine cut from a Himalayan peak. He never travelled without these two good-luck charms.

Latry was, meanwhile, taking a holiday in New York where he was honoured by America's leading chefs and gastronomes, with Oscar in the chair. At a banquet representing the best in American cuisine he gave flattering judgment on Minnesota turkey, soft shell crabs on swordfish, Pride of Virginia ham and cranberry sherbet.

In London, Sir George Reeves-Smith stressed the importance of making American tourists feel at home. In a frank speech he said, "A visitor from the U.S.A. is worth three from any other country, not because he necessarily spends more but because he usually stays at least nine days and the others only average three. Moreover, let us never forget that Americans have taught us all the hotel amenities—hot and cold water, central heating, air-conditioning and, of course, baths everywhere." That New Year's Eve, the hotel offered a tableau of George Washington cutting down the cherry tree of 1938. In New York's Waldorf-Astoria, long closely linked with the hotel through Reeves-Smith's friendship with Lucius Boomer, the Savoy's American office passed under the control of a live wire, Arthur Collard, who had started his service with the Company at Claridge's.

The Munich ordeal and the many problems of this period had

meantime brought the Managing Director and his freckled young assistant closer to one another, a mutual and instinctive warmth deepening while they worked together. Wontner now began to appreciate the buoyancy which had kept the Savoy afloat through so many crises. All kinds of improvements had been in progress, year after year. A new and vast telephone exchange and switchboard were in operation, and the largest gas-fired stove in the world had been installed in the Grill kitchens. An underground garage, soon to be requisitioned, was built to take five hundred cars on a single floor.

Confidence swept through that year of destiny. Queen Marie of Yugoslavia's chef arrived for another of his refresher courses with Latry. Lord Rosebery was host at the Derby Night dinner to celebrate Blue Peter's triumph at Epsom. From the ceiling hung a huge jockey cap from which coloured balloons cascaded. Fourteen hundred dinners and suppers were served after the Eton and Harrow match. That afternoon a party of Harrovians telephoned to book a table, explaining that they had no evening clothes in London. Would they be allowed in with morning coats? The answer was icily negative.

Tyrone Power and his new wife, Annabella, were almost trampled underfoot by hysterical admirers. To get into the Savoy the film star borrowed a taxi-driver's cap and coat, stuck a cigarette behind his ear and drove himself along the Strand and into the forecourt.

The needle of the hotel's barometer oscillated wildly between crisis and frivolity. Anxious to emulate Tom Mix's old stunt, Gene Autry rode into the ballroom on Champion who, alas, did not prove as well-behaved as his famous predecessor. Gilbert Beyfus, K.C. celebrated a birthday by climbing a pillar in the restaurant which proved his agility at 52 but, according to his friends in the Temple, finally killed all hopes of the High Court judgeship on which he had set his heart.

Fred Astaire held a Press reception and declined to talk about himself or Hollywood or indeed anything but salmon-fishing. Luise Rainer, on holiday after her triumph in *The Good Earth*, did not seem to enjoy the carefree gaiety of her fellow-stars. She hid in her modest room and evaded all the publicity vultures, unlike Gigli who installed himself in Suite 412 at six guineas a day and made light of depressing war talk. Like Zavattoni he had a touching faith in his Duce's ability to control, and even master, Adolf Hitler. Less exuberant was Winston Churchill, unsmiling but in good appetite as he lunched with the Duff Coopers. Back from a Territorial camp, Anthony Eden looked strained and worried when he addressed American newspaper correspondents, warning them of the German menace while their Ambassador, Joseph P. Kennedy, remained pointedly non-committal. The veteran airman, Eddie Rickenbacker, homeward bound from his tour of the Continent, was optimistic about Anglo-French military might. "If war comes," he said cheerfully, "Germany will soon be faced with a severe shortage of raw materials." His view was not supported by Colonel Joseph Beck, the dour Polish Foreign Minister who had already learned painfully that Hitler was less than reliable. Moody and nervous, he sat bleakly at lunch with Lord Halifax, Eden and Churchill who each asked blunt awkward questions about his country's defences and morale.

While the radio jangled with the world's hopes and fears, Thornton Wilder remained isolated and sad of face in his room, making notes for a new play On the same floor the volatile impresario, Sol Hurok, was closeted for hours with Lee Shubert and autocratic John Murray Anderson, devising mammoth productions which would rock Broadway and London, unless . . . War talk seemed almost a breach of etiquette. One hilarious guest demonstrated how a beard could be fastened with curling pins and tucked under a gas mask. In the foyer a woman's fur-lined mask, with separate sections for purse, lipstick and compact, dangled from her alsatian's neck. Arriving at the Savoy during a trial blackout, the second Duke of Westminster appeared to regard the crisis as a personal affront. Much more phlegmatic was Ezio Pinza, the future star of *South Pacific*, then singing at Covent Garden. To keep his waistline trim, he rode back and forth on his bicycle which he parked in the new garage.

The social occasion of that year was a glittering supper party in the restaurant to honour the Comédie Française company whose gala performance at the Savoy Theatre had been attended by the King and Queen. Lord and Lady Bessborough, with Sir George Reeves-Smith proudly wearing his Legion of Honour ribbon, greeted Madeleine Renaud and her fellow-artistes. They were out-dazzled by the voluminous dress worn by Lady Cunard who had flown back specially from Italy. At midnight in an atmosphere charged with emotion, six hundred and fifty guests stood to attention and joined in singing the Marseillaise.

Plans to celebrate the Golden Jubilee of the Savoy were stored away, like so much else, as peace drained out of Europe. On the morning of 4 September 1939, the hotel suffered a shock almost more profound than the closing of the restaurant. Air-raid sirens, even bombs, would have been taken for granted but none had ever expected to see Sir George Reeves-Smith walking through the Front Hall in a bowler hat and lounge suit. The reception clerks followed him with looks of dismay and returned incredulously to their books.

For over forty years the Managing Director's silk hat and frock-coat had been almost as much part of tradition as the bronze of Count Peter over the great forecourt.

LIKE THE rest of the country the Savoy put on its tin hat and waited for the blitz. Seventy members of the staff were fully trained as A.R.P. wardens, among them the veteran William Lawes from the Works Department who patrolled the roof, keeping out the cold in a two-hundred guinea raccoon coat left behind during the gay 'twenties by an American visitor who could not pay his bill. Others requisitioned the carriage attendants' heavy grey overcoats which, with their brass buttons, made an odd ensemble with A.R.P. helmets. Headed by C. C. Toye, who was normally in charge of the Bill Office and had joined the Savoy early in the Great War, the volunteer spotters came on in pairs for four-hour shifts. Two floors were shut down and the Restaurant, with its glass cupola, temporarily closed.

The 'phoney war', or *sitzkrieg* as the Germans called it, began. Women in London appeared in zipped one-piece siren suits, corduroys and cardigans, carrying white pekingese dogs in the blackout. Soon the grill-room was closed and for a time its clientèle melted away. Only one kitchen, presided over by Latry, remained in operation and the Grill's maître-chef, Virlogeux, departed sadly for the Dorchester. The restaurant was in a shelter at night and only open upstairs during the day. Here Santarelli persuaded lovers of *haute cuisine* that they would rather eat a powdered egg omelette than the roast beef which usually lasted only for a quarter of an hour.

Latry set himself the task of maintaining his reputation on an austerity budget that meant no cooking-oil, little sugar or butter and *ersatz* mayonnaise, and improvised grimly with turnips, vegetable-stuffed steak and mutton bacon. The man who was reputed to know two hundred ways of preparing an egg now practised almost as many enigmatic variations on the humble swede. Although he might well sigh, *"Où sont les sorbets neiges d'antan?"*, he had no sympathy for dowagers who mourned Lapsang Souchong or businessmen in reserved occupations cajoling for extras. His own son, Roger, fought at Dunkirk and later joined the Maquis. Captured and tortured by the Gestapo, he managed to survive the horrors of Belsen and even a death-sentence.

"Tell them it's steak or ships," Latry would shout fiercely at his waiters. His colleague, Alban, later invented a potato roll on which he was complimented by Lady Oxford and others who thought it deserved an austerity *cordon bleu*. Lunching with Lord Derby and Lord Halifax, the new Ambassador to Washington, Winston Churchill set an example by ordering the three-shilling Woolton menu of unrationed food; one sardine, a tenuous leg of chicken and a mysterious soufflé made from apples, but would not deny himself or his guests the compensation of a good cigar. Meanwhile, Latry and his pastry-chefs always tried to perform endearing miracles when a favourite guest had a birthday or came home on leave. Somehow he prepared a cake for A. P. Herbert, the only serving Petty Officer M.P., and his wife, a sergeant in the A.T.S., who were celebrating their silver wedding.

Few of the hotel rooms were occupied during the first months of the war when reservations were automatically made for 'dinner and a bed in the Air Raid Shelter', at that time no more than a straw mattress laid on the floor. None seemed embarrassed at the sudden loss of privacy. The improvised restaurant, soon reopened with evening dress optional, was crowded every night. Here, while Mr. Churchill was talking one evening to Lady Eleanor Smith, Anton Dolin and the Duff Coopers, he was summoned to the telephone by a page. A few minutes later, flushed and unusually excited, he was back. After a little while

Left, the Queen, then Princess Elizabeth, with her future husband at a wedding reception in the River Room at which every member of the Royal Family was present. The Princess was bridesmaid to her lady-in-waiting, Mrs Vicary Gibbs. *Below*, Princess Margaret enjoys Antonio's spirited flamenco dancing at a Charity Ball

Hugh Wontner, Chairman and Managing Director of the Savoy Group

he was called away again and returned, breathing hard but with a beaming face. "It's true," he said in a low voice, bowing to the ladies. "Good night, and God bless you." He was to take over at Number 10.

Often, during the strenuous war years, he would return to the Savoy to lunch or dine privately with members of the War Cabinet, Chiefs of Staff or the many foreign statesmen who made the hotel their wartime headquarters. Usually he chose the Iolanthe, the only Private Room which did not open into another. Too exhausted to return home, he asked one day if he might retire for his usual 'forty winks' which miraculously always seemed to recharge his batteries. A river suite was henceforth at his personal and exclusive service throughout the war.

The P.M.'s transport and attire were quite unpredictable. Never disturbed by air raids or alerts, he would arrive by limousine, armoured car and often on foot. Smiling or dour, he would stride through the foyer in uniform or, more frequently, in the well-loved siren suit. At table one evening, he called for an envelope and the waiter naturally asked if he also required notepaper. "Envelope, large," barked the P.M. but with a twinkle in his eye. When it arrived he carefully slid his portion of meat from the plate into the envelope which he handed to the waiter with a smile. "I don't need this," he said quietly. "Please take it home to your family. We're all in this together, you know."

Duties permitting, he was always reluctant to miss the meetings of The Other Club at which he could dine, relax and argue. Up from his village and dreading the evacuees who might descend on him, gouty Sir Alfred Munnings was asked to dine and confided afterwards to his diary, "Winston was clapped when he arrived. Lord Gort was given a tremendous send-off to France. H. G. Wells foresaw Bolshevism in Germany if Hitler is done with. Anyhow, it was a great evening . . ." Munnings showed his appreciation by decorating the Minutes with some delightful thumbnail sketches.

If, as sometimes happened, there were only thirteen at dinner,

Kaspar would be taken off his shelf in the Pinafore Room and ensconced in the vacant chair next to the President who carefully tied a napkin round the ebony neck. One Thursday evening, looking up at the familiar perch, Mr. Churchill noticed that Kaspar was not among those present. He was shocked to learn that the mascot had disappeared after a dinner party for the officers of No. 609 (West Riding) Squadron. For a joke one of the guests had removed Kaspar and installed him in their mess. To avoid trouble, he was smuggled back into the Savoy and restored to his shelf after a few days.

Some weeks later he was again kidnapped by members of the same squadron who were being entertained by Air Commodore Harald Peake. The host was quite unaware that 'Operation Kaspar' was being planned behind his back. The first step in the liberation of poor Kaspar was to stuff the tunic of a decoy with empty wine bottles. He was promptly challenged at the door by the head waiter. Another officer then followed with a heavy bag which he was requested to open before reaching the Embankment exit. It was full of oddments, not of course including Kaspar who had been evacuated under the raincoat of the Squadron's Intelligence Officer.

It has often been said that the cat was flown out to an R.A.F. mess in the Middle East, but the facts have recently come to light. According to Frank Ziegler, the guest with the raincoat over his arm, Kaspar spent the rest of the evening at the Suivi before departing for 609's station in Lincolnshire where he sustained facial injuries including a battered ear.

The Prime Minister and his fellow-members mourned in silence but word of the episode reached Air Commodore Peake, then Director of Public Relations at the Air Ministry. Embarrassed every time he lunched at the Savoy, he finally dropped a hint to 609 that they might spare his blushes by repatriating the prisoner. Kaspar duly reappeared in his old quarters at the hotel after the Squadron Workshop had performed some excellent plastic surgery on his face.

Although meetings of The Other Club are secret, there is

some evidence that the Prime Minister expressed warm pleasure at seeing Kaspar back again. Whether or not he said, "Bring me the cat," and lovingly sat him down to a full *couvert* on this occasion, cannot be confirmed, but it is in character.

Early in the war the Prime Minister's son-in-law, Vic Oliver, while appearing in the Savoy cabaret in the deep shelter, quipped, "We're employing very small waiters tonight to make the sandwiches look bigger." In the forecourt pocket torches winked in the blackout to guide taxis or, more often, guests on bicycles. With so many cinemas and theatres closed, people were even more eager to dine and dance between the steel girders in the Abraham Lincoln Room where Carroll Gibbons was back at his white piano but with only five in his orchestra. Although twice blown off his platform by bomb blast before V.E. Day, he could proudly claim that Hitler never made his band miss a beat. On holiday in America when war came, it had taken him six months to arrange a passage. When cross-examined by an official who asked why an American citizen and a neutral was so anxious to hurry back to England, he replied simply, "Because the people over there have been nice to me and this is no time to run out on them." He landed with a scooter which ran a hundred miles to the gallon and did not vitally impair the war effort.

In the Restaurant and the now reopened Grill, field-marshals and privates shared Woolton Pie which Latry had created at the suggestion of the Food Minister and named after him. The recipe for this vegetable dish was used by housewives all over the country and, in its way, had some effect in impressing the need for economy at all social levels. Many a celebrity was photographed at the hotel to lend prestige to austerity. Evening dress, siren suits and slacks jigged and swayed to the Orpheans; and the management, acting on the policy that none but the brave deserved the fare, offered Service honeymoon couples an all-in rate of three pounds a day which covered a luxury double room, breakfast, dinner, dance and cabaret.

In a letter to a friend, Lady Diana Cooper wrote, "A great deal of our welcoming took place at the Savoy Hotel where we had decided to perch until I could divest my house of its battle-dress. The Savoy was selected because now more than ever is the Grill the one place in London. Without music and apparently without closing time, you are certain always to find bits of the Cabinet there (for where else can late supper be eaten?). Workers off their shifts, actors, writers, the Press, Mayfair's hostesses who have abandoned their private houses and still want to entertain—they are all grazing in the Savoy Grill. Friends move from table to table—here a cup of soup, there a glass of wine. By living in this great hotel one need never wrestle with the blackout, which is blacker than ever."

One saw familiar faces in war paint; John Mills and Anthony Pelissier, cracking a bottle before joining the Army as rankers; Gilbert Frankau, nibbling a lunchtime snack before dashing back to his desk at the Air Ministry; Terence Rattigan, an air-gunner's flash on his shoulder, supping off potato roll and thinking wistfully of steak and kidney pudding and his favourite plover's eggs; Vivian Ellis, in R.N.V.R. uniform; David Niven, a Staff Officer chuckling at his arrest by over-enthusiastic Home Guards who had carried him off to Guildford Gaol; and the many volunteer pilots of the Eagle Squadron who had come over from the United States and Canada without waiting for America to come off the neutral fence. One of these airmen, still in flying kit, walked into the hotel lobby and sat down at a writing-desk. After a few minutes he fell asleep and could not be woken for quite a time. When he finally came to, he was still dazed but apologized to Victor at the Reception desk and stumbled into the Strand. At the bookstall, an Eagle pilot walked off absent-mindedly with the hotel's complete stock of that day's Sunday Times, thinking it was a *single* copy of one of his home newspapers and its bulky supplements!

As the false alarms receded, long queues waited for tables. The old homing instinct was strong and friends had the urge to gossip, grumble or celebrate. The hotel suites brimmed over with people quickly bored with country life but now without servants to take the dust sheets off their town houses. In that oddly unreal interlude between peace and war, the Savoy was like a spacious and comfortable limousine which had dipped its lights but still throbbed with the old power rhythm. Blinking from the blackout gloom, guests made for the encouraging fragrance of coffee and Carroll's nostalgic, sentimental piano. For many, 'Trust in God and keep your Martinis dry' became almost a signature tune, and the Nazis began to seem rather like a third-rate opera company playing Wagner and missing its cues.

The months of surmise, fretting and impatience ended with the shock of Dunkirk and the blitz on London. Latry invented *tarte de Gaulle* with parsnips instead of fruit, in honour of the austere general who was rallying *La France Libre* to his colours. On the seventh floor the management agreed to set aside suite 780 for a small Foreign Office department headed by Lord Bessborough. Soon it was busily stitching up parcels of comforts and giving advice to Free French refugees and their families. A river suite was transformed into a club where Canadian officers could relax while on leave. Before long the First American Eagle Squadron announced laughingly that they had transferred their H.Q. from 'somewhere in England' to suite 618-619 at the Savoy. The Eagles were rarely allowed to buy a drink and, after a gay night at the Suivi, the Nut House or the Four Hundred, often made their eyries in one of a dozen friendly bedrooms.

The hotel service seemed as composed and well-ordered as ever but in the kitchens and staff-rooms passions were simmering. Latry and many of his countrymen wept as they listened to General de Gaulle's impassioned plea to all freedom-loving Frenchmen, but others had less confidence in the Allies, and fierce arguments broke out when the Royal Navy attacked French ships off Oran. The atmosphere became even more electric when Mussolini entered the war, most people applauding Winchell's sardonic quip, "Italy looks like a boot and behaves like a heel." Many naturalized Italians had volunteered or been called up but feeling against them ran high. All over the country ice-cream parlours and cafés were wrecked by hooligans. In Soho, Fascists quickly changed the names of their restaurants, advertised 'new

181

Swiss management' and righteously expunged spaghetti from the menus.

Behind the scenes at the Savoy, a cold but inflammable war was in progress between French and Italians, a situation exacerbated by questions in the House of Commons and newspaper stories which angrily accused the Savoy of nursing a fifth column of foreign waiters. There followed a wave of arrests and round-ups which were short, sharp and inevitably a little haphazard. Even Latry was twice brought before a tribunal before being completely cleared. Fascists and men who had nothing but their Italian origin to condemn them were alike swept up into the net. The Banqueting Manager, Zavattoni, who had made no secret of his adoration of the Duce and used to keep a black shirt and dagger in his office at the hotel, was quickly interned. He was drowned with several other fellow-employees in the *Arandora Star* which was torpedoed, almost certainly by an Italian submarine, in mid-Atlantic en route to Canada.

Although a naturalized British subject, the gentle Santarelli was imprisoned, much to his horror and that of many Savoy patrons who wrote indignant letters to the authorities and even threatened to boycott the hotel in protest. It was obviously a miscarriage of justice and a cruel blow to a sensitive man who would never recover from the humiliation of being shut up in a prison cell. The Savoy directors and others were active in trying to get a fair hearing for Santarelli, who was transferred to an 'open prison' on Lingfield racecourse before the case was reheard and his innocence completely established. His troubles did not end with his release. A number of the staff, temporarily blinded by prejudice, threatened to walk out if he returned to the hotel. Despite the heavy demands of other duties, Wontner had several frank meetings with the men before finally convincing them that this was indeed a case for fair play.

When Santarelli walked into the Restaurant for the first time after his ordeal he was cheered by everyone present, and many shook him warmly by the hand. It was an astonishing gesture at a time when Italy was almost as much hated and despised as

Nazi Germany. Unhappily, poor Santarelli had sustained inner wounds from which he never fully recovered. He became highly nervous, he could not keep his hands from trembling and had lost the old effortless authority. Suddenly taken ill at the hotel in 1944, he died soon afterwards.

Another victim of a hasty security order was Luigi Donzelli who, despite his baby face under a casque of white hair and a mild manner, was much more durable. After managing the grill-room at Claridge's he had opened a successful restaurant in Jermyn Street. On being released from internment on the Isle of Man, he was anxious to return to the Company. Wontner agreed to employ him in the Savoy Grill where he was to become an outstanding manager when the very popular Manetta resigned to start his own establishment in Mayfair.

Among several Savoy misfits on the confused Isle of Man was Fortunato 'Wilf' Picchi, a bald little man standing no higher than five feet, who had been Zavattoni's assistant in the Banqueting Department but did not share his political views. He spent six wretched months behind barbed wire before being released. Although 47 and far from robust, he volunteered as a parachutist to lead British airborne commandos behind the enemy lines in his homeland. He made his jump and helped to accomplish a major act of sabotage and demolition in Southern Italy but was captured and condemned as a spy. He did not crack under torture although promised leniency if he would give information about the raid. After weeks of silence, Rome Radio announced that he had been shot by a firing squad on Palm Sunday, 1941.

Picchi had many friends among the old Savoy regulars who were not alone in paying tribute. A fund was started and donations began to pour in from many strangers all over the country who were touched by the heroic story. His memory is preserved in a cot endowed at the Queen Elizabeth Hospital for Children in Hackney.

Staff shortages, food rationing and the blackout were already routine when the first bombs rained down on London. Much of the Savoy's valuable silver, glass and china was stored in cellars under Waterloo Station and had to be replaced by oddments from closed-down hotels. None of the special Irish linen could, of course, be bought and sheets were no longer changed daily, although a tiny reserve of the best linen was kept for V.I.P.s in some of the River rooms. While 'utility' in quality, stocks had still to reflect the reputation of a hotel to which Rupert D'Oyly Carte would later point proudly in his Report: "Our visitors included most of the great figures of the war. We provided a temporary home for most of the sovereigns or presidents of the nations overrun by the Germans." They would accept Latry's improvisations on Spam and the dreaded dried egg, but the hotel insisted to the end on its basic choreography of soap, towel and crisp table napkin; and the Savoy Laundry, hit by several bombs and almost destroyed by incendiaries, continued miraculously to live up to its telegraph address, 'Unblemish, London'.

Income from rationed meals and empty suites had dwindled, while overheads mounted for running repairs and a huge A.R.P. and black-out budget. The Group showed a loss in 1940 for the first time in its history, and a raid on Reserves quickly became imperative. Before long, cash resources were exhausted and salaries had to be cut, from the Managing Director's downwards. By this means something like £80,000 a year was saved. A welcome gesture by debenture-holders was a moratorium on the payment of interest, but the crisis was not over. Part of the preciously hoarded linen had to be sold, and eventually many of the cases of fine Havana cigars which would be sorely missed in the years to come. Somehow, the wage bills were met and the Savoy managed to avoid the straits of most London hotels who found it impossible even to pay their ground rents.

When the heavy raids began, the problems of wear and tear and the endless arguments with Ministries over manpower and food came to seem almost trivial. Overnight the Savoy became Blitz Hotel; informal, gayer and inevitably more human. The Restaurant was closed except for luncheon, but evening meals were served in the River Room now turned into a bombproof fortress with a tiny corner for Carroll Gibbons and his men. As

Right, Johnny Johnson, for many years mine host in the American Bar. *Below*, Joe Gilmore, the head bartender who internationally famed for devising special cocktails in honour of celebrities and historic occasions

Above, a service of Royal Worcester porcelain depicting characters from cele-brated Gilbert and Sullivan operas. *Below*, Mr Coggan, head of the China and Glass department, keeps a constant check on stocks. This is quite a task since the banqueting service alone, known as 'The Savoy Garland', has over eleven thousand pieces and a year's reserve

Split-second timing and liaison between kitchen and table are essential. Orders range from a dinner-party for eight in the Sorcerer Room to election nights when two thousand five hundred full-course meals may be served. *Above*, *Commis*-waiters at the ready during luncheon service. *Below*, Alban, Maître-Chef of the grill-room (now retired), supervises a special dish

Alban checks the appearance of fancy baskets of spun-sugar fruits and flowers

Assisted by a dough-mixer and two young helpers, Maître Laplanche and, right, head pastry chef Emile Dufay, stir a huge Christmas pudding

the sirens wailed, guests trooped down to the converted Abraham Lincoln Room where the former makeshift palliasses had been replaced by numbered and pink-curtained bunks. A section of the shelter was set aside for the Duke and Duchess of Kent who usually dined at the Savoy when he came home on leave from R.A.F. duty. Although small and simply furnished, the staff managed to transform it into a 'Royal Suite' with the help of a little paint and a few fresh flowers.

V.I.P.s, interrupted at dinner by air-raid alarms, were given corner alcoves, practically soundproofed by heavy curtains, where they could continue in private conference throughout the night if necessary, with coffee, sandwiches and drinks served from an upstairs bar.

Special arrangements had also to be made for the snorers who became known to their victims as 'Hitler's Secret Weapon'. At first a sheltermaid used to go on nightly patrol and tickle the soles of culprits, but as this was considered both undignified and largely ineffective, a separate compartment, shrouded and remote from the others, was set aside for the stertorous.

In the main lounge from half past eight onwards, already changed into dressing gowns, pyjamas, siren suits and slippers, guests would settle down placidly to a book or newspaper before bedtime. Soon the descent began, a convoy laden with writing pads, eye masks, diaries, novels, magazines, pills, jigsaw puzzles and packs of cards. Earplugs were specially welcome when bombs and ack-ack became unpleasant.

Among those who steadfastly declined to go down to the shelters was Lady Oxford who had been bombed out of her house in Bedford Square. On Frank Owen's advice she moved into the Savoy where she remained until her death at the end of the war. Incredibly rigged in full white evening gown with train and wearing high Russian boots—an ensemble known to the staff as 'Lady Oxford's battle-dress'—she held nightly court in the foyer, tiny but imperially stiff-backed, playing a rubber of bridge or chatting with her son, Anthony, and a chosen circle as if she were back in her old drawing-room at Number 10.

When a bomb gave its high-pitched whistle followed by a crash of glass, the staff used to implore her to take shelter. Instead, she went up and stayed at her desk writing letters to her family and friends until her usual bedtime when she would retire under a couple of Shetland shawls, sleep until 4 a.m. and often read until breakfast. She never drew the blackout curtains which gave the management continuous nightmares and always meant a double-check on her room.

Although much shaken by the death in Rumania of Elizabeth Bibesco, her beloved daughter, Margot Oxford retained her sense of humour to the end. She was much amused by an incident when rationing was particularly fierce and the voice of the mock turtle plainly heard in the land. To dine with her she once invited a young R.A.F. officer, Sir Hamilton Kerr, who was blessed with the appetite of an Oxford Blue and looked forward to a change from his Squadron Mess.

"I only have a simple meal, just scrambled eggs," explained his hostess, "but *do* ask for anything you like." The head waiter took Sir Hamilton's expansive order and returned within a few minutes solemnly bearing two plates of scrambled eggs.

Hector Bolitho, another Squadron Leader who liked meeting fellow New Zealanders at the Savoy and was 'unofficial Consul-General' for countless American journalists and Eagle pilots, tells many a good story of those days. He had managed somehow to pick up a lemon, the first in months, and it was suggested that he might care to present his treasure to Sir George Reeves-Smith who was ill at the time and would welcome a slight change of diet. Alas, Bolitho had already given away half of his lemon but gladly donated the rest. Delicately segmented, it was carried up to the Managing Director's suite on a silver salver.

The so-called 'luxury' hotels were obvious targets for agitators and opportunists of every breed. Wendell Willkie, who had come over to observe British morale and report to his government on Lease-Lend, was almost due to arrive for luncheon with Sir Harry MacGowan and other business leaders when a crowd of angry women, yelling Communist slogans, marched from the forecourt into the lobby and made determinedly for the Restaurant. Some opened their fur coats to reveal incongruous banners proclaiming, 'Our Children are Starving' and 'Ration the Rich', and a number had even arrived in taxis to storm the barricades.

A warning from Hansen, the Head Porter, led to prompt action by 'Willy' Hofflin, the newly-appointed General Manager, who deployed porters to repel the invaders. Hugh Wontner was also quickly on the scene and ordered that the doors leading to the Restaurant should be closed. Half the women were thus cut off from those who had meantime sat themselves down at the tables with arms folded, screaming abuse or demanding to be served with food. Others wrapped themselves round pillars, tied their scarves to chairs and clawed at waiters who asked them to leave. Their sisters on the other side of the doors raised a frenzied protest and clung to brass rails in the best suffragette style. The police arrived and declined to interfere, but the Carnera-like figure of Hansen had its effect. With majestic firmness he convinced the ringleaders that they must either leave or be forcibly removed, and the rank-and-file at last departed after assaulting some of the hapless porters who yet managed to keep their self-control.

If the demonstrators hoped to impress the poker-faced Willkie, who had arrived during the closing stages, they were disappointed. He declared at the luncheon that a similar free-for-all in the Waldorf-Astoria would have brought out the riot squad, armed with tear-gas.

While the new American Ambassador, John G. Winant, was lunching with The Pilgrims, ack-ack guns started to bark on the Embankment. He turned to his neighbour and said quietly, "I now know why the Nazis can't win. Today in Islington I came across a woman in the ruins of her poor home. She was arranging a few sprays of lilac in a broken vase which she filled from a fireman's hose. What chance has Hitler got against her?"

The United States had not yet entered the war but millions of Americans echoed Dorothy Thompson's eloquent broadcast, "When you speak, Churchill, brave men's hearts everywhere go out to you; there are no neutral hearts, except those that have stopped beating have gone into neutral. There are no neutral prayers."

A small but touching gesture at this time is characteristic of America's reaction. A few employees of the Hotel Pierre in New York, who had formerly worked at the Savoy, sent Sir George Reeves-Smith a cheque for a thousand dollars which they asked him to share among any of their old friends who had suffered in the raids.

To keep the public informed of the Battle of Britain and the blitz, American newspapers and radio networks sent over their top reporters. The Savoy's American Bar was soon a bazaar for gossip and a convenient Press rendezvous for almost a hundred war correspondents. One by one, starting with the *New York Times*, their London offices were blitzed or suffered such damage from blast as to become unworkable. With a shortage of clerical staff and an erratic or overloaded telephone service, they found it convenient to move into the Savoy which became office and club, round the clock. Reporters deposited their bags and laundry and took off on flying missions or in naval convoys, assured of a room, a bath (with the regulation five inches of hot water) and their favourite corner in the bar, if and when they returned.

They brought a warm gusty humanity with them, even if a few old-fashioned eyebrows were raised at their shirtsleeves, the bottles of Jack Daniel's bulging from hip-pockets, and the earthy dialogue that used to rattle 'The Glasshouse', as they renamed the lounge. They played impassioned stud poker and marathons of chess, or clenched their fists in fierce games of matchstick 'spoof' for which helpful waiters looted every ashtray in sight. Drinking and talking shop into the small hours, they waited impatiently for Press releases but always with half an eye on all the comings and goings past Victor's desk in the Reception.

The procession was quick-changing and often rich in drama. Late one night Katina Paxinou, 'the Duse of Athens', swept in dishevelled and hollow-eyed after being torpedoed on her way to New York. With a coat over her pyjamas she had spent hours in a lifeboat before being rescued. The Duke of Kent, a dashing figure in R.A.F. uniform, would arrive for dinner with his lovely young wife, so soon to be widowed when his Sunderland crashed in the north of Scotland. An excited babble of French announced the arrival of grandmotherly-looking but intense Madame Tabouis, the political writer, who made for her room where she dictated at breathless speed to a relay of hotel stenographers. Henri Bernstein, the playwright, still looked the debonair boulevardier although he had just landed in the last British ship to leave Bordeaux; and tall, angular General de Gaulle, sparing of words and gesture, cut a monosyllabic swathe through any reporters and admirers who tried to stop him.

Dr. Benes, General Sikorski, Maharajahs in the War Cabinet, and representatives from Greece, Holland and Belgium all jostled in the foyer but a respectful path was quickly cleared for Winston Churchill whose cherubic smile and 'V' sign always brought a cheer. In his wake one saw another bulldog figure, that of Hilaire Belloc in a flowing Spanish cape with a cigar jutting from his mouth, or Sir William Beveridge arriving to lunch with Lloyd George with whom he liked to discuss the blueprints of the future Welfare State.

The elderly but high-spirited Sultan of Johore provided an unexpected news story which went round the world. After lunching at the hotel he was stopped in the Strand by a pretty blonde who was selling Red Cross flags. He bought the entire stock and chatted pleasantly with her for a few minutes. That evening the Rumanian-born Marcella Mendle dined with the Sultan. They were married three weeks later.

A few of the American correspondents would go up on the roof to join the fire-spotters and watch the flares, gunbursts and bomb flashes on the Embankment until the sickly-sweet carrion breath of rubble and ashes sent them below to their typewriters or the warm reassurance of alcohol and friendly gossip. Fire-watchers coming off duty with smarting, bloodshot eyes were always shanghaied and plied with restoratives.

Tich's Bar, a small room reserved for residents 'and friends', and named after Arthur 'Tich' Massara, a cheery waiter cum bartender who later left to join the R.A.F., developed into an all-night club for some of America's hardest-worked and most endearing citizens. Here met staff men on the *New York Times*, chunky Drew Middleton of *Associated Press*, who had the latest baseball scores cabled to him from New York, and the fast-talking chess addict, Larry Rue of the *Chicago Tribune*. The most lovable of them all, waiflike Ernie Pyle, was later killed in the Pacific. He made numerous friends in England, while in his own country a remarkable tribute was paid to his memory. During a War Bond Drive in Indianapolis, one of his manuscripts was auctioned and knocked down, after spirited bidding, to an insurance company for over ten million dollars.

Open-handed with their liquor, cigarettes and candy bars, always laughing, drinking, wisecracking and ready to throw dice on the carpet for a week's pay, these correspondents seemed carefree but, between spasms of fun, all of them worked selflessly to give America a true and vivid picture of wartime Britain, often in the face of unsympathetic or isolationist editors back home.

Ed Murrow lay in the gutter outside the Savoy so that his microphone could pick up the wailing sirens and the actual thump of German bombs for his countrymen across the Atlantic. On the roof, gruff Quentin Reynolds wept as London smouldered in the ashes of a thousand fires but, later in the bar, quaffing mighty draughts of gin, he would quickly have his friends rocking with stories in imitation Cockney slang. He used to keep three goldfish in his bathroom *bidet* until they were accidentally drowned by a maid. It was a perfect excuse for a gay all-night funeral party. His hotel bills were often in the neighbour-hood of £200 a week. Propped up by pillows, with a typewriter between his knees and a bottle of the old fortifier beside him, he would tap out the wonderful radio scripts which proved to 'Mr. Schickelgruber' and the world that London could indeed take it.

A great camaraderie, linked by a traditional thirst and the freemasonry of printer's ink, developed early between the American newsmen and Fleet Street editors who munched hot cheese sandwiches between editions or settled down in the

American Bar with a glass when their papers had been put to bed, the inseparable telephone always within reach. When almost every line in Fleet Street was out of action, and only that of the *New York Times* in the hotel seemed in working order, it was unhesitatingly offered to rival newspapers, apart from hard-pressed British colleagues.

Their four-page newspapers spiked or blue-pencilled by Security, D-Notices or plain bureaucratic ignorance, these London editors and their staffs needed a safety-valve like the Savoy where they could rely on a relaxing drink and the sympathetic ear of a fellow-sufferer. And always commuting between the Americans and his own colleagues was the inevitable Swaffer, commentating on the war news but ever-ready to help and advise any newspapermen who might need his astonishing contacts in high places.

The hotel was now almost an international Press Club with its growing corps of Americans and Australians; here Aneurin Bevan, 'The Bollinger Bolshevik' of *Tribune*, would argue with gruff but kindly John Gordon, editor of the *Sunday Express*; and the handsome editor of the *Sunday Chronicle*, Jimmy Drawbell, would often be mistaken for Leslie Howard who used to creep unrecognized to his corner table in an old tweed coat and unbecoming horn-rims. Drawbell was always surrounded by politicians, celebrities and writers like Sir Philip Gibbs and Beverley Nichols, while Monica Dickens often came in to rest one pair of weary feet from her nursing unit. His star contributor was Dorothy Thompson who settled into the same suite she had last occupied in 1928 when she married Sinclair Lewis. Always dynamic and groomed to the very last eyelash, the confidante of statesmen and Cabinet Ministers and the first journalist to be honoured by a private dinner and an interview with the P.M. himself, Miss Thompson reigned as the Overseas Press Queen of the Savoy. Her suite was like a star's dressing-room at Drury Lane and always crammed with cables, invitations and huge bouquets of flowers which she would take round personally to London's hospitals. "Being married to Dorothy was like living permanently

191

in a newspaper office," her husband used to complain, and wartime London offered even less respite. Her three white telephones jangled incessantly while she dictated letters and articles, gave interviews and posed for newsreels. A thousand guests attended the reception which Lord Kemsley gave in her honour at the Savoy.

While some guests slumbered in the shelter, teleprinters and typewriters clattered in every other room, and the night owls, jocose or lachrymose, hooted in the bars, it was wise to "batten down all blondes, brunettes, red heads and two-toned jobs," recalls a reporter. There was a late-night collision in the darkened forecourt of the hotel when the night porter heard someone shout, "Is that you, Quent.?", followed by an unmistakable growl, "It isn't F.D.R."

A waiter in the bar picked up another scrap that has been preserved. Two correspondents were arguing so fiercely that a rough house seemed inevitable. "What makes you think you won the war, anyway?" demanded a blurred Georgian. There was an angry silence until his friend replied, "What the heck! So it was a *moral* victory for the South."

A remarkable number of sprightly guests were to be seen in the River Room, dancing cheek-to-cheek with most attractive nieces. After a raid, usually shaken and looking rather less debonair without their dentures, most of these uncles seemed painfully anxious to avoid Press reporters and, above all, photographers.

When *The Lady is a Tramp* had been played a dozen times and the last-ditch dancers had drifted off, Carroll would make for Tich's Bar for a drink, a hand of stud poker or a night-long game of chess with Larry Rue. He suffered from insomnia, due probably to delayed shock after the bomb that blew him off his dais. He had picked himself up with a grin and drawled his usual, "Hallo, everybuddy." In a moment or two, while the shuttered windows rattled like peas and the lights clicked on and off, Noël Coward sat down nonchalantly at the white piano and started to sing a number from one of his shows. The audience demanded encores and firmly refused to go on dancing. For almost an hour and a half, while enemy aircraft ploughed the sky like heavy tractors, Coward gave a non-stop cabaret until his voice had dwindled to a whisper.

Incendiaries straddled the roof that night but the high-explosives which had rocked the hotel were all near-misses, leaving only broken windows. The luck ran out a few nights later when a bomb struck the parapet over the entrance in the Strand, close to Count Peter, laying a carpet of masonry over the rubber forecourt. The same night, another cracked a corner of the building overlooking the Embankment, killing two people, one of them a Belgian Deputy, of the thousand or more who were in the hotel at the time. Four stained-glass windows of the Savoy Chapel were destroyed by blast, but the lovely altar-silver presented by the Royal Family was safely housed in the Cathedral of St. John the Divine in New York.

In less than an hour and armed with hand torches while the bombers droned overhead, the staff had inspected each of the five hundred rooms for slivers of light and adjusted any flapping blackouts. Windows were quickly replaced but with little hope that they would survive more than a few days. Meantime a much-reduced Works Department inspected damaged rooms, closing down several or giving first-aid to buckled window-frames and cracked ceilings. A.R.P. workers and nurses, often with a minimum of sleep, returned to their normal duties with eyes a little bloodshot but rarely without the Cockney twinkle.

The tiny pages, neat as new pins with buttons, hair and shoes shining, more than proved their worth in those feverish days when quick thinking and a willingness to run errands for every-one, from wardens on the roof to nervous or fretful guests in the basement shelter, relieved an overtaxed staff. Nothing seemed to convey a sense of normality more than the daily inspection parade of these lads, standing like midget guardsmen among the wreckage of a previous night's raid. Grateful old ladies would reward them with sugar lumps or their precious sweet ration, and many of them would become hopeless addicts of Hershey chocolate nut bars. One smart youngster, Charles Ruel, who had migrated back from the country like so many other London sparrows, took the eye of the Argentine millionaire, Dodero, who later found him a post in his shipping firm in Buenos Aires.

Like an experienced boxer the Savoy had soon demonstrated its ability to roll with the punch, but the fight had only started. The year 1941 would prove the most testing in the whole history of the hotel.

On New Year's Day, W. A. Hofflin had taken over as General Manager. He had come to the Savoy in 1928, on Friday the 13th, a fortunate day as it turned out. Like so many of the world's great hoteliers, he was a Swiss who had trained at the famous school in Lausanne, having first become interested in the business through his father who used to supply meat to local hotels and restaurants. Starting traditionally by peeling potatoes, he went through every branch until he could talk technicalities with chefs, wine waiters and almost any other specialist. He began his career with the Company in the reception office at the Berkeley where he impressed the management by his tactful handling of guests and an instinct for both thinking and acting quickly in crises. He never forgot a lesson from Reeves-Smith whom he rashly telephoned late one evening. The Managing Director would only be disturbed on the rarest occasions by telephone calls which he disliked, but Hofflin explained breathlessly that a fire had broken out at the Berkeley.

"Well," answered the cool voice, "you're in charge. Put it out."

He had succeeded to his new post, the key position in every large hotel, after many years as assistant to Gilles. Tall and handsome with the physique and bearing of a soldier, Hofflin had a clipped manner which sometimes startled guests expecting gallant courtesies from an hotel manager. He could be derisive, sardonic and abrupt with personnel but every decision bore the trademark of the dedicated artist. I was not surprised when he once told me, a little wistfully after a long and hard day, that

194

he had sometimes regretted not having trained to be an architect, as his family had hoped.

In his twenty years as General Manager he could claim to have been, almost literally, wedded to the hotel. In fact he and his wife, Greta, were married from the Savoy in 1932. The war years, during which they lived in the hotel and worked incredible hours—Mrs. Hofflin was in charge of the Red Cross nurses—brought him to grips with every kind of staff and rationing crisis, apart from the careful handling of V.I.P.s. "I have always regarded myself as an innkeeper," he reminded me shortly before his retirement. "This office is like a confessional box and I never betray a confidence. To run an hotel's working life is not nearly as difficult as to make guests feel at home."

Few situations ever found him at a loss but he liked to recall the occasion when Winston Churchill was leaving the hotel one night and casually asked if he might buy a dozen of the Savoy's large white ashtrays. They were most convenient, he explained, for cigar smokers. Completely baffled, Hofflin tried not to look surprised and suddenly realized that the Prime Minister was referring to the metal waste-paper baskets in the Pinafore Room. The following weekend a dozen of the huge 'ashtrays' were sent off to Chartwell with the compliments of the management.

The strenuous war years would have killed a less resilient man, but Hofflin thrived on the stimulus of contact with the many statesmen and celebrities he welcomed. "The greater the man, the easier to receive," he always insisted. "I have known a bad film actor to expect much more ceremony than a Royal Prince." He was, nevertheless, a very worried man indeed at a *Quatorze Juillet* reception for General de Gaulle. Members of the Fighting French had been invited with their families, and the Lancaster Room was gay with tricolour and charged with emotion as old friends embraced and drank to better days. Tumultuous applause greeted the general who was quite unaware that Hofflin was fighting a desperate rearguard action. The Lancaster Room was being stormed like the Bastille by frenzied patriots all eager to pay tribute simultaneously to their leader. Hofflin, normally

195

as calm as a Swiss lake, was swept aside by two thousand people, many of whom had dispensed with formal invitations. At last the doors were closed, much to the angry disappointment of several hundred who had to wait outside until their leader departed.

Royalty, ambassadors and V.I.P.s of every kind are often at the mercy of cranks who need to be handled firmly but with the minimum of fuss, a technique of which Hofflin was the complete master. During the war, his calmness sealed off a number of awkward situations. At the first hint of disturbance, he would shoot his snowy-white cuffs, square those broad shoulders and walk unobtrusively into the lobby, a short distance ahead of the hotel detectives. They rarely had to be called upon after he had said his few well-chosen words. Some years later, the light flashed on the dashboard in his office to inform him that a crowd of men with some obscure political grievance were in the lobby, intent on presenting a petition to a Cabinet Minister who was due to arrive for a private luncheon. Hofflin quickly intercepted their spokesman and promised that the Minister would receive the petition before he left. The men withdrew quietly, few in the Front Hall having the least suspicion that an ugly little 'scene' had been smoothed away.

A convivial man, he could hold his own with Frank Owen, Quentin Reynolds, Negley Farson and other formidable characters, and liked particularly to relax from harsh protocol in the company of men like these, who worked and played hard. During the wearing, but exciting, war years he made an enormous variety of friends. One of them, now a distinguished architect in Los Angeles, wrote to him just before his retirement, "Since my wife and I plan to be in London soon it occurred to me that this souvenir would be of more use back with its rightful owners. Many years ago, in a burst of boyishness, I purloined a *demi-tasse* spoon while dining at your establishment."

In those difficult days of rationing, some guests were not content with such little mementoes. They 'requisitioned' the hotel's soap, towels, bedside lamps, sheets, brushes and even corridor carpets. Souvenir jackdaws, practical jokers and, above all, intrusive photographers were wartime hazards which Hofflin denounced fiercely and privately accepted with good humour, but he was in a terrifying rage when awakened, in the very small hours, with the news that a naked man had been seen prowling along the corridors on the fourth floor. Overpowered and hastily wrapped in a blanket, he pleaded his complete innocence and begged the management not to call the police. As it happened, he had a perfectly reasonable explanation which was checked and verified.

The 'prowler' was an American pilot who had missed his last train back to camp after a late bottle-party. A newspaper friend had given him a key to his room at the Savoy where he had quickly crept into bed without troubling to look around for a spare pair of pyjamas. Soon afterwards he awoke with the familiar thirst and went off to the bathroom—as he imagined—for a glass of water. Instead he found himself in the corridor with the lock snapped behind him. He was wandering about, naked and bemused and trying hard to remember the room number, when a floor waiter brought him down in a rugger tackle and called for reinforcements.

While Hofflin was popular with Americans whom he treated like a broadminded uncle but also, at times, with the firmness of a regimental sergeant-major when they became too exuberant, their special favourite was petite pretty Jean Nicol who was in charge of the hotel's Press and Publicity Office and later wrote a most entertaining book recalling her experiences. She listened sympathetically to the highly-strung journalists, soothed away their troubles and made them feel at home when war anxiety and strain could not be subdued even in Tich's Bar or at West End bottle-parties. It was fitting that she should be asked to edit *The Savoy Standard*, which appeared on Thanksgiving Day just before Pearl Harbour.

I have before me a copy of this unique four-page newspaper which was printed in Fish Street Hill and published by the hotel who underwrote its cost. Larry Rue, Eric Baume, Hector

Bolitho, Mollie Panter-Downes and all the other more or less resident journalists contributed without fee. They wrote in flippant New Yorkerish style of life in blacked-out London and shared the private backroom jokes of off-duty hours.

This one-issue only newspaper, as sentimental-tough in tone as an early Hemingway story, had to be reprinted in a few hours but further supplies soon gave out. Residents, visitors, embassies and Fleet Street offices eagerly snapped up copies which soon found their way to the White House and even into foxholes in remote battle zones. One went to Winston Churchill who read it in bed and chuckled over its gay irreverence.

From Russia Quentin Reynolds cabled: "Am fine except for conjunctivitis, boils, dysentery and boredom. Stop." Carroll Gibbons was earnestly encouraged to learn a new tune. The hotel's medical officer offered helpful advice on the infection carried by the parasite known as 'American Barfly or plasmodius alcoholicus'. In extreme cases he recommended complete immobilization of both hands, arms in Plaster of Paris and a liberal diet of Vitamin B1, or alternatively amputation of both arms and permanent abstention from alcohol.

From the Ministry of Information Brendan Bracken wrote warmly to Jean Nicol, "The Savoy Hotel has ceased to be just a hotel. It's a Newspaper House . . . It's most fitting that this publication of yours should be appearing on Thanksgiving Day . . . but I think it's really we British redskins who should be giving thanks that the Pilgrim Fathers have come back and installed themselves on their original Strand."

Within a few months of Hofflin's appointment as General Manager, Sir George Reeves-Smith died at the age of 86. He had been Managing Director of the Savoy for over forty years and almost a symbol of its tradition and continuity. During his last illness he had come to rely all the more on Hugh Wontner whom he regarded as his natural successor. Unlike Hofflin who had already served as Assistant General Manager for thirteen years and moved with expected ease into his new appointment,

Sir George's deputy was scarcely known to many of the staff and even less familiar to the guests. Although he had joined the Company barely three years before, Reeves-Smith had known him very much longer and appreciated his business and administrative sense allied to a remarkable memory. To many he appeared rather an aloof figure, sparing of words and gestures, but Sir George had absolutely no doubt of his calibre. Now that the post of Managing Director was vacant for the first time in over forty years, Rupert D'Oyly Carte did not hesitate. He appointed 32-year-old Wontner as Managing Director of the Savoy Group, with Thornewill as Vice-Chairman.

During the night of 16 April 1941, a land mine fell outside the Embankment entrance rocking the hotel and shattering every window facing the river. A grinding crash of masonry was followed by a rumble like the echo from a dynamited quarry. Men and women, with faces cut and eyes smarting from dust, rubble and cordite, crunched unsteadily over glass. That night poor Don Minifie of the *Herald Tribune* lost an eye while watching the scene from his window. Scores of others were bleeding from ugly gashes which were quickly bandaged by Mrs. Hofflin and her Red Cross helpers. Eric Maschwitz was lying face downward on a stretcher receiving first-aid for a lacerated back. Mrs. Kate Butler, bruised and suffering from shock but instinctively erect with dignity, came down from her room covered in black dust from head to foot and with literally only the whites of her eyes showing. She declined first-aid, conferred briefly with Hofflin and went off to change. Within a few minutes she was back, her white hair miraculously coiffured, a brooch at the neck of her crisp black dress, calmly directing her staff of housekeepers on salvage operations. Chamberlain, the Embankment Head Porter, was blasted off his feet and pressed against the bomb-proof wall, and had to be taken to hospital by ambulance. The nurses were meanwhile tending dozens of casualties from the Strand who had been brought into the hotel for treatment.

More than sixty suites were put out of action, apart from all the bathrooms, the Pinafore and several other banqueting rooms, and many offices. The restaurant was a pulp of smashed tables and chairs, and the kitchen a completely unusable shell. Over 5,000 glasses and pieces of china were destroyed.

Armed with a pocket torch, Miles Thornewill was to be seen everywhere, calming the residents, the majority elderly and in a state of shock, helping to co-ordinate the Control Room, and gently advising members of the staff anxious about the welfare of their families and homes in other parts of the city. Imposing as ever, even in a siren suit covered by debris, Hofflin directed a squad of waiters and porters, many of them bruised and cut, in salvaging bits of furniture which were hastily moved into the former grill-room. A scratch staff took over the disused kitchen and by first light, hot breakfasts were already being served. At noon, guests who had braved the rubble and stepped gingerly over broken glass, sat down to an emergency luncheon menu redeemed by spotless napery and almost the customary service.

It was the worst raid suffered by the hotel but by no means the last of many near-misses. During a Board Meeting at which Rupert D'Oyly Carte presided, a heavy bomb landed nearby with enough force to blast the curtains from the windows. There was a moment's silence and fleeting glances were exchanged. The Chairman gave his little cough and said calmly, "Gentlemen, to continue . . ."

IN HIS capacity as Managing Director and later Chairman, Hugh
Wontner was to exercise more power and responsibility than any
other single figure in the history of the Savoy Group. Although
the wartime stresses and shortages would be followed by threats
of mergers and take-overs, strikes, intensive competition in the
hotel trade and a volcanic international landscape, the first twenty
years and more of the new régime have proved outstandingly
successful. In the spring of 1941 when Sir George Reeves-Smith
died, the prospect looked anything but bright, with profits at
vanishing point, most of the hotel rooms empty for long stretches
of the year, and key personnel either in the Services or interned on
the Isle of Man. Understandably despondent, the shareholders
could hope for little more than a holding operation by the new
Managing Director, still an unknown quantity to most of them.
They expected him to keep the books in order and to tread
cautiously in the footsteps of his predecessor.

He slipped very quietly into gear; indeed, so smoothly unobtrusive was the transition that veteran members of the staff
who had come to regard Sir George as a synonym of the Savoy,
felt the quite unexpected sensation of no change. The hotel
continued to run on rubber tyres like the trolleys which slid
noiselessly along the corridors on each floor. Those who met the
freckled and bespectacled young man for the first time came
away impressed by an orderly mind which adjusted effortlessly to
problems. The whispering gallery echoed with reports of a tireless
worker behind the heavily-boarded windows of Sir George's old

office, but always with a quick practical sympathy for members of the staff and their families who had suffered through the call-up or been bombed out of their homes.

The impression of 'no change at the top' was reinforced when the Managing Director wisely took over Reeves-Smith's very capable secretary, Miss Olive Barnett, and promptly appointed as his assistant Reginald Bentley, who had served Sir George for so many years and had the workings of every department, in particular the important cellars, at his fingertips. And always at hand with the wisdom of long experience was the Vice-Chairman, Miles Thornewill, highly respected by the staff and aware of all the pitfalls and snares which threatened the new chief. The latter was in the position of a junior Counsel who, tugging diffidently at his leader's robe in Court, finds himself suddenly asked to take over an important brief halfway through the proceedings. Familiar with the case and its general strategy, he has nevertheless to apply his own style of advocacy.

Austerity had banned turn-ups, cuffs and so many other refinements in men's suits that a waggish former dandy commented sadly, "*Ex nihilo nihil fit*," but the practised eye can always detect a rare touch of style. Aided by the resourceful Hofflin, the new Managing Director was determined to maintain a Savile Row cut at the Savoy even with the skimpiest of utility materials. In happier days the hotel buyers at Smithfield would order two tons of the finest cuts of prime quality meat with a casual nod and the tick of a pencil. Every week the restaurant kitchens had consumed two hundred gallons of cream, a ton of butter and 14,000 eggs. The pink slips were still hooked to a board indicating order, time and table, but the days were long past when twenty-eight varieties of cheese were on offer. The hors-d'œuvres trays were laden but only with vegetable titbits, rarely relieved by sardines or anchovy. Under French names, Spam and snoek linked arms in a grisly can-can and cavorted with dried egg, bacon rind stews or bogus rissoles. The machine for whipping cream mourned beside elaborate baskets bare of toothsome petits-fours. Veiled was the tank in which well-bred trout had glided back and forth, and Latry's mighty open ranges where proud barons of beef had once spluttered now stood bleak and silent. The maître-chef himself had finally decided to abandon the unequal struggle and retired to grow fruit and vegetables at The Little Farm, near Maidenhead. His successor was the serious Dutrey.

As the air raids ceased, theatres and cinemas began to reopen and the restaurant was soon so crowded that bookings had to be made well in advance but always with priority for Service guests and prewar patrons. Never before or since has the clientèle been more cosmopolitan or polyglot. In the bars one saw Australians drinking sundowners, Americans and Canadians imbibing rye and bourbon, and small groups of thirsty, volatile Free French, Greeks, Poles, Czechs and Norwegians.

America's entry into the war had started a rash of bookings for rooms, suites and receptions. The radio and Press correspondents were now reinforced by many more, including Raymond Gram Swing and burly William Shirer who broadcast a daily diary to the United States. Demanding, cajoling and pleading for accommodation were Lease-Lend officials and observers, American Red Cross leaders like Arthur Hudson, businessmen and trade delegations, with bemedalled generals and admirals from a dozen Allied and neutral countries. Taxis, embassy limousines and staff cars flowed endlessly into the courtyard. Presided over by Gottfried Keller, the Foreign Press Association entertained Turkish and Swedish journalists and at one luncheon, attended by every diplomat in London, offered King George of the Hellenes a menu far removed from Royal banquets of the past. The party settled down to a feast of oratory after a sketchy meal of lobster patty, potato rolls and rice pudding.

Meanwhile, over Wontner's hand lay a skein of statistics, reports and memoranda of all kinds. Every day a batch of documents arrived on his desk, including the regular analysis of stocks, consumption of all kinds, breakages, wear and tear, wages and other outgoings. The curve on his graph was showing a slow rise after the early slump in trading profits when the Company's shares were at their lowest, but even with an excellent balance-sheet grave problems in administration had still to be faced. The five-shilling, three-course limit on meals was an anxiety and often meant a financial loss to first-class restaurants and hotels with traditional standards to maintain. Not the least of their problems was the climb in all expenses, including wages for staff which, even viewed charitably, was scratch in quality but still at a premium. Thanks to Wontner's previous experience in the secretariat of the trade, he became spokesman and go-between in the many complicated negotiations with government departments all through the war. The five-shilling Meal Order was an example of his diplomacy in meeting the public interest whilst protecting the essential needs of the catering industry. Where proof was forthcoming, hotels and restaurants with inescapably high over-heads were grudgingly permitted to charge something extra on a graduated scale, plus a little for minor luxuries, like oysters, when available. If music and facilities for dancing were pro-vided, an additional charge could now be included. Without these concessions, few of the leading hotels and restaurants could have continued.

The Savoy became more and more a hub of affairs, the venue of Kings, statesmen and most of the Service V.I.P.s, who brought with them additional problems over security arrangements. In the grill-room one saw Lord Louis Mountbatten, dining on his return from the Dieppe raid; Jan Masaryk, de Gaulle and the Soviet Ambassador, Maisky; General Wavell, briefly back from Africa and snatching a hurried luncheon on his way to report to the War Cabinet. At Claridge's the picture was much the same but with a regal varnish from King George of the Hellenes, the King of Norway and Queen Wilhelmina of the Netherlands. In his third floor suite King Peter of Yugoslavia dressed for his marriage to pretty Princess Alexandra of Greece, and the Presidents of Poland and Czechoslovakia were among many other exiled Heads of State. General Catroux arrived to confer with Charles de Gaulle after his talks with General Giraud in North Africa, soon to be followed by General Montgomery who was home on short leave and insisted austerely on the most modest room in the hotel. Another guest back from Algiers was Archbishop Spellman. A few days later an American, the Rev. James L. Blakeney, Chaplain-General of the United States Army, preached for the first time in the Savoy Chapel.

Although the house-list was gratifying, the directors would not permit austerity as an excuse for inferior attention. The menu might be dull and the pink tablecloths and napkins stored for the duration, but the white linen was always crisp and fresh and no explanation accepted for half-emptied ashtrays or chipped glasses. The cruets, crockery and silver were stacked neatly in the service rooms on each floor, the skeleton staff of silver-smiths constantly cleaning and replating. As in prewar days, no room was let without the preliminary ritual of oiling locks, testing each tap and a fastidious inspection made of bed linen, carpets, lights, bolts and curtain hooks under Mrs. Butler's sharp eye. Every Monday, following a practice which dated from the first opening of the hotel, each of the hundreds of clocks, one in every room, was carefully checked. One of them was missing from the mantelpiece after the departure of an American colonel who returned it only when the Managing Director himself sent a polite reminder. His reply was almost disarming; apparently he had found the pretty clock quite irresistible.

Despite the small extra charge permitted for meals and enter-tainment, it was no surprise that the catering side could not avoid a loss, even allowing for an increased demand for wines and spirits. Although the Company had started the war with vast reserves, all the normal sources of wine had now been cut off and it was only possible to buy comparatively small parcels at auctions or from private cellars and at prices which became more and more inflated with scarcity. A glance at the Savoy's wartime wine list demonstrates that a wide and balanced variety of the traditional wines of Europe was maintained, although some unusual ones unavoidably found their way into the cellars.

Spurious and very odd wines and liqueurs would be submitted

hopefully to the Company but hastily rejected by meticulous judges like Hugh Wontner, Reginald Bentley and J. M. Eggle, head of the cellars and one of the hotel's most unusual characters. A native of Linz, he was small, swarthy and intense with a dedication to his craft which took no account of normal working hours. From noon until often well past midnight he would occupy himself with a thousand details which a lesser man might have delegated to others. Often with cause he trusted few, waging ceaseless warfare against all varieties of petty larceny. His notes addressed to the management concerning those who threatened his cherished wines and cigars were always explosive and highly personal. "There is only one difference between a waiter and the devil," he used to mutter darkly. "A waiter has two tails."

Himself the very embodiment of rectitude, he suffered a profound shock when stopped in the early hours during a blackout while crossing Savoy Place. A detective in plain clothes took one look at the little figure, coat turned up under a black hat and grasping an attaché case, and promptly demanded his identity card. Eggle burst into incoherent, guttural protest but was taken in charge before he could find words. With Olympian rage he at last stammered fiercely, "I am the head of the highest profit-producing department of the Savoy Hotel." The detective hesitated, made a quick enquiry and released him.

Many were surprised to discover that, for a country traditionally more interested in beer than wine, a reasonable quantity and variety of hocks, moselles, clarets and burgundies were still on sale at the end of the war. This was evidence of the large stocks in England when Hitler swept into France and sealed Europe off from the British Isles. One of the most notable was the Glyndebourne cellar of fine German wines, purchased by John Christie, and temporarily not required. A stock of champagne was released after the tragic night when a bomb destroyed the crowded Café de Paris. There was also the cellar of the Langham Hotel which had closed its doors for ever, as it turned out.

The shortage of good whisky was almost as acute as that of

wines but the Savoy had some advantage since it was already in the whisky business, in a small way. This had begun many years before the war as a result of the close contact between Lucius Boomer of the Waldorf-Astoria in New York and Sir George Reeves-Smith. They had agreed that the Savoy should supply the Waldorf with a rare and fine blended Scotch of good age and pedigree. Shipments being halted by the war, the accumulated stocks were retained for the Savoy, Claridge's and the Berkeley. As a result of this and of purchases on a large scale of single whiskies, blended for the Savoy to its own recipe, the hotels in the Group were thus in the enviable position of not having to ration Scotch.

The Managing Director was responsible for starting the hotel's poultry farm, which had a curious background. A summons was suddenly received from the Ministry of Food accusing the Savoy of buying chickens above the controlled price. This greatly incensed the management which had scrupulously kept to the letter of the law, despite a growing black market on every side. Dealers would draw up after dark in Savoy Hill in vans loaded with carcases which they tried vainly to sell to the hotel. The black marketeers were peremptorily turned away, although the kitchens would have been more than grateful for any supplement to their minute rations. At a time when guests had to be satisfied with the official ration of a pennyworth of butcher's meat per meal, one of the Company's directors had the bitter experience of lunching with a friend at a West End club where a waiter offered him a steak which would have served half a dozen diners in the Grill.

It was therefore additionally irritating for the Savoy to be exposed to an ill-founded prosecution. The case was heard at Bow Street before Sir Laurence Dunne, the Company being represented by Gilbert Paull, K.C., now a High Court judge, with H. H. Maddocks for the Ministry of Food. The result entirely vindicated the Savoy which was awarded costs against the Ministry. As so often happened at that time, the advance gossip established guilt in the public mind while the decision itself attracted little notice. Deciding to risk no more one-sided experiences of this kind, Wontner had started the farm in Surrey. Here for the rest of the war and some years afterwards, Savoy chickens were born and bred, free at least from the terrors of Bow Street, and large quantities of their eggs sent to the packing stations for sale to others.

The Savoy remained a tempting target for snipers, not all of whom acted from high-minded or patriotic motives. Some journalists seized every chance to caricature the hotel as a Grand Babylon, cynical and replete, while the less fortunate pinched and scraped along on their puny rations. Fairly typical was the action of a Fleet Street diarist who became a habitué of the grill-room in the war years. After his meal one evening he asked for cigarettes, then in very short supply. He gave a handsome tip to a waiter who slipped him a packet from his own private hoard. Next morning, the country was informed in explosive headlines that cigarettes were unlimited at the Savoy for those who could afford them.

Bombs and rations were the unavoidable trials of war but, far more irksome, were the niggling and often unreasonable restrictions drafted by various Ministries. One of the most irritating to the already hard-pressed hotels and restaurants was an Order by the Ministry of Fuel and Power regulating the use of electricity by the area to be illuminated. This Ordeal by Wattage meant, in the case of an hotel as large as the Savoy, that tens of thousands of electric light bulbs had to be unscrewed, examined and less powerful ones substituted, where necessary. When this was done in the small Residents' Lounge, it became obvious that knitting or reading would henceforth be quite out of the question, and the management decided to keep to the former modest lighting.

Within a short time an Inspector appeared from the Ministry, mounted a ladder and solemnly examined each bulb in the Lounge. A summons was duly served on the hotel for the misuse of electric light, which gave some advance satisfaction to gossip-writers, apart from a waiter whom the management strongly suspected of having reported the 'scandalous evasion'.

The Managing Director gave some thought to the matter. Having noted that the glass wall in the Lounge permitted its electric light to illuminate an area beyond, he decided to fight the case. At Bow Street, counsel for the Ministry pointed out that the illumination in the Lounge of 818 square feet was 1,180 watts, or 953 in excess of the regulations. With some confidence he sat down to await a conviction and fine. The defence then drew the attention of the Court to the glass wall which allowed lighting from the Lounge to penetrate into the foyer and part of a staircase beyond. The magistrate, Mr. McKenna, not only dismissed the summons but awarded 40 guineas costs against the Ministry. The crowd of interested spectators included a certain waiter who hurried away, looking extremely put out.

Among those most severely hit by the shortage of butcher's meat was the famous old English restaurant of Simpson's whose celebrated sirloins of beef and saddles of mutton disappeared from the trolleys and were not seen again in their full glory until long after the end of the war. Partial relief came from an agreement made by Hugh Wontner with Cameron of Lochiel to supply venison from Scotland. He also paid visits to Aberdeen to buy herrings for smoking. At the same time, in his kitchen at the Savoy, Dutrey grappled with a dozen and one strange expedients. When someone proposed owls as a possible supplement to the rations, he gave it his usual worriedly intense consideration. "What do I do with an owl?" he asked in despair. "Stuff it?" suggested a *sous-chef* innocently.

Like Sir George, Wontner also found time somehow to keep an eye on the Laundry which remained a cornerstone in preserving first-class service. Throughout the war and even after setting up his H.Q. in North Africa and France, General Eisenhower continued to send his linen to the Savoy in sealed aluminium containers.

Waiters might look impressive in starched shirts, collars and cuffs but Hofflin and his department heads had their moments of dismay. Staff training was now inevitably sketchy, and many of the waiters and porters were either physically unfit for war service or had emerged from retirement. Even so, they were in such short supply that it was decided to supplement them by waitresses who had never before been employed in the service of food and wine in the Savoy. Great care was taken in their selection and many were the wives, sisters and daughters of present or former members of the staff. They proved excellent and looked exceptionally smart in uniforms designed for them by Captain Molyneux, at Miles Thornewill's request.

Luigi, the courtier and diplomat who had so miraculously restored gaiety and charm to the Grill, was horrified to learn one evening that two of his waitresses were dropping plates. It was all due, apparently, to the disturbing presence of handsome Clark Gable in the uniform of the American Air Force. The film star was embarrassed by this attention and always dealt severely with autograph hunters and the many hostesses who tried to turn his war service into a social circus.

The prewar Green Room atmosphere was back, with a strong American garnish. Service men on leave, dining with their families or dancing to the Orpheans, found themselves surrounded by a glittering all-star cast. From Broadway and Hollywood flocked all the celebrities on their way to entertain the troops. The men, crew-cut and in battledress, were not always recognizable and often preferred to remain anonymous, but they were rarely allowed out of camera range, much to the annoyance of Hofflin and Victor, the Reception Manager, who shared a fierce distaste for flashbulbs and hysterical film fans.

It was Jean Nicol's task to keep the Press happy without irritating the stars or, equally important, other guests. She had a sympathetic touch in dealing with show people who could be exacting and over-sentimental, but usually good-natured once their confidence was won. Almost as shy as Gable and James Stewart was Al Jolson, clearly ill-at-ease with reporters and anxious to be off to the army camps with his party of entertainers. A seaman in the First World War, Edward G. Robinson was an anglophile and anything but the aggressive 'Little Caesar' of his films. He liked to wander about the back streets and joked cheerfully with bomb victims and A.R.P. workers. On the roof where he had once played the bagpipes, in happier days, a uniformed Heifetz now sat for hours chatting to the nurses and bomb spotters before departing for the war fronts.

Bob Hope and many others passed through, but every eye was on the actresses who managed to look glamorous even in battle dress. Delysia had kept her old quarters on the fifth floor and always disdained, like Lady Oxford, to go down to the shelter even during a raid. Now back in residence between army tours, she spent most of her time working in the suite reserved for the Free French Committee. With an eye perhaps on the chic Hollywood beauties, she had designed her own Ensa uniforms, two for weekdays and a becoming creation for Sundays and gala occasions. Nobody was her equal in squeezing cheques and gifts for the Red Cross from wealthy diners when their resistance was low. While touring the Middle East she once jumped from her jeep to wish good luck to some soldiers on the road. One of them, a waiter from the Savoy, she recognized and kissed on both cheeks in the French fashion. "What about my mates?" he suggested. Delysia promptly went down the line, kissing each man in turn, with a finale for their captain.

Dinah Shore, Patricia Morrison and other stars led some of the earliest parties to the American war camps. After doing their 'smalls' in the hotel's hand-bowls, they would somehow emerge bewitchingly and with the Hollywood lacquered finish intact. Blonde Carole Landis fell in love with a dashing Eagle Squadron pilot during one of her camp shows. Being a Roman Catholic, she had to await the Church's dispensation which arrived at the hotel only a few short hours before the time arranged for the wedding. Wearing a gown designed by Hartnell, with Kay Francis as her dresser and Mitzi Mayfair as maid of honour, she was the most photographed bride of the year. The Savoy prepared a small but exquisitely-decorated cake which she cut to a chorus of exploding champagne corks and flashbulbs.

Behind the scenes at this Hollywood-style celebration was

Jean Nicol who shortly afterwards married an Intelligence Corps officer, Derek Tangye. They had met by chance for the first time in the hotel lobby. After the war they retired to grow flowers and vegetables on a Cornish farm, the setting for several of Tangye's delightful books.

Marriages, engagements and sweet-sour leave celebrations kept up the tempo of dining and dancing. No evening ended without a toast to 'absent friends', many of them missing or in prison camps. Hofflin, Luigi and Amanda managed to keep tally of birthdays and wedding anniversaries, but bouquets of cut flowers now replaced the elaborate cakes and table decorations of peacetime. It seemed almost like the old days, however, as Noël Coward came in with a large party after the première of his film, *In Which We Serve*. The Prime Minister, back from the United States, was given a thunderous welcome in the restaurant when he arrived to dine with his wife and some friends after the first performance of *The Life and Death of Colonel Blimp*.

The hotel was now London's inevitable setting for official dinners, receptions and the numerous meetings to promote war charities and welfare causes. After the opening ceremony of the 'Wings for Victory' week in Trafalgar Square, the Lord Mayor drove to the Savoy where Thornewill handed him a cheque for £10,000 on behalf of the Company. Enormous sums were also raised by charity raffles in which the first prizes were no longer a Cartier pendant or a portrait by Lavery but a lemon or a precious tin of sardines.

At all hours of the day and night, the hotel bristled with actors, journalists and Service folk, always assured of seeing a familiar face and eager to exchange news of friends. Peter Daubeny, a former actor, had lost an arm while landing at Salerno with the Guards and was back on sick leave just before being invalided out. On his first night home he was dining alone in the grill-room when Ivor Novello, an old friend, walked in. Before long Daubeny had confided that he was planning to become a theatrical manager. Novello listened sympathetically but warned him of the dangers of challenging the strongly-established firms.

Calling for a pad, he began to sketch out costings and estimates until they were the last in the room. Although busy with successes of his own, like *The Dancing Years*, Novello there and then offered to write a comedy for Peter Daubeny Productions. He kept his promise and *We Proudly Present* at the Duke of York's helped to get the new management off the ground.

A few months later Ivor Novello was to reappear in the grill-room in less happy circumstances. At the height of his popularity, idolized by audiences and enjoying an income of £35,000 a year, he was nevertheless in a state of depression. Overworked, inconsolable at the death of 'Mam' (Madame Clara Novello Davies) and barely recovered from the effects of pneumonia, his one relief was to escape after the Saturday night curtain to his lovely country house near Maidenhead. However, he was careless and foolish about the petrol regulations and had apparently made improper use of coupons for his short weekend trips. The fact that he drove a Rolls-Royce did not help his cause in official eyes. He was prosecuted and sent to prison for a month, a crushing and humiliating blow to a man of his temperament. He came out of gaol convinced that he was ruined and disgraced for all time. Characteristically and in spite of his depression, he arranged to send a piano as a gift to Wormwood Scrubs and also signed a handsome cheque for the after-care of discharged prisoners.

Although many of his faithful admirers had written him comforting messages, he was still very nervous of risking insults and sneers in public. It took much personal courage, after some persuasion by MacQueen Pope and other friends, for him to agree to sup in the Grill on the very first night after his release. As he walked in, the handsome profile seamed by pain and anxiety, Luigi greeted him with a smile and a warm handshake and led him to his usual table. Heads turned sharply and the room, so recently buzzing with chatter, stopped to catch its breath. Suddenly people stood up and clapped and Novello, now weeping unashamedly, was surrounded by friends. He was too moved to do more than peck at his meal but, with his usual courtesy, scribbled Alban a thank-you note for thoughtfully sending up some cold rice pudding, always his favourite sweet.

He was in the first and very welcome Ensa unit which crossed the Channel soon after D-Day. Following him, among others, was Gertrude Lawrence who had flown over from America clutching a dozen precious eggs for her old friend and former secretary, Evie Williams. A sudden lurch made an omelette in the lap of her next-seat neighbour, Ernest Hemingway. They were both egg-stained but roaring with laughter when the plane touched down at Croydon. 'Gee' headed at once for the Savoy and was fortunate to find even a small single room, while the heavily-bearded writer, then *Collier*'s chief war correspondent, went to the Dorchester where, in exuberant moments, he liked to empty his revolver into the toilet.

Hemingway, so soon to 'liberate' the Scribe in Paris, lost no time in invading the Savoy's American Bar for sessions with Irwin Shaw and the gay, good-looking photographer, Robert Capa, who had survived every dangerous assignment since the Spanish Civil War and would meet his death in a minefield in Indo-China. They were often joined by 'The Kraut', Hemingway's nickname for Marlene Dietrich, who managed to look like a Parma violet even in khaki. Hemingway would give her a crushing bear-hug, bury his beard in her neck and go around pumping hands with everybody in uniform, promoting them all on sight.

"Always call a colonel a general," he laughingly advised his brother, Leicester. "That's what he's intent on becoming and he'll think well of you for knowing what's on his mind."

As D-Day approached one could feel the tension in the hotel. The very air seemed taut with rumour and speculation. Impatiently poised to take off, war correspondents would return gloomily to the bars. In the cloakroom, Townsend and his staff were now accustomed to handling anything from a borzoi to a bazooka and remained impassive when the buzz bombs and rockets came roaring over from the Pas de Calais. As in the days of the blitz, the A.R.P. staff would slip on overalls, reach for tin hats and go serenely to their posts. The control room was in full-scale operation once more, the roof spotters alert, with Mrs. Hofflin and her nurses ready to deal with casualties. Apart from blast and the inevitable crash of glass, a few hundred broken windows were now routine.

No other London hotel suffered the air-raid damage sustained by the Savoy. Scarcely a major raid during the early blitzes failed to leave its mark on the buildings. It took three separate direct hits by explosive bombs, the last striking the cupola at the corner of the Strand frontage. The wreckage though considerable was less extensive than that from a high explosive bomb which hit the coping in Savoy Court. Here the enclosed area contained the blast and caused heavy damage, but repairs were again carried out with almost magical speed.

The secret lay in the hands of Mr. Webb, the soft-spoken and courteous head of the Works Department. Years of working with Rupert D'Oyly Carte on schemes of modernization, decoration and alteration had given him a detailed knowledge of every part of the building. In charge of the carpenters, bricklayers and all the different grades of building staff, he also controlled the Furnishing Department which handled carpets, curtains and upholstery work. In a key position to mobilize repair forces, he had the advantage of large stocks of materials, including window glass bought when hostilities began and distributed at different places in London. Handiest of all were the hotel's premises in Drury Lane which, though severely damaged by incendiary bombs, still provided valuable storage space not far away. At the end of the war, all the Embankment window frames, even those made of gun-metal, were so twisted that it was difficult and often impossible to straighten them to take new glass.

Even with a Works Department which performed minor miracles when much of the hotel hung almost literally on its hinges, the Savoy would have been forced to close its doors but for the cool heroism and devotion of so many members of the staff during the raids. Typical was the action of a pageboy,

Sammy Mitchell, who tore off his uniform and flung it over the first oil bomb to fall on the roof. Both his hands were badly burned and he was taken to hospital where he soon recovered. Later, he left the staff to become an apprentice jockey.

Meanwhile, the hotel's revolving doors never stopped spinning. Gertrude Lawrence staggered into the crowded Front Hall late one night, hollow-eyed and gaunt, with her hair stringy and unwashed for days. Only a few weeks earlier she had crossed gaily to Normandy and given two shows a day in wrecked towns. Sleepless, snatching canned meals and always on the move, she had to be sent home, suffering from dysentery and battle-front fatigue. She was lying outstretched on a bed, still in her faded Ensa uniform and barely conscious, when her husband raced up to her room. The overworked hotel doctor did what he could and the chambermaids, who had always adored her, looked in anxiously but were being run off their feet, like the nurses. Worse, her former secretary was tied down by civil defence work and could not leave her post. Commander Aldrich had to return immediately to his duties in Southampton and was sick with anxiety until an angel appeared in the shape of a little woman, a complete stranger to him, who announced herself as Lou Hollis and one of Gertrude's devoted fans. She had learned that the star was ill—rumours flickered at lightning speed in those days—and volunteered to nurse her until other arrangements could be made. Wasting no time she took off her coat and stayed all night. Every night after her work, Aldrich recalls gratefully, she would spend a few hours by the bedside until her idol was fit to go back to America.

Although the flying bombs had closed all but eight of London's forty theatres, the hotel was soon reacting to the tonic of war news from the Continent. Among the gayest parties was a surprise dinner and reception in the ballroom, arranged by two hundred American naval officers to celebrate both Admiral Stark's birthday and his forty-two years' service in the Navy. Soon afterwards, General Jimmy Doolittle gave a cocktail party

Gloria Swanson, one of many Hollywood stars who make the hotel their London head-quarters

Seen here in a scene from *Private Lives,* Noël Coward and Gertrude Lawrence were always the centre of attraction in the Savoy Grill, the traditional rendezvous of Show Business personalities

Above, John Wayne does a stetson hat trick for a page-boy fan

Below, Charlie Chaplin gives his wife, Oona, a Savoy rooftop guide to some of the London landmarks he knew as a boy

Danny Kaye, a great favourite with the staff, can rarely
resist good-natured clowning

Non-stop telephone calls and a mountain of mail are handled when Liberace is in
residence. One gift was this miniature piano fashioned from flowers

A thousand guests attended the party to celebrate the ten-year London run of *The Mousetrap*. Aided by Peter Saunders, Agatha Christie cuts the half-ton birthday cake prepared by the hotel's *pâtissiers*

for British and American airmen on the third birthday of the U.S. Army Eighth Air Force. The Line-Shooters Club of R.A.F. fighter and bomber pilots, formed in 1943, dined once again in a private room. They swapped stories and drank nostalgic toasts but there was also a practical side to the reunions. Each of the members made a weekly contribution to a fund which helped the widows and children of old comrades over hardship.

Nothing enlivened those last months of the war more than the record number of white weddings in the Savoy Chapel when the guests would usually walk the short distance to a reception in the River Room, cheered the whole way and pelted with confetti even by complete strangers who happened to be in the hotel.

The shape of things to come also seemed brighter when Lord Woolton presided at a luncheon when the gas industry outlined cheerful plans for post-war kitchens and cookers. The guests sat down to fish flan, roast venison and ice-cream, now allowed to be manufactured after a ban which to many had seemed eternal. Made from skimmed milk, synthetic cream and egg-powder, its taste and effects could be anaesthetized by a glass or two of 'bubbly' and a bravely-named Sauce Melba.

As news of the Nazi collapse came through, the demand for tables grew quite overwhelming and many had to wait three days or more for a reservation. The management was swamped by bookings for Victory Night dinner-parties, adding to those made by optimists almost from the outbreak of war. Already hard-pressed for accommodation, the Reception reluctantly refused many old clients in order to absorb high-priority delegates to the Commonwealth Conference. For some days the hotel became almost an imperial G.H.Q., with floor after floor taken *en bloc* for offices and rooms required by statesmen from India, Australia and New Zealand.

Amid all the comings and goings and a victory fever that almost burst the social thermometer as news crackled in from the very suburbs of Berlin, it was announced suddenly that the long years of black-out were at last over. Some buildings, including the Houses of Parliament and many in the City, hesitated before switching on, but not the Savoy. At dusk on 23 April 1945, after 2,061 nights of darkness, the curtains were left undrawn, and every light in the hotel burst radiantly over London's ancient river, almost like a carillon of thanksgiving.

THE FIRST New Year's Eve after the war was an understandably
gay affair of bagpipes, balloons and Bollinger, with many of the
two thousand diners and revellers determined to forget Winston
Churchill's shock defeat at the polls. After a painful strenuous war,
some had expected an early return to the old voluptuous standards
of comfort, others a political millennium; all were soon disillusioned by even tighter rationing and soaring taxes. Nevertheless,
despite the first gloom over the General Election, everything
pointed to a bullish period for the principal hotels. Partly in
protest against austerity but more to please guests seeking relief
from years in drab uniform, evening dress again became obliga-
tory in the Savoy Restaurant. The hotel suites were quickly filled
with people waiting hopefully for first-aid to their town houses.
There was also the anticipated rush of American tourists, starved
of foreign travel and the remembered delights of a London Season.
The lines from New York hummed with pleas for bookings from
former patrons. Every liner and aircraft was freighted with
market-hungry business contractors and contact men, most of
whom made for London's dozen leading hotels but usually ended
disconsolately in furnished apartments remote from the centre
and let at exorbitant rates.

Gertrude Lawrence had to accept a single bedroom at the
Savoy instead of the suite she had so gaily asked 'Binkie'
Beaumont, the impresario, to reserve for her. With no room for
her trunks and even the bathroom ceiling-high with bouquets,
she reported plaintively to her husband, "I can't unpack anything

but the two suitcases I had on the boat." She passed the time seeing old friends and knitting mittens for Bernard Shaw before moving into a tiny flat in Park Street. However, each of her entrances into the Grill ranked as a performance equalled only by that of Marie Tempest gracefully pouring afternoon tea in the foyer. After her triumph in Daphne du Maurier's *September Tide*, she was again the idol of London's West End and every night a solid crush of admirers waited for hours outside the hotel. Signing autographs she would call out blithely, "Anybody going my way?", and seat herself beside the chauffeur as her delighted fans piled into the Rolls-Royce.

Only a truly great actress could have carried off a scene while she was lunching one day with her husband and Fanny Holtzmann, her volatile New York lawyer. An elderly peeress stopped at their table and made a cutting remark which the star ignored with obvious self-control. The feud dated back some years when the woman's son had proposed marriage to 'Gee' who was invited to call at the mansion in Mayfair. She was greeted there by Lady X., who waved a cheque book and asked coldly, "Miss Lawrence, how much do you want *not* to marry my son?" Years later in his very moving book, *Gertrude Lawrence as 'Mrs. A.'*, Richard Aldrich recalled the incident which was over so quickly that nobody else in the grill-room could have had an inkling of the drama. He took his wife's trembling hand in his, and the next moment she was laughing and blowing kisses to her many friends.

The hotel's switchboard hummed with so many enquiries that the reception staff had finally to insist on application by letter. A room was found only with difficulty for Léon Blum, peering sadly through thick-lensed glasses, a forlorn and broken figure after his two years in Buchenwald. High-ranking officers turned in surprise as Hofflin himself ushered to the lift an unrecognized, crewcut little figure in plain G.I. battledress and heavy combat boots. A few minutes later, in a river suite and not waiting to unpack his valise, Heifetz was gently nursing his precious Stradivarius back to life.

Supping in the Grill after concerts were Jeanette Macdonald, Grace Moore, so soon to be killed in an air crash on her way to Sweden, and Gigli who supplemented the slender menu with dishes specially cooked by his wife and flown in from Rome. José Iturbi brought his own supply of eggs and always ate half a dozen hard-boiled, swearing that they settled his stomach before a recital.

The famous River Room, long cut off from its superb view of the Thames by a brick wall built in zigzag fashion as a bastion against blast, was quickly restored to its original shape by removing the wall. The Abraham Lincoln Room was stripped of its battle-dress as an air-raid shelter. The adjoining Green and Pink Rooms were ingeniously divided between floor and ceiling to create the entirely new Manhattan Room and The Parlour. The hotel's architect, Sir Howard Robertson, was responsible for the conversions and the new names, as he was for designing and christening the Berkeley Buttery and Claridge's Causerie.

Reopened immediately after the war, the Banqueting Department was very soon at full stretch again under a new manager, Paolo Contarini, who rivalled Zavattoni in efficiency but also contributed great charm of manner and a lively sense of humour. Genially he supervised Victory dinners for famous generals like Wavell, Montgomery and Alexander, countless regimental reunions, film parties and diplomatic receptions. One of his first and most amusing tasks was to arrange a Ministry of Information dinner in honour of its Chief Censors. The souvenir menu was formally headed, "Released times: Dinner—submitted by Savoy Hotel at 20.00 BST." Of its thirty courses all but three had been crossed out by a blue pencil.

Contarini had first joined the staff as a young man. Combining professional and technical skill with a shrewd business head, his advancement was inevitable. Today he shares the position of General Manager with Beverley Griffin who, after serving in the Royal Navy and while still in his early twenties, applied to the Savoy for training in 1945. His apprenticeship in the kitchens and various other departments, including that clearing-house of

221

talent, the Reception Office, was followed by a further year's practical experience in Switzerland. On his return, he was appointed assistant to the much-loved Manager of Simpson's-in-the-Strand, Freddie Heck. After exceptionally good work there as joint-manager, he moved back to the hotel in 1955 as assistant to Hofflin.

Santarelli had seemed irreplaceable but Amanda, who now took charge of the Restaurant, was an immediate success as Manager. Handsome and almost as admirably tailored as his predecessor who rarely appeared in anything but fifty-guinea suits, Amanda had great organizing ability and a civilized forbearance under stress granted only to restaurant managers who are outstanding. He quickly won the confidence of his highly-qualified staff and an equally critical international clientèle.

His maître-chef was Auguste Laplanche, successor to the gifted Payard who had died suddenly from a heart attack. A native of Rouen, Laplanche began his career as a ballboy for tennis-playing guests at a nearby château where he was given snacks by the cook and also picked up some of his secrets. Apprenticed to a local hotel, he soon made for Paris and later the Trianon Palace at Versailles. His first post in England was at the Hotel Metropole before moving to the Savoy Grill where he held the position of third chef under Virlogeux. The war brought some remarkable changes and he left to run a wartime Anglo-French mess, never to be forgotten by its lucky members. For a time he worked at the Hotel de Paris at Bray, rejoining the Savoy Restaurant kitchens at the end of the war. A true Norman, he was passionate about vegetables and devoted most of his weekends to his cottage garden in Hampstead. He had considerable respect for the best English dishes, if expertly prepared, and rather less veneration than Latry for the elaborate recipes of prewar days. Meanwhile and for some years to come, Laplanche and Alban, his opposite number in the Grill kitchens, had to meet the daily challenge of serving an average of two thousand *couverts* with meagre rations of sugar, meat, fats, cream and eggs.

The highly talented Abel Alban could scarcely speak a word of

English, like his master, Escoffier, under whom he had served as *chef saucier* before coming to the Trocadero in London in 1922. After shopping one Sunday morning in Soho he was on his way home heaving a basket laden with chicory, leeks and other vegetables, and fell into conversation with a distinguished-looking man who spoke very good French. Alban said his basket was intended for his family's *pot-au-feu* and mentioned that he was a cook by profession. They parted most amicably. Some weeks later, Alban became a *sous-chef* in the grill-room kitchens. Summoned one day to the Managing Director's office, he was astonished to discover that the man behind the long boardroom table was George Reeves-Smith, his chance acquaintance.

He was to stay almost forty years at the Savoy where he quickly established himself not only as a chef of great finesse but a 'character' who could make even General de Gaulle unbend. Fernandel once advised him more than half-seriously to give up cooking and join him on the stage. Ebullient and kindly, he had a droll sense of humour. One day a puzzled waiter came down to the kitchen with an order from a client who had asked confusingly for *Consommé Madrilène, English, en gelée, très chaud*. Alban served very hot tomato soup which was well received.

When a journalist asked him how he regarded women, Alban replied with a straight face, "From head to foot, since my mother was a milliner and my father a shoemaker." Both, incidentally, were excellent cooks. A tremendous worker, he found no opportunity in all his years in London to see either the Tower or Westminster Abbey. Only three times in his life had he worn a dinner jacket, so it is said; first, on his wedding day; later at the opera after Chaliapin had been down to the kitchen and presented him with a ticket for *Boris Godounov*; and finally at the great dinner in his honour when he retired.

There were new faces in several other departments. Chubby, genial Victor had retired from the Reception Office where Charles Fornara, for many years at Claridge's, was now in charge. He and his staff had to handle a very full house-list, apart from the numerous visitors who besieged the hotel's couriers at Cherbourg,

Southampton and the airports, and a daily flock of cables and letters from film stars and their retinues asking for accommodation. After he left in 1950 to take over the management of a South Coast hotel, Fornara was replaced by his assistant, Michon, who was tragically killed only two years later on his way to meet his family on holiday on the Continent.

Another key post also changed hands soon after the war when Mrs. Kate Butler, the Lady Superintendent, retired after over thirty years' service. Her successor was Mrs. Pugh whose appointment was one of Rupert D'Oyly Carte's happiest inspirations. Recovering from an illness, he was much impressed by the poise and efficiency of the Scottish matron and finally persuaded her that soothing awkward or temperamental hotel guests and controlling a staff of housekeepers, chambermaids, valets, cleaners and others would be child's play after a hospital. By a curious coincidence, Mrs. Butler's predecessor also owed her appointment to a chance meeting. Sir George Reeves-Smith, when visiting Uppingham at half-term to see his son, had noticed Miss Chapman at the hotel where he usually stayed and persuaded her to come to the Savoy as Head Housekeeper. She was a great success and later married the General Manager, Pruger. Their son, Michael Chapman, is today in charge of the Imperial Hotel, Torquay.

John Hannay, a lively personality with excellent contacts in the business and social worlds as well as Fleet Street, had joined the Company before the war. He returned after service with the Cameron Highlanders, became personal assistant to Thornewill and applied himself again to Business Promotion, now more than ever an essential part of every major hotel's activity in a highly competitive business. The movements of important clients and V.I.P.s have to be carefully followed and their special demands noted and, wherever possible, anticipated. Celebrities, particularly those with glamorous names on stage or screen, have obvious prestige appeal, and some managements have not hesitated to offer attractive inducements for their patronage, even to the point of under-cutting terms or persuading them to cancel bookings already made with rival hotels.

Scarcely a day passed when the Savoy did not appear in newspapers or periodicals. The bulky volumes of clippings, studded with Royal and social gossip, soon demanded the attention of a separate staff who had also to keep pace with the many reporters and photographers invading the Press Office in search of news. Winston Churchill's every appearance was covered enthusiastically and with as much affection as in wartime. When he and his wife paid their first post-war visit to the Savoy Restaurant everyone stood up and cheered them all the way to their table. It was acknowledged with the familiar, unforgettable V-sign and a buoyant wave of his cigar. After the General Election, when so unexpectedly he had to leave No. 10, he found himself with no London home and sent a message to Hugh Wontner to ask if he could make temporary arrangements for him. Arriving at the Prime Minister's wartime residence behind Downing Street, Wontner took Mrs. Churchill to Claridge's to see if his personal suite there might be suitable. On the way they passed Buckingham Palace where a crowd stood awaiting Mr. Attlee. Perhaps Mrs. Churchill shed a tear. The verdict of the General Election seemed a strange reward for all her husband had done.

The Duke of Palmella, the Portuguese Ambassador and an old friend of England, greeted Mrs. Churchill as she passed through the hall at Claridge's, but the shock of recent events had greatly affected her and she quickly entered the lift. Very soon afterwards, her husband moved temporarily into Hugh Wontner's rooftop suite, taking with him his detective and his secretary. Here he received many visitors including the members of his former Cabinet and Service chiefs. It was characteristic of his thoughtfulness—and confidence—that, during his residence, he insisted that his host should remain in the suite, in a room next to his own. Nearly eighteen years later, when Mr. Macmillan was taken ill and resigned as Premier, he too was suddenly left without a London home, and again it was to Claridge's and to the same suite that the retiring Prime Minister went, with Lady Dorothy.

All through the war and afterwards, Sir Winston rarely missed a dinner party with The Other Club, unchecked by smog or doctor's orders. On occasion he even flew over specially from the Riviera to dine at the Savoy and went back by the first plane next morning. Escorted by his private detective, he would be greeted by Hofflin or Contarini and taken up by lift to the first floor. He would then either ride in a wheelchair or walk to the Pinafore Room where Marc, who was in charge of the private dining-rooms, smoothly took over. Whatever else was served in between, the club's founder-President insisted on his favourite soup *La Petite Marmite Savoy*, and liberal helpings of ice-cream. On one occasion the menu included a piglet from the litter of a sow which Sir Winston had presented to an old friend, Harry Viener, the mayor of Medicine Hat, Alberta. The piglet was prepared by Laplanche and served with full porcine honours, including a rosy apple in its mouth.

Sir Winston attended many official receptions and banquets, among them the moving occasion when fellow-politicians and statesmen honoured his half-century as an M.P., but more often he preferred to dine quietly with a variety of friends. After seeing *Fifty Fifty*, he invited Harry Green and his wife to supper in a private room and stayed very late, enjoying the American comedian's repertoire of conjuring and card tricks many of which Green would pass on to Prince Philip.

Nothing gave the hotel staff more pleasure than to welcome Sir Winston in the Restaurant, the Grill or occasionally in a private suite for birthday and wedding anniversary celebrations. His tastes and remarkable appetite varied little over the years. Often he would start with oysters, when in season, while Lady Churchill had mussels. On occasion he ordered mussels as well, proceeding to two plates of *petite marmite*, chicken, game or roast beef, and the essential *bombe glacée*.

He dined no fewer than five times at the Savoy in a single fortnight. To celebrate one of his birthdays, he and Lady Churchill gave a small luncheon party in a fifth floor river suite, their only guests Pamela, Countess of Lytton and Anthony Montague Browne, his private secretary. The suite was decorated with a beautiful arrangement of roses and poinsettia, a bowl of red roses forming the table centrepiece. The head pastry chef, Emile Dufay, prepared a special layer cake adorned with one red candle and 'Many Happy Returns' in chocolate icing. Soon afterwards when the veteran Marc retired to his villa in the South of France, he was much touched by a letter of good wishes from Sir Winston and a warm invitation to visit him in Monte Carlo.

The long period of post-war shortages coincided ironically with a crowded house-list and some of the most dazzling celebrity functions in the hotel's entire history. War damage estimated at over £250,000 was unlikely to be made good and compensation paid for some years to come. Although smarting under restrictions which gave British hotels and restaurants little chance to compete with State-encouraged rivals across the Channel, the directors were determined to maintain the Savoy's standards of service and taste. The porters were once more resplendent in new whipcords; the five-shilling limit on meals decreed in the summer of 1942 would persist for eight endless years but the pink cloths and napkins were quickly back on tables adorned by gleaming silver and crystal. If the fare were simple and a nagging frustration to the maître-chefs, guests were beguiled by gay flowers and artistic table decorations, while curtains, carpets and candelabra had the semi-splendour of ingenious make-do-and-mend.

Most comforting during this frugal twilight was the promise of a skilful professional staff after the inevitable shortcomings of recent years. Backed by Thornewill, the Managing Director was enthusiastic to resume and improve the hotel's training schemes. For many years part of the Company's profits had been set aside for a superannuation fund, and plans were ready to make the pension scheme even more liberal. Conditions of employment and pay, despite all the difficulties of the war, were among the best in the whole of the industry. With key figures at the top like Hofflin, now joined as Assistant Manager by Arthur Collard formerly at the New York office, with Amanda and Luigi,

Fornara and the already inestimable Mrs. Pugh, Laplanche, Alban and Contarini, the Savoy seemed assured of a loyal and efficient staff. It came therefore as a shock when, barely a year after V.E. Day, the whole framework was suddenly threatened by a series of extraordinary strikes.

These followed a campaign seeking to impose on the Savoy (and as a consequence on all other hotels) recognition of the catering branch of the National Union of General and Municipal Workers of which Arthur Lewis, M.P. was the London district representative. One of his powerful allies was an Italian junior grade waiter called Piazza, who obtained employment in the Savoy Grill and barely a few weeks after joining the staff, was describing himself as Chairman of The Savoy Staff Committee.

Within five days of his arrival, there was an unofficial strike which was quickly settled. However, the management considered that his activities had begun to interfere with his work and decided to suspend him for indiscipline. Although he remained on full pay, several of his supporters promptly started a second wildcat strike. While negotiations dragged on and tribunals, official and otherwise, attempted to sit in judgment, the majority of the staff made it clear that they would refuse to work with Piazza if he were reinstated. Many resented his claim to speak for the Savoy with its thousand and more employees, belonging to almost twenty different Unions. There was a growing suspicion that political capital was being made from a manufactured grievance which did not warrant a strike.

The situation became so confused that the management decided to discontinue Piazza's employment, particularly since he had not been working since his suspension. This ignited yet another strike, thanks to extremists in the Union who delightedly seized the chance to make trouble and propaganda during Royal Wedding week, when London hotels were crowded with visitors and hundreds more arrived daily by sea and air.

The Savoy was soon picketed by men and women singing *The Red Flag*, practically none of them with any link at all with the hotel. By this time, the strikes had attracted so much publicity that all manner of cranks joined in the picketing, but the hotel carried on smoothly, with visitors coming and going as usual. Dissatisfied with results, the extremists then went further; having failed to stop supplies of food from Smithfield and Covent Garden or seriously to interrupt the business of the hotel, they lay in the road outside the Savoy to prevent the tankers carrying fuel oil from reaching the point where they could discharge it into the hotel's tanks. Characteristically, A. P. Herbert offered to drive in one of the lorries but was restrained. At a film reception, attended in the middle of one strike by leading Hollywood stars, a picket burst in, snatched the microphone from Bob Hope and yelled for support.

Outside the hotel, particularly in the small service road leading from Savoy Hill, crowds of agitators and their supporters gathered night after night in mounting numbers. They were confident that the reserves of oil within the Savoy could not last much longer and expected the management to capitulate. It was common knowledge that the hotel depended on fuel and diesel oil to make the electricity which lit not only the whole of the Savoy but worked all its lifts, pumps, machinery of every kind, apart from the steam turbines for space and water heating. The last strike having by now been declared official, Union pressure caused the virtual withdrawal of fuel supplies.

It has never been disclosed what secret steps the directors took but tankers continued to arrive at the Savoy at all hours, and from all points of the compass. Their only problem was to get near enough to discharge their load. Attempts were made to waylay them on the Embankment, in the City, the West End and the Strand; but finally, while guests, including several M.P.s, watched from the windows of the hotel, the police, mounted and on foot, held back the shouting crowds as each tanker came in sight. The vital oil was delivered time and again.

In this remarkable battle, unlike any other in hotel history, the Savoy carried out its services with only minor interruptions and little inconvenience to guests. American visitors, accustomed to strike-breakers and violence, came to regard the strikes as rather a joke and advanced good-humouredly through surly picket-lines, irrepressibly taking photographs for their albums. They were unaware of either the passions festering below the surface or the grave political implications. The air of normality inside the hotel was due to the loyalty of the overwhelming majority of the staff who resisted every kind of intimidation and quickly filled temporary gaps in service. A large volume of volunteer helpers also came from the outside, among them the Earl of Airlie's son, Angus Ogilvy, now the husband of Princess Alexandra. He enrolled as a temporary waiter but, as he cheerfully admitted later, his 'career' ended after only two days when he dropped an omelette at the feet of an important guest.

Among many old patrons, Winston Churchill ignored the whole affair and insisted on having his usual birthday dinner in the hotel. During Royal Wedding week, when some newspaper accounts reported a 'beleaguered' hotel, over five hundred people were in residence, and a thousand dinners were perfectly cooked and served one night in the Restaurant.

It was extraordinary and almost without precedent in Britain for an official strike to suffer such a defeat. From the outset, the Company's directors had stoutly insisted that it did not spring from genuine grievance or hardship but was, in fact, a politically-inspired attack not directed specifically at the Savoy—a convenient status symbol—but against the whole of the catering trade. At the height of the battle one or two of London's leading hoteliers had become faint-hearted and critical of Wontner's leadership. As the dust died away and the strikes (which had also affected the kitchens of some other London hotels, including Claridge's, the Dorchester and the Berkeley) receded into the background, there was a calmer assessment of it all. A Court of Inquiry set up by the Government issued its report which included a recommendation that Piazza be found suitable employment outside the Savoy Group. More important, the leaders of the hotel industry now saw the whole wildcat affair in perspective.

It was announced that each member of the staff, who had

loyally helped to maintain essential services during the disputes, would be made a shareholder in the Company by the gift of ten Ordinary shares. One old lady, a cleaner, soon afterwards approached Hugh Wontner in some agitation, explaining that she had handed in her share certificate at the local post office only to be told that they could not cash it! Luckily, she had second thoughts about selling her shares which would soon double in value. Many, like the chefs and heads of departments, were already shareholders and a number had shrewdly invested most of their savings in the Company. But the gift of shares to several hundred members of the staff, throughout the whole Group, proved more than a generous gesture on the part of the management. It was a fillip to staff morale after one of the most violent interludes in the history of the Savoy, ending very differently from the way it had been planned by its organizers.

FILM STARS, journalists and tourists from every part of the globe converged on the capital for Princess Elizabeth's wedding. Like her parents, who had often danced at the Savoy in their younger days and invited Carroll Gibbons and his orchestra to play at Buckingham Palace for their Silver Wedding celebration, the Princess had a warm feeling for the hotel. At the most fashionable wedding of 1946, attended by the King and Queen and every other member of the Royal Family, she acted as bridesmaid to her lady-in-waiting, the Hon. Mrs. Vicary Gibbs, whose first husband had been killed in action while serving in the Grenadier Guards. The bridegroom was the Hon. Andrew Elphinstone, son of the 16th Baron. Following the ceremony at St. Margaret's, Westminster, a reception was given in the River Room, a glittering Royal occasion but, at the same time, delightfully gay. Among various informal photographs was one of Princess Elizabeth standing beside a young naval lieutenant, her future husband, until then quite an unknown figure to the British public.

Almost since her teens, the Princess had enjoyed going on to sup and dance at the Savoy, often after a visit to the ballet or the opera. She and Princess Margaret never expected any special arrangements to be made for them. The Manager waited at the private entrance in Savoy Hill and quietly led the party to their table, with the Palace detective and the hotel's chief security officer unobtrusively in the background. With a minimum of protocol and often at short notice, Princess Elizabeth would sometimes arrive with her friends for a small supper party in one of the private suites from which they could watch the lights across the Thames.

In the ballroom sixteen-year-old Princess Margaret danced in public for the first time to the music of the Orpheans, pleaded to be allowed to stay "just a little longer" and hid behind her very tall partner, Lord Blandford, hoping to delay the curfew. She paid many subsequent visits and made a point of going to the Savoy when Lena Horne was leading the cabaret in the Restaurant. Fond of dancing, particularly to Latin-American rhythms, Princess Margaret used to wave her long gold cigarette-holder in time to the music between dances.

At one Charity Ball, Carroll Gibbons had to exercise all his good-humoured diplomacy. Princess Margaret constantly requested sambas and rumbas while her cousin, Princess Alexandra, sent over little notes for old-fashioned waltzes and Scottish reels. Before the dance ended at 5 a.m., he had tactfully compromised by playing each Royal request in strict rotation.

Not long after their marriage, Princess Elizabeth and her husband attended one of the most memorable banquets ever held in any hotel. It was arranged by The Pilgrims to commemorate the unveiling of President Roosevelt's statue in Grosvenor Square. The project took root in the historic Abraham Lincoln Room where an appeal committee was formed and Sir William Reid Dick entrusted with the design of a bronze statue. The magnificent banquet at which Mrs. Roosevelt, the guest of honour, was formally presented with a replica of the fine monument, was attended by several members of the Royal Family, the Archbishop of Canterbury, ambassadors, all the wartime Service leaders, and political representatives from the United States and the Commonwealth, with Winston Churchill paying eloquent tribute to his old friend and colleague.

For some weeks previously, the Savoy's heads of departments had carefully planned the dinner which was held in the Restaurant to enable a thousand guests to be seated, instead of five hundred, the capacity of the Lancaster Room. On this unique occasion, the wives of Pilgrims were invited. Arrangements were also made for an international broadcast of the main speeches. Sir Campbell Stuart, formerly Managing Director of *The Times* and Chairman of The Pilgrims' Executive Committee, was determined that the evening should be remembered with pleasure for many years to come and lost no time in discussing his ideas at several meetings with Hugh Wontner. Under the latter's direction, the smallest details were meticulously thought out and executed, from the order of precedence and the complicated seating arrangements to the new silver service in use for the first time, the microphones and other equipment, and the split-second timing of the speeches to be broadcast. As it was very unusual indeed for a banquet to be held in the Restaurant, and never before on anything approaching this scale, ingenious arrangements had to be worked out for the placing of tables to ensure that one thousand hot and perfectly cooked dinners could be served smoothly by waiters working in unfamiliar conditions. The liaison between kitchen and restaurant had therefore to be fool-proof. While Amanda and Laplanche shared the main honours, their task would have been impossible without the most skilful dovetailing of all departments.

The banquet was a complete success and carried through with the ritual calm expected at a dinner for a dozen leisurely guests in one of the smaller private rooms. There was, meantime, no interruption of the normal service in other parts of the hotel, except that those who came to dance were directed to the River Room which had been converted for this one evening only into a charming substitute ballroom.

A smaller and more private dinner was held a few months later when King George VI became the first reigning British Monarch to dine in a London hotel. The staff was on its toes, the red carpet in place, and Hofflin concealing his nervousness behind a composed mask as he waited to welcome and escort His Majesty to the Lancaster Room. With three hundred officers of the Royal Marines, the King dined at a table decorated in the Corps colours and glittering with ten sets of massive silver candelabra. The music was provided by the Royal Yacht

Orchestra who, by request of the guest of honour, played his favourite tunes from Novello and Noël Coward. Within a year the King again dined privately at the hotel, this time with former fellow-cadets from Osborne and Dartmouth.

The formal Evening Courts having been replaced two years after the war by Royal Garden Parties at which 'Presentation' was simply by attendance in the afternoon, the Season lost a little pageantry but none of its gaiety. Many of the débutantes and their escorts now had daytime jobs but the atmosphere in grill-room and restaurant was as relaxed and elegant as in the 'thirties, with the round of Ascot, Henley, Goodwood and the Eton and Harrow match spiced by glamorous stage and film premières and the revival of Covent Garden.

The pleasant tradition of Derby Night celebration parties was soon renewed by winning owners, among them the Aga Khan who proposed a toast one evening to Léon and Suzy Volterra, both looking rather rueful. Often they had stood, hand in hand, at the window of their suite over the Thames, dreaming of the day they would lead in a Derby winner. The prize seemed theirs in 1948 but for a cruel twist of fate.

That year the Aga Khan had entered the well-bred Noor and seemed only to fear his friendly rival, the Maharajah of Baroda, whose fine colt, My Babu, had equalled the course record in the Two Thousand Guineas. Aly Khan had different views and warned his father that M. Volterra's My Love had a speed and stamina which could be dangerous if the going became heavy. Still unconvinced but determined to win his fourth Derby, the Aga Khan offered to buy a half-share in My Love, if he could run it in his own green and chocolate colours. Léon Volterra, secretly confident that his other entry Royal Drake had a better chance, accepted against his wife's advice. The race was smoothly won by My Love who overhauled Royal Drake, leaving Noor and My Babu to plod into third and fourth places. That night it seemed that every waiter, porter, chambermaid and page in the hotel had backed My Love.

The following year the Volterras looked even more certain to

235

achieve a lifelong ambition with two powerful entries, Val Drake and the big bay Amour Drake, the latter ridden by Rae Johnstone, My Love's jockey. The Aga Khan would dearly have loved to buy the pair whom he considered far superior to his own entry, Hindostan, but M. Volterra was determined not to repeat his mistake. Although rain clouds were gathering, only a few trusting souls, among them Aly's wife Rita Hayworth, backed Mrs. Glenister's outsider, Nimbus.

On the morning of the race Madame Volterra arrived at the Savoy, looking anxious and strained. She had come to London without her husband who was ill with heart trouble but had urged her not to miss the Derby. Respecting his chronic fear of aeroplanes, she travelled more leisurely by the Golden Arrow. At the reception desk she was handed a telephone message that Léon Volterra was dying. This time she had no hesitation in flying back and gratefully accepted Jack Hylton's offer of a charter plane. As she landed, the French airfield staff were already switching off a radio commentary from Epsom. Amour Drake had been beaten by Nimbus in the first photo-finish in the history of the race. Her husband, desperately ill, had listened to the broadcast without apparently hearing the result of the photo-finish. Suzy Volterra kissed him and whispered the merciful white lie that their horse had won. He seemed to rally a little but died a few hours later. Six years passed before the Volterra colours triumphed in the Derby on Phil Drake. In her suite that evening, the Epsom victory a little frayed by painful memories, Madame Volterra dressed with her usual elegance and smilingly went down to greet her dinner guests in the American Bar.

G.B.S. once joked that he was the one male celebrity in England who had never rested his foot on its rail, and ladies were only admitted in 1947, under protest from some regulars. Here Britain's driest Martinis and quick-healing potions were dispensed but Joe Gilmore declined to follow Harry Craddock's precedent of inventing a new cocktail every week, reserving that honour for national events and celebrities. 'Four Score' celebrated Sir Winston's eightieth birthday, and Princess Margaret's marriage inspired 'Wedding Bells'. To welcome President Truman on a State Visit, Gilmore prepared a special cocktail of 60 per cent bourbon and 30 per cent applejack, topped up with Crême de Menthe. Alas, the President declined his 'Missouri Mule' and instead demanded a straight bourbon and water.

Mr. Truman could be delightfully informal. Although he had his 'royal suite' on the fifth floor, he refused to eat his meals in private. "I like to see people," he said firmly. "Nobody's going to fence me in." On one of his later visits he startled the young ladies in Room 205 by putting his head round the door and calling out cheerfully, "I hear there's a barefoot Democrat from Kentucky working here." He was referring to Jeanne Gilbert then in charge of the Press Office. Mr. Truman also surprised one of the assistants in a nearby Strand outfitter's when he went in to buy a tie. The young man fumbled rather amateurishly until the ex-President, an old hand, gave him a free lesson in folding a tie to impress a customer.

Certain other 'guests' used to be a great trial to the Savoy barmen who, over the years, have learned to spot and discourage a pest that is endemic to most luxury bars. Languid young men, usually well-dressed, will spend an hour or so reading the newspaper and making a liberal snack of olives, potato crisps, onions and other nibbles. Giving every sign of waiting for a friend who is delayed, they rarely order a drink and every few minutes or so ask the barmen if they are *sure* the clock is right. Gilmore and his colleagues have cultivated a secret technique to make this type of patron unwelcome, with of course the greatest politeness.

Immediately after the war Reginald Bentley had the task of replenishing the Company's cellars, despite import regulations and currency restrictions. Contact had again to be made with the Continent, not only to renew the former close links with the wine centres of Europe, easier in France than in Germany, but also to start up again the importation of, among other things, sardines from Portugal, cheeses from France, ham from Italy, quails from Egypt and *foie gras* from Strasbourg.

The tourist trade had once more to be created, despite British austerity which contrasted with the much more attractive conditions in some European countries. Taking a small aeroplane from Croydon, Wontner flew to Belgium within a few months of the end of the war. Landing there at an airfield heavily damaged by bomb craters, he was met by a car sent for him by the Century Hotel in Antwerp, not long freed from German control. By previous arrangement a number of European hoteliers assembled under the same roof at the same time. France was represented, as were Switzerland, Holland, Belgium and Denmark. With Wontner was Sir Francis Towle, the only surviving European hotelier who had been President of both the International Hotelmen's Association and the International Hotel Alliance. Meeting now for the first time in six years, the representatives of the industry decided that every effort was necessary to revive international travel by lowering the barriers made inevitable by war. Wontner proposed the foundation of a new International Hotel Association to combine the functions of the two previous bodies. This was unanimously agreed and he drafted the resolution on which the world organization of hoteliers and hotel associations rests today. (In 1961 he became President of the International Hotel Association and re-elected two years later.)

Notwithstanding austerity and shortages of all kinds, the Savoy and the others in the Group were doing an expanding business, with more and more dollars coming in from American visitors, but it might not be easy to maintain the tourist flow. As Rupert D'Oyly Carte grimly reminded his shareholders, with one eye on an unsympathetic Government, "travellers to England may be interested in viewing war scars but not in inadequately equipped and shabby-looking hotels." As he had decided to take his famous Opera Company to New York, a practice the war had interrupted, this also offered the opportunity for a look at the hotels there. The Chairman and Managing Director left together for America and spent the Christmas of 1947 in New York, before going on to Washington to see its latest hotel. It was stimulating to be released temporarily from the inescapable drabness of wartime shortages and restrictions in England, but neither D'Oyly Carte nor Wontner had realized the effect of six years of rationing until they were confronted with the normal quantity of food eaten in America, which they found much beyond their capacity or desire.

Some months later, Rupert D'Oyly Carte was taken ill while on holiday in France. He was flown back to London from Geneva, with a specialist in attendance, and not long afterwards died in his suite at the Savoy at the age of 72. His estate was valued at more than £300,000, including all the performing rights in the Gilbert and Sullivan operas, which passed first to Hugh Wontner and A. F. Moir, his executors, and then to his daughter and only surviving child, Bridget. Among his bequests were one thousand Savoy shares each to Wontner and Thorne-will. The manuscript of Arnold Bennett's *Imperial Palace*, a gift from Sir George Reeves-Smith, was left to Bridget D'Oyly Carte.

Now without a Chairman, the Board of the Savoy decided to appoint Hugh Wontner, thus combining the offices of Chairman and Managing Director for the first time since these were held by Richard D'Oyly Carte. Still only 40, the new Chairman was now in a position of overall responsibility on policy and administration. An employee whose service dated back to the days of César Ritz welcomed the appointment with the comment, "He seems to understand every section of the hotel, and even knows the price of string beans." Only a few close colleagues were, however, aware of the new chief's grasp of finance and international trade, a quality rare in an hotelier.

The Company's policy was perfectly defined at one Annual General Meeting by a shareholder, the well-known surgeon, Lord Webb-Johnson, who said that the hotels aimed to knit "modern new-world efficiency with old-world courtesy." The young Chairman's respect for tradition was equally emphatic. He once declared, "The Savoy really is history and we have come to feel this is an asset, not something to be discarded like a worn rug. We feel we can afford to acknowledge the past." Under his régime the hotel would wear many a gay ribbon in her hair but never a wig.

The Savoy celebrated its Diamond Jubilee in 1949 with record business but predictably small dividends. For the following year, the Company's net profits were only £73,000, owing to the heavy expenditure needed to catch up wartime neglect. Staff overheads had also soared with the Catering Wages Act, and the cost of materials of all kinds was inflated by heavy Purchase Tax. Bomb scars had to be treated long before War Damage claims were leisurely settled by Whitehall. Few places on the Continent had London's soot problem which meant that first-class hotels needed almost round-the-calendar washing-down and repainting, almost like the Forth Bridge. As a leading dollar-earner and a magnet for the luxury tourist trade, the Group had quickly asked permission of Government departments, then still in control, to allow the replacement of out-of-date equipment. In addition to restocking, refurnishing and painting the hotel inside and out, it was considered vital to restore the cuisine, wines and service to former standards. To maintain its tradition for entertainment, the Savoy had also to engage international stars like Hildegarde at fees of £1,000 a week and more.

It took courage and vision to pour out so much capital on improvements and re-equipment, and incidentally to set the pace for all British hotels for many years to come, a policy which would pay handsomely in tourist expansion. Heavy bookings for suites and a thriving postwar demand for the public and private dining-rooms could have induced complacency or, worse, a narrow economy. Instead of retrenchment, the Chairman decided to invest in the future. High on his priorities list was the programme for training executives of the future. Enthusiastically directed by the management, ably assisted by Olive Barnett, the three hotels resumed and consolidated their position as the most sought-after hotel school in the world. Then, as now, trainees came from all parts of Europe, with a few from the United States, among them the sons of famous British, French and Swiss hoteliers. Upwards of sixty students were accepted to pass through each department, from the kitchens upwards, the most promising British students then being sent on to 'finishing schools', various selected hotels abroad. They received basic living and travel expenses but, equally important to morale during their long and hard months of training, was the personal interest shown by the directors who, from time to time, gave informal tea parties and encouraged *esprit de corps*. Hofflin and other heads of departments could be stern masters but they always showed understanding of youngsters easily intimidated by the grandeur of a hotel like the Savoy. Hofflin never forgot how scared he himself had been on his first day. "Even so long ago," he told the trainees, "I regarded it as a fabulous place. I contented myself with walking round for hours and looking at the staff entrance."

Like Sir George Reeves-Smith, who founded the Hotels and Restaurants Association in 1910, the Chairman has played a prominent part in its activities and in many other bodies on travel and tourism. Although shy by nature and always happier in committee than on the public platform, he was persuaded to face a challenge at Cambridge in a Union Debate. The hall was packed with undergraduates and others and not a seat was to be had even in the gangways when a motion, "That British hotel catering is a disgrace," was proposed with gusto by Gilbert Harding, attired in a bottle-green dinner suit. His attack was in this case fortified by a genuine devotion to good cooking.

In replying, Hugh Wontner saw a useful opportunity to impress some home truths on those who sighed for French hotels with Michelin's coveted forks and rosettes. Extracts from his speech give some picture of what the Savoy and others still had to endure six years after the end of the war.

"Before rationing was introduced, an hotel chef of the highest professional standing would use an average of two and three-quarter ounces of butter for each meal he prepared. Now, under rationing, the allowance is only nine-twentyeighths of an ounce. That, I may say, is not of butter alone, but of all fats. The butter permitted is no more than three-twentyeighths of an ounce; and the remaining six-twentyeighths of an ounce has to be taken in margarine or cooking fat.

"Do you know that, before the war, a leading London hotel would take between five and six thousand shell eggs per week in its kitchens, and that the present allowance is 180 eggs? Even those eggs are only received in respect of residents in the hotel who surrender their ration books. Separate restaurants have no eggs at all.

"Then there is the question of meat. The present allowance will purchase in weight about one ounce for each main meal, which compares with an average of six to eight ounces per meal before rationing was introduced. Where, may I ask, is the offal? What has happened to the kidneys, the liver, the sweetbreads?

"No country in the world, I would say, has a wider choice of raw materials of first-class quality than Great Britain. Who can say with truth that Scotch beef or Southdown mutton have any equal in France or in any other continental country? What about the variety of game, the Aylesbury ducklings, the Colchester oysters, the Stilton cheese? I hope your mouths are watering.

"Bad meals there are in England, and I may say, on the Continent and in America; no country has a monopoly of good cooking nor of bad cooking." The motion was narrowly carried, at a time of course when the country was irritated by rationing, and every other self-respecting chef suffered from high blood-pressure or returned home to grow his fruits on less stony ground.

Hugh Wontner went determinedly ahead with his plans for expansion. He now had a new asset in Bridget D'Oyly Carte, whom he had invited to join the Board soon after the death of her father. Dark, slim and vital, with an appropriately Gilbertian sense of humour, she studied drama in her earlier years and developed a strong artistic sense. For some time before the war, she had been her father's assistant in dealing with décor until most of the work of the furnishing and decorating departments came to a standstill in 1939. In the intervening period, she had been engaged in work for the London County Council in some of the poorer districts. She now inherited not only her father's Opera Company but the work he had enjoyed so much in the hotels.

'Miss Bridget' dislikes publicity, but evidence of her successful flair soon became evident. There was much to be done after so many years of enforced wartime neglect; wear and tear had been heavy and the freshness of curtains, covers, carpets, paintwork and the like had to be renewed or restored. It was in many ways frustrating to attempt to bring back prewar standards, since restrictions were not modified or abolished for many a long year. Great efforts, however, were made. The American Bar was refurnished and the heavily-damaged parts of the hotel gradually rebuilt or repaired. Extensive alterations to the eighth floor were carried out so as to open more suites with that superb panorama south over the Thames, an attraction for the visitors arriving for the Festival of Britain. Many other schemes were set on foot but only became possible after an everest of forms had been completed for submission to the Ministry of Works, the Board of Trade, the London County Council and many other departments. It became almost a full-time occupation for some members of the Company's staff to get permission to do even simple things. When, finally and with the support of the Sanitary Inspector, the Savoy renewed a Gentlemen's Cloakroom, a Question was actually asked about it in the House of Commons!

It was part of Wontner's plan for future development that the principal specialized departments of the Savoy should be separately organized and directed. In the war, he had formed the Strand Power Company to take over all the engineering services, including the Savoy power station responsible for the generation of electricity. The hotel supplied a small area in the Strand, a survival of Richard D'Oyly Carte's original engine to provide the electric light for the Savoy Theatre. As the hotels had become increasingly filled with machinery, the staff of the Strand Power Company, directed first by Leslie Sayer and then by H. H. Morton, included experts in many fields of engineering; electrical, mechanical, structural, lifts, pumps, boilers and kitchens. Only in this way was the maintenance of a high standard possible in a new age.

The idea of specialized subsidiary undertakings was not new to the Savoy. For some years, in its factory in Drury Lane, carpets had been stored, furniture made and repaired, and curtains, covers and so forth manufactured. Directing this very active and varied department, was Rupert D'Oyly Carte's former assistant, Miss Peggy Rudd, who still continues to do so, under 'Miss Bridget'.

A third subsidiary was now set up to control building operations, and also to take over the Works Departments at the Savoy, Claridge's and the Berkeley. A search for suitable premises led to the purchase of a timber merchant's yard just south of Waterloo Bridge. The premises were rebuilt to house administrative, technical and drawing office staff, and to provide storage for building materials. Machinery was installed in the carpenter's shop and equipment of other kinds bought. Directing this undertaking was E. C. L. George, who had succeeded the veteran Mr. Webb, and quickly established himself as a very able organizer and most efficient technically. This subsidiary has since become responsible for many building and decoration schemes, both in and out of the hotels, its success leading after some years to the acquisition of one of London's oldest firms in plaster work.

Meanwhile, John Hannay had joined the Savoy Board. With expanding business in the hotels and a heavier strain on the management, both the Chairman and Vice-Chairman needed his help in their various responsibilities. One entirely new venture he took over and has since managed. Apart from renewing the Savoy's policy of meeting visitors at the seaports, it was necessary to look further ahead. After the war, travel by air was still on a small scale, with London Airport a jumble of wooden huts and Northolt operating only European flights. On a bitterly cold day, with the wind whistling across the flats, Rupert D'Oyly Carte and Hugh Wontner had stood looking at the desolate scene with Hannay at hand for consultation. It was decided that a Savoy Office should be opened at London Airport, the first of its kind anywhere in the world. Today, it is one of the most important links in the chain of travel, with over ten members of its staff working there full-time.

Soon after the war, guests came more often but for shorter periods, which added to the strain on the Reception and House-keeping departments. There was no lack of variety among visitors. Mae West arrived and professed astonishment that the R.A.F. had named their famous life-saving jackets after her. Nevertheless, she lost no time in telephoning a local gymnasium for a supply of weights which she needed apparently for uplifting exercises. Like a galleon she sailed into the hotel, blazing with jewels; a thick bracelet shackled her wrist, and her luggage included a hundred and fifty dresses and sixty pairs of shoes with six-inch wedge heels. She was flanked at her Press conference by four stalwart leading men who also acted as bodyguards but failed to prevent a thief raiding her theatre dressing-room and making off with most of her jewels. She had to go on in 'prop' diamonds but rightly assured the audience, "They can't take the sparkle out of Diamond Lil." A more demure figure was the seventeen-year-old Elizabeth Taylor, sharing a suite with her mother and the woman tutor who gave her lessons, three hours a day, between takes at the film studios. A year later she was back at the hotel, honeymooning with the first of her husbands, Nick Hilton. The suite seemed to glow with flowers, baskets of fruit and ice-buckets.

In the grill-room after seeing *Perchance to Dream*, Garbo sat hunched under a sombrero, talking earnestly with Ivor Novello. Yvonne de Carlo arrived at the hotel with a jewel-case containing twenty pairs of ear-rings, while Charles Boyer, a little plumper since his prewar visit, still had a gratifying reception from faithful matrons. Robert Montgomery had difficulty in avoiding his admirers and was mercifully rescued by the Reception Manager, Charles Fornara, who was almost his double in looks and used to muffle up in a teddy-bear coat with a hat over his eyes to act as decoy while the film star made off by a side-exit.

On General Election nights, Lord Camrose would take over the ballroom and all the public suites on 'the river side' for his two thousand guests who were entertained to champagne and a buffet supper while the results were flashed on a mammoth board. The banqueting rooms were often booked weeks in advance. A thousand guests, headed by Their Majesties, attended a reception after the marriage of the Earl of Derby to Lady Isabel Milles-Lade. At a farewell dinner to the popular American Ambassador, Lewis Douglas, five hundred Pilgrims sang *For He's a Jolly Good Fellow*. There were receptions for visiting Americans as varied as Dean Acheson, Dorothy Lamour and Sister Kenny, the last an unforgettably gracious figure as she greeted in turn hundreds of polio victims who had come to welcome and thank her.

The gramophone magnate Sir Louis Sterling, a regular patron for forty years, was joined at his famous Saturday luncheons by friends who were aware that they would almost inevitably be asked to contribute to one of the many charities under his wing. On the Saturday before Christmas he would summon Luigi or Amanda, call for a list of the staff who had served him through the year and sign a dozen or more liberal cheques, each enclosed with a friendly message. He and his wife, Cissie, also kept open house at his home in Regent's Park but he was a little shaken when a stranger once accosted him as he was crossing the Savoy lobby and said warmly, "Don't tell me your name, I *know* you. Yes, now I remember; I met you at the Sterlings." "Very likely," laughed Sir Louis. "I'm so often there." In his will he left £100 to each of his favourite waiters and several other members of the staff.

Prowling grill-room and bars, the gossip-writers missed two attractive young women who were quietly chatting in the foyer one afternoon. The Shah of Persia's lively sister, Princess Shams, had asked a lovely girl then at finishing school near London to join her for tea a few days after meeting her at an embassy dinner. Impressed by her vivacity and charm, the Princess sent her brother a note which said bluntly, "She is one of the most beautiful girls I have ever met. A good wife for you." Photographs followed, and before long Soraya Esfandiary was on her way home for betrothal to the Shah.

Queen Soraya's next appearance at the hotel was at a banquet given by the Iranian Ambassador for sixty guests, including the Duke and Duchess of Gloucester. From the Caspian came vodka and caviare, while fresh rhododendrons and azaleas were specially despatched from the Riviera. Wearing a gown lined with mink, a glittering tiara and emerald ear-rings carved like miniature bunches of grapes, the 21-year-old Queen stood with her husband on a vast Persian rug in the Lancaster Room to greet the five hundred guests at the reception which followed. The occasion was a social and diplomatic success but the hotel detectives were more than relieved when the last of the limousines left the forecourt. At a modest estimate the women guests wore jewels worth over a million pounds sterling. Before returning home, the Royal couple came in once or twice to dine informally and dance the tango. They were delighted when Laplanche, alerted by the restaurant manager, sent up a basket of spun-sugar flowers in the Shah's national colours.

There was no lack of material for reporters in search of news. One night while proposing a toast after dinner, Sir Noel Curtis Bennett had a heart attack, slumped forward and struck his head on the microphone. Doctors from an adjacent banqueting room were called and vainly applied artificial respiration. Although much shaken, Lady Curtis Bennett asked the other guests to continue with the dancing but most were too grieved to do so. White-faced and shocked by the tragedy, many recalled that the dead man's brother, Sir Henry, had died in almost identical circumstances while making a speech at the Dorchester, and similarly their father, the Chief Metropolitan Magistrate, at a Mansion House banquet.

In 1950 Carroll Gibbons left his white piano to become entertainments manager responsible for the orchestras and cabarets at both the Savoy and the Berkeley. For many of the faithful it seemed almost a personal loss. Hundreds of nostalgic farewell messages arrived for him, including one from a couple who first waltzed together at the Savoy in 1935 and had since danced regularly twice a week to the Orpheans. One of the orchestras replacing them was led by Ted Heath who remembered that his first Savoy 'engagement' had been *outside* the hotel when, at the age of 17 he marched up and down the Strand playing his trumpet as a very frost-bitten 'busker'.

When Gibbons married the actress, Joan Alexis, a few months after taking up his new appointment, all London's band-leaders came to drink their health. Among the hundred guests at the reception were his specially-invited colleagues, including maître-chef Laplanche, twelve bartenders and every porter who could take time off. The hotel pages adored the genial bridegroom and arrived in relays for a glass of champagne and a slice of wedding cake prepared by the restaurant's head *pâtissier*. They had quickly returned to prewar standards of smartness and discipline; their smooth hair was parted dead centre twice-daily by the hotel barbers; and every evening they wore two gleaming white waistcoats and two clean pairs of white gloves. Once again the strenuous training schedule was resumed; elocution lessons to teach a boy how to summon guests distinctly but without disturbing others, and the correct way to knock on a door. There were night-school courses in languages and deportment and for boys who showed promise and wished to continue in hotels when their voices broke or they burst their shiny buttons, classes in catering or accountancy to help them move on to the filing, audit or other offices. Many of the Savoy's best couriers and enquiry clerks have started under the signal board at the Reception counter, entering the times of every visitor's summons from the floors above. They lived briefly in an exciting world of celebrities who rewarded them with handsome tips and often friendship. A dozen very proud pages were invited to a birthday tea-party by Mary Martin's small daughter, Heller, and presented her with a bouquet specially made up by the floral department.

Before the opening of *South Pacific*, Mary Martin stayed at the hotel for several weeks and won all hearts including that of the usually immovable 'Willy' Hofflin who went to the opening

Above, the bedroom of a river suite reflects the Savoy's blend of traditional and contemporary décor. The hotel makes its own mattresses while expert craftsmen on the premises handle all maintenance from carpets to bed-lamps. A card index is kept of guest's individual tastes. *Right*, the Savoy's marble bathrooms, each with telephone and a variety of Irish linen towels changed daily and specially woven to company specifications, are world-famed

Above, soon after dawn a squad of cleaners is at work in the front hall as the night-clerks in Reception go off duty. *Below*, the electric lift in the gentlemen's cloakroom which was suggested by Reeves-Smith. It runs at 70 miles per hour and can handle over a thousand hats and coats an hour

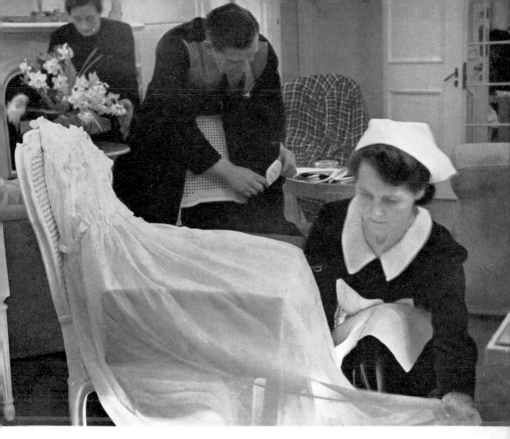

Above, in a second-floor suite a valet and chambermaid lay out the guests' evening clothes. In the background the floor housekeeper gives the finishing touches to an arrangement prepared by the hotel's florist department. *Below*, while their owner lunches in the Savoy, these pets are aired in the Embankment Gardens by Eric Holmes

Left, in the hotel's underground garage, one of the largest in London, a thoroughbred is given a shampoo and set. *Below*, this power station supplies all the hotel's electricity, air-conditioning and the exhaust steam needed for room and water heating. Half a million gallons of water are used on a peak day

night and cried like a baby. After the première, at a mammoth supper party in the Restaurant given by Rodgers and Hammerstein, three hundred guests stood up and cheered frantically when the star walked in to the strains of *Some Enchanted Evening*. The party continued in her suite on the fifth floor where she sang and danced for hours. Her audience sat on the floor and included the Oliviers, John Gielgud, Diana Wynyard and a score of celebrities from the American colony in London.

Hollywood stars were arriving in force, not all as diffident as John Wayne who whirled each of his partners, including Margot Fonteyn, expertly round the floor but took to the hills as soon as fellow-dancers began to applaud. Chain-smoking Hoagy Carmichael, in shirtsleeves and scarlet braces, lazily played the piano in his suite, one of the few guests who never visited the hairdressing salon and preferred to cut his own hair with the barber's scissors he had brought with him. Gloria Swanson crackled with excitement over her come-back in *Sunset Boulevard*. She ate extract of seaweed 'for extra energy' and had a secret hoard of malted coconut, dates, figs, dried nuts and a remarkable variety of other foods not chemically treated. She brought her own bread, herb tea and essence of sesame oil and garlic which her friends sampled with varying degrees of appreciation. Swathed in chinchilla and perfume she presided over a celebration party at which Dietrich danced cheek to cheek with Michael Wilding. Eva Bartok cycled up to the hotel in lens-catching, black silk tights, low-necked sweater and a lace cossack cap. Tallulah was back in London after nearly twenty years to make a recording for *The Big Show* and proved that she had not lost her old exuberance by loudly calling out to a friend, "What's the matter, dahlin'; don't you recognize me with my clothes on?"

Patricia Morison shook her dark tresses, five feet long, for the photographers, and actresses like Anita Ekberg made their pneumatic way up to the roof. One young woman, posing buxomly over the parapet, signed a statement, "I will not hold the Savoy in any way responsible for any damage to myself or my equipment." They were all swept from the front page when

Colonel Esmond Drury, a famed fly-fisherman from Wimbledon, settled a £1,000 bet for two angling enthusiasts who wagered on whether he could cast a two-ounce lead from the roof into the Thames. Strapped to a stanchion by a window-cleaner's belt, he swung his ten-foot-six salmon rod and landed his line well and truly in the river, 105 yards below.

The Festival of Britain brought a new surge of visitors. At the Festival offices in Savoy Court the King and Queen inspected a model of the South Bank Exhibition and soon afterwards, defying her doctor's warnings of a possible chill, Queen Mary watched the lights from a fourth floor window until well past midnight, when to the surprise of her equerry and the lady-in-waiting, she declined to go home and insisted on driving to see the floodlit St. Paul's Cathedral. Having enjoyed her evening out and the glass of Chablis and *marrons glacés* Hugh Wontner had provided for her, Her Majesty next day sent him her photograph, with a warm letter of thanks.

King Haakon of Norway was another guest fascinated by the sparkling view over the Thames and obviously delighted when joined one evening by Sir Winston Churchill who had been dining with members of The Other Club. One of the few visitors unimpressed by the spectacle was Billy Rose, the American show-man who had put on the World's Fair. Looking apathetically from his window, he asked, "What's that?" That, replied an indignant and patriotic floor waiter, was the great Festival of Britain. "I'd like to help it," said Rose sympathetically.

The hotel was in carnival mood. A party of coal miners from Leeds wrote to the Savoy pleading that their annual visit to London for the Rugby League Final at Wembley would be made memorable if they could meet Carroll Gibbons. The management gave them a small reception and, after drinks, Hannay showed them round the hotel before taking the whole party of thirty to dinner at Simpson's where Carroll sat down at a piano and led a lively sing-song.

The five-shilling limit on meals was at last abolished and licensing hours at the Savoy and the Berkeley extended to 2.30

a.m. To please visitors, mainly American, who did not always care to change or arrived by air with only a small suitcase, evening dress was no longer *de rigueur* in the Restaurant but, in the way of human nature, very few took advantage of the option.

Carroll Gibbons had settled in smoothly and engaged cabarets which suited the mood of sophisticated gaiety. Bea Lillie's opening night attracted almost every celebrity in town, among them Douglas Fairbanks and his wife, Orson Welles and Markova, who surprised Danny Kaye by her brilliant ballroom dancing. A few evenings later, Princess Elizabeth came in to supper and enjoyed the cabaret so much that she brought Bea Lillie back to repeat *Maud*, a traditional favourite with the Royal Family.

The Coronation and its pageantry attracted the largest number of visitors in London's colourful history. To prevent confusion which could have marred the occasion, a Coronation Accommodation Committee was formed well in advance, with Hugh Wontner as Chairman. His experience as Secretary to the previous body, established for the Coronation of King George VI, was now reinforced by his years with the Savoy Group.

The Coronation brought a record number of bookings to the hotel, but one well-loved figure was missing. Taken ill in New York during the phenomenal run of *The King and I*, Gertrude Lawrence had been full of plans for a new play which Daphne du Maurier was coming over to discuss with her. Sitting up in bed, flushed and excited but very near to death, she had called out to her secretary, "Be sure to write the Savoy and make certain of my room on the Route." When the sad news reached London every theatre and cinema flashed off its lights in tribute, and many of the grill-room staff, who had known and loved her since the early Charlot revues, were in tears.

With the flags of all nations shimmering in floodlight on the eve of the Coronation, the hotel seemed to invest itself with the dreamy magic of Count Peter's ancient palace. Next morning, the tinkling of spurs muffled by waves of velvet, satin and taffeta, many guests left for Westminster Abbey; peers and peeresses in crimson and ermine; maharajahs in jewelled turbans and coats of lustrous gold tissue; princes looking like exquisite chandeliers, with fine marzipan skins over their high diamanté collars; and silver-haired Prime Ministers from the Commonwealth wearing vivid sashes and orders with their Court dress.

That night the hotel staged what has become known as 'The Ball of the Century'. For some weeks a Committee, under Hannay's chairmanship, had been busily arranging a Coronation Ball in aid of various charities with the Duke of Edinburgh as patron. The tickets at twelve guineas each were over-subscribed months in advance, and the 1,400 guests who drove to the Savoy on Coronation Night through the packed singing crowds in the Strand were greeted by a spectacle of remarkable beauty.

For almost two days a team of workmen had carefully assembled the decorations designed by Cecil Beaton with the assistance of Miss D'Oyly Carte and others. The restaurant had been transformed into an Elizabethan pavilion, a vast domed tent fashioned from 4,000 yards of specially dyed and fireproofed silk and muslin in flamingo pink, grey and turquoise. Coronets of ostrich feathers hung from the chandeliers, the pavilion effect enhanced by hundreds of bay and camellia trees, flanked by over two tons of box-hedging in the shape of peacocks. Arriving guests passed into the restaurant between 150 heraldic emblems, while fitting vividly into the décor were sixteen Yeoman Warders from the Tower of London in full-dress uniform. The entrance to the ballroom was hung with mock ermine and every door on the ground floor had been covered with studded red velvet.

The guests sat down to a superb dinner prepared by Laplanche and his staff, the menu itself a work of art in the form of a parchment scroll with its red ribbon and heavy blue seal. Dancing together were old racing rivals like M. Boussac and Madame Volterra. Many guests favoured Elizabethan fancy dress while famous soldiers like Generals Omar Bradley and Marshall and Sir Claude Auchinleck looked magnificent in gold-braided full-dress uniform. From the Commonwealth had come the Australian Prime Minister, Robert Menzies, and Dr. Borg Olivier of Malta. The American Ambassador, Winthrop Aldrich, entertained a large party, among them Governor Earl Warren of California, while Sir Frederick Browning's table guests included Margot Fonteyn, Nadia Nerina and Frederick Ashton. Film stars had for once to play the unaccustomed role of sightseers, goggling at the many foreign Royalties like Prince Takadi of Japan and Prince Chula of Siam, and the vividly-turbaned Maharajahs of Darbhanga and Faridkot, while even without the diamond-studded collar which he had worn in the Abbey, the Nawab of Bahawalpur was still a striking figure.

The four dance-bands were reinforced by pipers from all the regiments of which the Queen is Colonel-in-Chief, including two Pipe-Majors of the Argyll and Sutherland Highlanders who had come from Canada at the special invitation of Buckingham Palace. Soon after nine o'clock, the popping of over 3,000 champagne corks was temporarily muted by Her Majesty's Speech, relayed throughout the hotel. An hour later many guests crowded to the windows or exuberantly climbed fire-escapes to the roof to watch the gigantic firework display on the South Bank across the river. A roar of applause greeted Sir Winston Churchill as he entered arm-in-arm with his old friend, the white-robed Pasha of Marrakesch, who had dined with him at Number 10. As Big Ben tolled midnight, a great shower of Elizabethan favours cascaded from the ceiling. Tiaras were gaily crowned with wimples; ruffs suddenly appeared on Abbey gowns designed by Balmain, Dior and Hartnell; and princes, generals and diplomats in roundhead and cavalier hats joined an endless conga-line, waving flags and jesters' dolls. For an hour Maurice Chevalier and Noël Coward led a sparkling cabaret which included sword-dancers and members of the Sadler's Wells Ballet. Hundreds of the guests were still dancing at dawn when a breakfast of bacon and eggs was served.

On that memorable day the Savoy kitchens provided more than eleven thousand meals, without ignoring special requests like that from El Mahdi of the Sudan whose bread had to be baked without salt, or the numerous guests from India and Nigeria who ate in their suites sitting on the floor because their religion forbade them to use leather chairs. Hollywood was represented by Bing Crosby, Bob Hope, Paulette Goddard, Spyros Skouras, Sonja Henie and many more; while from Paris came Claude Terrail and Sacha Guitry with his fifth wife, Lana Marconi.

There were other visitors like Roger Dolese who had brought his family over from Oklahoma and, finding the accommodation too small for them all, asked the management to knock down a wall between his suite and the one adjoining. Enjoying the hotel and its service, they ultimately extended their visit to include the birth of a new baby and promptly asked Dr. Gordon, the Savoy's much-liked doctor, to become godfather. They stayed altogether for two and a half years, their bill averaging nearly £1,000 a week. Soon afterwards the Nickles clan, eighteen strong from Calgary, drove up in a huge private coach which jammed all traffic in the forecourt. It had to back out and move round to the Embankment entrance where a van unloaded forty-five pieces of luggage.

The seasoned reception clerks and janissaries, many of them trained by the majestic Hansen, so long a classic figure at the Savoy, pride themselves on the smooth handling of all baggage problems, from the safe transit of a suitcase of bullion to arranging quarantine for a guest's private menagerie. When members of a Firestone Company Convention reached the hotel they were astonished to find four hundred trunks and valises already checked and awaiting them in their apartments. Unfortunately, the record was marred by the late arrival of a fourth truck; it had been 'arrested' for speeding on its way from London Airport! The Head Housekeeper was already arranging for the pyjamas, nightdresses, cosmetics and shaving gear always provided for guests in any emergency.

This party had reserved 219 rooms, the largest single booking in the experience of the Savoy, which has always declined to follow the practice of 'block' reservations by Conventions who like to take over entire hotels in the United States. There are always the exceptions. When the American Bar Association decided to hold its meeting in London, to be attended by five thousand lawyers and their wives, the leading hotels combined to make this possible and arrangements worked perfectly. The Savoy was chosen as the headquarters and a very large number of lawyers and their wives stayed there, including Chief Justice Earl Warren and many others. Apart from these special occasions, the management considers that residents and long-established patrons have a priority, like the members of a club or regiment who have met for reunions and celebrations over the years. It is quite different in America where too many hotels have been built, some so huge that there is no other way of filling them except by Conventions, which necessarily destroy any personal bond between guest and hotelier.

Partly for this reason the Company has declined a flattering series of invitations to purchase or advise on projects for new hotels in various parts of the world including the Far East, Africa, India and Brazil. "Whilst we appreciate the compliment," Mr. Wontner has replied, "it has been our policy to confine our thought and attention to our business here."

His strong feeling for tradition is allied to a personal warmth known only to his family and a few close friends and colleagues. It prompted him to give a reception in honour of Madame Ritz who was in London for the Coronation, and a fitting occasion to welcome her back to the hotel after more than half a century. The white-haired old lady, still very active for her years, was received at the entrance by the Chairman who conducted her to the Pinafore Room where she was greeted by Lady Reeves-Smith, who had come from Claridge's, and by Madame Schwenter, widow of the head of the Meurice Hotel in Paris, who had been Assistant Manager at the Savoy soon after Ritz departed. All the department heads in the Group were present. With some emotion, Madame Ritz recognized and embraced old employees who had been at the Savoy with her husband, like James Townsend, Harry Williams and Walter Hore, the Company's Secretary, whom she clearly remembered as a junior clerk.

She chuckled when Townsend, the very dignified Head of the Gentlemen's Cloakrooms, recalled that her husband had discharged him sixty years ago when he was a pageboy at the hotel. Summoned to run an errand, he was nowhere to be found and Ritz had angrily given orders that he was to be dismissed. The following day he was back at his post but the Managing Director had not forgotten and ordered him to leave at once. Young Townsend explained that he had been sent out to find a hansom cab for some guests and had run as far as Northumberland Avenue before he was successful. Ritz smiled, congratulated him on his enterprise and promptly reinstated him.

Madame Ritz's memory was surprising as she chatted vivaciously of amusing incidents during her husband's régime and enchanted Laplanche and Alban with some racy anecdotes about Escoffier. What had begun as a semi-formal reception became a family party which ended long after curfew.

Another gesture was inspired by the Fuchs-Hillary expedition. When Vivian Fuchs arrived at Scott Base, he and his party were welcomed by a complimentary case of champagne and 4 lbs. of caviare, flown out to New Zealand and taken on by a U.S. Navy aircraft. Originally, it had been planned to send a fully pre-cooked five-course banquet but Fuchs wired back: "I don't think we can do justice to a Savoy meal on a primus stove."

Nothing did more, perhaps, to bring Hugh Wontner closer to the staff than the dramatic 'Battle of the Berkeley'. For many years he had moved almost invisibly between his sixth floor suite at Claridge's and his Savoy office when he was not abroad on business or a delegate at international hotel conferences. Crisp of manner but judicially fair-minded, he had seemed austere to some employees who saw a tall lean man in a dark suit with a thin gold chain across the waistcoat, and a gravely ascetic face over a gleaming white collar. Few were aware of his shyness and simplicity once outside the demanding worlds of hotel business and finance.

From both his parents he inherited a knowledge of the theatre, his interest in acting continuing since his schooldays at Oundle.

In 1937 he was elected a member of that fine amateur dramatic society, The Old Stagers, with whom Ellen Terry once appeared, and has very often played in their annual production during Canterbury's Cricket Week. Before the war he used to appear with The Windsor Strollers at the Theatre Royal. On family holidays abroad, he has preferred quiet and modest hotels out of the public eye and always escapes the attentions of local photographers by looking the completely average tourist in shorts and sandals with a camera slung over a casual checked shirt. After one holiday in Greece, enraptured by the amphitheatre in Epidaurus and architectural treasures in Athens and elsewhere, he was much affected by the elusive principles of good proportion in design and their effect upon those who live and work in such an environment. "I altered the shape of an office or two," he recalled soon after his return, "and now I find people happier at work there."

His mood was far from easy-going and relaxed when the hotels came under direct threat. The Savoy Group's growth in prestige and prosperity—the trading profit for 1953 had reached a record figure of £654,438—inevitably attracted speculators, but even more tempting to some was the chance of seizing control of the immensely valuable freehold properties owned by the Company. The first significant signs of mysterious buying of Savoy shares were noticed in the autumn of 1953. Before long two well-known property men, one a specialist in 'take-over' bids, were heavily engaged in trying to obtain a controlling interest. The battle raged for months during which millions of pounds' worth of shares changed hands.

Confronted with this trojan horse and firmly convinced that there was a duty to the public, the staff and loyal shareholders to prevent the destruction of the Company, Hugh Wontner was determined to resist. He and his colleagues on the Board suspected that the Berkeley was the real hidden target of 'the enemy' and, acting on expert legal advice, took effective counter-action with one bold strategical move. Wontner, with the Board's approval, arranged for the transfer of the Berkeley to a specially-formed subsidiary Company. By an ingenious arrangement, the Savoy Staff Benevolent Fund, a charity, was thus charged with the duty of ensuring the use of the site for an hotel and restaurant.

This move, which now has a prominent place in Company Law text-books, caused a sensation at the time and attracted so much critical comment in the financial columns of some newspapers that a debate followed in the House of Commons and finally a Board of Trade Enquiry. By this time, however, one of the property men had sold his shares to the other who, within an ace of securing control, now realized that the prize had slipped from him. He decided to withdraw and offered his block of shares to Wontner who, after intense and secret negotiation, was able to raise the enormous funds needed to beat off the challenge. The rival share holdings were finally bought out for well over £1,250,000. Although the source of this capital has never been disclosed, despite much guesswork, it is certain that the City, which had wrongly been considered critical of the Berkeley move, came to the rescue and saved the Savoy Group. It was a triumph for Hugh Wontner and his directors, after many months of strain and anxiety, but carried off with no flourish of trumpets.

Symbolic of the Savoy's proud tradition was the new Wedgwood table service which soon afterwards came into use. Reserved for the 'river' or restaurant side of the hotel, and made from fine gold-edged white bone china, it commemorates the ancient link between the Savoy and the Thames. Silk screens delicately reproduce the Royal Barge, its golden superstructure gay with coral flags and pennants and floating serenely on a river of turquoise. It was designed by the artist wife of Sir Howard Robertson, a President of the R.I.B.A., who was responsible for the hotel's forecourt and many other schemes for decoration and rebuilding, and later joined the Board.

In the grill-room a new Doulton china set of 5,000 pieces was put into service. The now-familiar decoration consists of a band in medium grey between two fine lines, with a dark grey 'S' badge engraved on each piece. More recently the hotel ordered for the Banqueting Department what is perhaps the largest set of china ever made. The service of Royal Worcester porcelain, known as 'The Savoy Garland', has 11,200 pieces, together with a similar number as a year's reserve.

With the end of austerity, the Savoy reverted quickly to its traditional French cuisine. Glazed *truite au bleu* reappeared, *paté de foie gras* from Strasbourg and Bayonne ham, green corn for the hotel's famed salad and the countless delicacies, many specially imported, which Laplanche and Alban demanded. The head chefs tasted each dish before submitting it for the approval of epicures, but of equal importance were appearance and presentation, particularly in hot weather when palates have to be wooed. The cold buffet glowed in still life with *poussins* in aspic, galantines of capon, pink salmon with a glint of parsley and lemon, and *caneton glacé*. The chief pastrycook gave loving care to some special creation for a party; perhaps a miniature pagoda of cream and marzipan, an exotic fruit salad or a gracefully beribboned basket of colourful roses made from spun sugar.

While the maître-chefs prepared the dishes of a classic *haute cuisine*, each kept his own jealously-guarded refinements with sauces, stuffings, herbs and spices. The restaurant chef from Rouen coloured his palette with Norman subtleties and often served *tripes à la mode de Caen, canard à la rouennaise* and highly sophisticated fish stews. Alban, a true son of Burgundy, flattered clients with remembered magic from the Côte d'Or. His *coq au vin, escargots* and the finesse of his sauces made the grill-room a tabernacle of gastronomy. One of his famous dishes, *sole surprise de Gaulle*, now has an honoured place in the kitchen lore; it was lovingly fashioned from fillets of sole and lobster mousse and sealed in a pancake decorated with truffles.

The chefs were painstaking over the regional or national dishes ordered by a cosmopolitan clientèle. They prided themselves on being more than equal to orders ranging from *shashlik* to strawberry shortcake, Alaska crab, crawfish bisque, exotic curries and Salzburger *nockerl*. Both were aware, nevertheless, of a distinct change in eating and drinking habits. Diners would never again take to multi-course meals, while an increasing number consulted diet sheets and called for grills and salads. The trend was for simpler but excellently cooked food with sound clarets and a spry *rosé* rather more in demand than the magisterial wines of the past. Traditional British fare was requested more often than quail and truffles; kippers became suddenly popular; film stars like Cary Grant asked for sausage and mash; roast beef, mutton and even the humble tripe and onions were in constant demand, with tea more favoured at breakfast than coffee, even by Americans.

In a diet-conscious and less gracious age, gastronomic flattery has become rare and not always appreciated. As that charming epicure, A. J. Liebling, reported sadly, "If an actress had a dish named after her now, the recipe would be four phenobarbital tablets and a jigger of Metrecal."

OVER THE years the organization of the Savoy has been firmly based on the mechanics of a smooth, self-contained unit geared to all demands *within* the Group. One of the directors, G. B. Potts, has remarked, "We are the only hotel in London where every whim of the most exacting guests can be gratified at four in the morning as satisfactorily as at four in the afternoon." Such a claim has meant a rigid limitation of other services, however tempting or profit-making in the short term. The Savoy is one of the few major hotels in the world which sturdily declines to undertake outside catering.

Nevertheless, early one Sunday morning on 3 October 1954, the hotel felt compelled to break its own rule and accepted an unique challenge. It was swathed in sleep, save for the night staff of sixty alert for any sudden orders for service. The ballroom had closed and only a few lamps burned in the grill-room where breakfasts would be served from seven onwards. The main hall was cool and silent but for the ticking of an ormolu clock. The familiar daytime aroma of cigar smoke, exotic perfume, flowers and rich leather had faded. The reading-room was empty behind its glass panel but now and then a chandelier in the hall played on a silver inkstand or the scalloped edge of an escritoire.

The two always-illuminated signs, 'Reception' and 'Enquiries', picked out the figures of a few night clerks making notes in smooth copper-plate. At the shadowy swing-doors, tall grey-coated porters stood immobile like temple buddhas but watchful for late visitors, and with one eye on the cards over the Head

Porter's desk showing arrivals and departures for Atlantic liners.

The arteries of the hotel were pulsing smoothly, with the night-report noting little of unusual interest, when at 2.30 a.m. a light flashed on the switchboard and the call was instantly passed to Marini, the Night Manager. At the other end, the polite voice of Mr. Eden's secretary at the Foreign Office apologized and announced an emergency. He went on to explain that the Nine Power Conference at Lancaster House had been scheduled to end on the Saturday but was to be extended by a day owing to last-minute differences between the Ministers. Luncheon for 150 delegates would therefore have to be provided that very day and Mr. Eden had personally suggested that the Savoy might come to the rescue since the firm normally responsible for official catering could not cope at such short notice.

It would have been almost routine to serve such a meal in the hotel but Mr. Ashley Williams regretted that this was out of the question. To save time and bring the Conference to an end that afternoon, the luncheon would have to be held at Lancaster House. In case it was a hoax, the call was discreetly traced back and quickly confirmed as genuine. The Night Manager promised to give an answer within a few minutes.

The difficulties were obvious. Since no equipment was available at Lancaster House, it would all have to be specially transported. The hotel staff, normally reduced at weekends, would also be later than usual in reporting for Sunday duties. Finally, the problem remained of choosing and preparing a suitable menu and making the necessary arrangements for extra supplies.

Bedside telephones were soon ringing throughout the hotel and in the homes of department heads enjoying their sleep after late Saturday night duty. The Banqueting Manager, Contarini, soon recovered from the shock news and decided that the luncheon must go forward. Luckily, extra waiters would be coming in for a Green Room Club dinner that evening and could be recruited. Laplanche went down to his glass cage in the restaurant kitchens and seized pencil and pad. Once he had agreed to prepare a cold buffet for 150 important guests in addition to the Club banquet and normal meals in the hotel, he summoned his night cook (always on duty for floor-service after the Restaurant closed) and instructed him to roast turkeys, chickens, beef ribs and saddles of lamb so that they could be cold and ready by morning. The menu was quickly composed; smoked salmon or melon would be followed by cold meats and salads, fruit salad and cream, French pastries and a variety of cheeses. Additional supplies of fresh fruit and vegetables were rapidly ordered by telephone, and the baker alerted to increase his usual Sunday quota by 300 fresh rolls.

Within half an hour of the S.O.S., the Ministry was told that "luncheon would be served." Mr. Ashley Williams would arrange transport through the Ministry of Works. The choice of wines and spirits was discussed and agreed, and the price of the meal settled at £2 a head. From long experience of diabetics, vegetarians, Moslems and other special guests, the meticulous Laplanche had already noted details of any individual preferences, like that of M. Mendès-France for fresh milk.

Shortly after dawn, the head of Stores was called from his bed in the suburbs and arrived within the hour to supervise the packing of china, glass, silver and linen. Not wishing to disturb the General Manager at his cottage in Westerham, this call was postponed until 9 a.m., to give him a little much-needed rest as he was due back in the afternoon for the Green Room Club banquet. Hofflin listened carefully to the arrangements so far made, tied up a few loose ends and stressed that, once undertaken, the luncheon must in every way live up to the hotel's reputation.

The complicated operation moved with controlled frenzy by chefs, waiters and table men. In his kitchen Laplanche was supervising with Napoleonic thrust but without thought of a possible Waterloo. Two sides of smoked salmon were being sliced while a squad of helpers carved the various cold meats. Meanwhile, all the bar equipment, the soft drinks, the wines and liqueur brandy, the lager beer, ice, mint and so on were in readiness. From the Banqueting Department's stores, neatly arranged for smooth transport, emerged a pyramid of china, milk and cream jugs, cruets, cutlery, ladles, sugar tongs and bowls, wine, cocktail and liqueur glasses, buffet cloths, table cloths, doylies, napkins, ash-trays, matchstands and every other item of equipment required for 150 discerning *couverts*. Miss Marshall of the Florist Department was already busily arranging dainty sprays for the buffet and three colourful centrepieces to decorate the main table. At 10 a.m. Contarini and his assistants drove to Lancaster House to inspect the dining-room and decide on the site of the buffet and the general layout. The Ministers would be seated and the remainder of the guests served from the buffet.

Back in the hotel all was going to plan, but transport still needed very careful attention. The Ministry of Works van would clearly be inadequate and a second, complete with driver, had to be requisitioned from the Savoy Garage. Since all goods could only be delivered through the main entrance at Lancaster House, where the Foreign Ministers and their parties would be arriving for the first conference at 11 a.m., split-second timing was essential to avoid traffic hold-ups.

Before 10.45 the vans had delivered most of the basic equipment and supplies. A shuttle-service of private cars then transported the head waiter, fifteen waiters, two barmen and three platemen who at once began to prepare the room and buffet. Everyone concerned in the operation had to produce special passes issued by the Ministry's security officer. The last van left the hotel at 12.30 p.m., and the buffet at Lancaster House was completely ready with everyone at action stations by three minutes to one.

As the clock struck the hour, the British Foreign Secretary entered the dining-room with Mr. Dulles, followed by the other Ministers and their staffs. They rose just before 3 p.m. when the Agreement was ready to be signed. Before leaving, Mr. Eden shook hands with Contarini and his assistants, informing his guests for the first time that the luncheon had only been arranged at a few hours' notice; "a masterpiece of achievement on the part of the Savoy Hotel."

WITH VARIATIONS in flavour, the sugar icing on the hotel's layer cake has always been piped on by operatic, stage and film stars. In the heyday of Covent Garden and the Royal Albert Hall, Melba, Caruso, Chaliapin and Tetrazzini had made the Savoy their headquarters; between the wars, when Novello, Cochran and Noël Coward were in the ascendant, the grill-room was both rendezvous and market-place for the Stage; in the 1950s, although opera and the legitimate theatre were still traditionally represented, the scene was dominated almost entirely by Hollywood and Broadway.

Television had yet to snuff out the candlepower of film studios, cinemas and music-halls. Lavish premières, Royal Command Film galas and the London Palladium's appetite for American artistes brought a non-stop flow of celebrity names and promotions. "Under the Union Jack, the Stars and Stripes, the massed chandeliers of the Savoy, the waiters stand at attention by the great glass doors . . . a touch of religion, a touch of family, the mixture goes smoothly down," dryly recalls Graham Greene after a rather solemn M.G.M. luncheon to celebrate Louis B. Mayer's decision to produce films in Britain. Scarcely a day passed without some banquet or party to mark the glory of screens, wider still and wider, and colour more desperately beautiful than ever.

Film stars clicked in and out of the Savoy like strips of celluloid through a moviola. Many came only for a Press reception, a studio luncheon or the opening of a personal appearance tour, but they travelled with retinues of agents, publicity experts and personal attendants. The beautiful red-haired actress, Maria Montez, arrived with her husband, Jean-Pierre Aumont, and made a regal entrance with nineteen pieces of luggage in addition to twenty-two hat-boxes, carried in by a relay of pageboys. This was required for only a week's stay in London.

Stars like Chaplin, Liberace and Danny Kaye received hundreds of letters and telephone calls, quite apart from the not always welcome attentions of hysterical admirers. When Frankie Laine and Johnnie Ray were in residence a special force of detectives and bodyguards had to be recruited to keep bobby-soxers in order and prevent the more lovesick from forcing their way in. Pat Boone, the mildest of crooners who liked nothing more stimulating than deep-breathing exercises and quarts of milk, entered his suite one night to find a young woman breathing heavily and intent on stripping off her clothes. He fled to the inner room and called for help.

'Schnozzle' Durante bounced into the hotel with hundreds of cigars and a beautiful girl. In his exuberance he rushed to the window of his river suite, admired the view and started to turn a lever. As the huge windows opened he stepped back hastily and muttered, "I toight dat handle was going to pervide moosic." Equally uninhibited was Victor Mature who liked to greet visitors in a red and white flannel nightshirt and tasselled cap. One evening he appeared in the main hall wearing bush shorts, a safari shirt and moccasins, having just returned from filming in Africa. He demanded his usual fifth floor room and bath but was politely reminded that he had arrived two days early and the hotel was quite full. In vain he pleaded, argued and protested. Rather than stay anywhere else, he flew home to New York for the weekend and returned to claim his old room. He also brought a hip bath, "just in case," as he told the Reception with a wink.

Groucho Marx booked the same suite he had last occupied a quarter of a century ago. He needed no script-writer. When a reception clerk asked how long he intended to stay, he snapped back, "till it stops raining." One reporter asked, "What would you like to be if you were not Groucho Marx?" "Dead," was the reply, as he loped unmistakably into a Press conference in the Gondoliers Room, roaring *Take a Pair of Sparkling Eyes.*

Interviews with film stars usually vary from the fatuous to the offensive, but Brigitte Bardot proved more than competent in dealing with them. Sheathed by Balmain, she was asked between wiggles what she did with her evenings. "Crossword puzzles," she replied sweetly. When questioned about make-up by a woman reporter she said, "I hate lipstick because it makes troubles." Shelley Winters, who later departed because the hotel's amenities did not include a turkish bath, had little patience for formal interviews. She received one reporter, while in bed and using a hairdryer which she handed to him with the suggestion, "Here, you dry and I'll talk."

At that time and before the crisis wave of economy, studios lavished money on an endless series of receptions which were arranged with automatic precision by the hotel, not always an easy matter. Flowers, catering and special photographic facilities all needed care but these were routine to the banqueting staff who would undertake two or even three such affairs in the same evening. More difficult were certain stars who had little sense of punctuality and sometimes behaved with less than dignity when they finally arrived half-way through the reception or, more embarrassingly, put in a perfunctory appearance for a few minutes. One cowboy hero was usually so inebriated that the studio tried to keep him out of sight. He was cooking a hamburger in his room late one night when the saucepan began to blaze and touched off the curtains. He rushed out into the corridor, almost in the nude, searching for a fire-extinguisher. Next morning he was politely asked to leave. Another film actor did not endear himself to the staff whom he kept hopping to his whims. He always left by the side-entrance to avoid the inconvenience of tipping.

On the credit side were unspoilt actresses like Jean Simmons who declined to sign autographs but delighted journalists by offering her own album for their signatures. Errol Flynn tipped liberally, but more significant was his kindness and consideration towards the staff. At the hotel he did not practise the wild behaviour which was reserved for night clubs. Many others also behaved quietly and with modesty. Arriving at the hotel in a hurry, Gene Kelly had the misfortune to trap his finger in the car door. His hand and arm went septic and he had several shots of penicillin before he could attend a Press reception. He amused journalists by clowning and tap-dancing and without saying a word about his accident.

The pattern varied little; gossip-writers and critics were injected with alcohol, canapés and high-powered publicity. The prize exhibit would then jump through the customary hoops. Women writers made notes on dress and jewellery; others chatted about the star's house and bathing-pool in Hollywood and quizzed her on a rather fanciful genealogy; while a few of the more earnest even showed a little polite interest in the forthcoming epic. Soured by experience and cynical of all publicity, the majority ignored the guest of honour and attacked the buffet until the waiters announced wearily that the bar was closed.

Occasionally a touch of novelty pumped a little blood into even those hardened arteries. In a packed Lancaster Room, Marilyn Monroe exhibited a nylon midriff at a Press reception at which Sir Laurence Olivier, her co-star in *The Sleeping Prince*, presided with great skill and charm. Her replies to questions were clear, intelligent and entertaining. She then departed to Englefield Green to go for a 'quiet' cycle ride with Arthur Miller, attended by only fifty photographers.

Studios usually paid dearly when they attempted to change the tradition of unlimited food and drink for something less conventional. After her marriage to Aly Khan, Rita Hayworth was unwisely projected as semi-royalty. Embossed invitations had been sent out to critics who were asked to form an orderly queue for the privilege of a few gracious words from the deity. Many declined, and poor Miss Hayworth was left marooned among liveried attendants and hand-wringing publicity men.

An unrehearsed incident also marked the appearance of Marlene

Dietrich at one lavish luncheon in the River Room. Always a favourite with the photographers, she had posed with her usual ease and delivered some astringent and quotable comments while chain-smoking between courses. The red-coated master of cere-monies came forward, banged the table extra hard and called for the loyal toast. He then intoned with great solemnity, "My lords, ladies and gentlemen, you *now* have your chairman's permission to smoke." An enormous cigarette-holder in mid-air, Dietrich blushed in a silence as thick as a studio handout. She recovered superbly and made a pretty apology.

Away from the gossip-writers, most of the film celebrities liked to enjoy themselves in their own way. Ava Gardner would spend all day in Suite 505, reading scripts and playing gramo-phone records. Behind enormous dark glasses, she often dined in the restaurant before slipping away to a night club. Passionately fond of dancing, her solo flamenco once cracked the glass floor at the Don Juan in Mayfair. When the club closed at 5 a.m., she took the entire Latin American 'combo' back to her suite where she changed into slacks and sweater and danced mambos and cha-chas barefoot with Esteban, the band leader, for another two hours.

Like most of the glamorous actresses, she received an avalanche of love letters and offers of marriage. One practical amorist sent a lavish bouquet up to her suite with a passionate plea for audience. When this was denied, he angrily asked a chambermaid to reclaim his flowers. Miss Gardner's misfortunes were not yet over. After the Royal Film Performance, she made the embarras-sing discovery that her form-hugging, black velvet gown did not permit her to curtsy to the Queen. Julie Wilson was another artiste whose couturier had made locomotion rather precarious. She hobbled about in what she called "my income tax dress, because I can't sit down in it, which proves that it's for singing only."

Dorothy Dandridge arrived in a Rolls-Royce to appear in the hotel cabaret with a £10,000 wardrobe which filled her suite, but room had also to be squeezed for her small zoo of stuffed poodles, spaniels and bulldogs and a library of books on psycho-analysis. Another cabaret success, Lena Horne, always turned up the central heating in her suite to near boiling point and relaxed in a bath-robe fastened at the neck by a huge safety-pin which had been her lucky charm for twelve years. Along the corridor Eartha Kitt lay curled up on a sofa, surrounded by Christmas presents which she had brought from Sarah Churchill in New York for Sir Winston and his family.

An actress who appeared more recently in cabaret at the Savoy was Juliette Greco. Her first visit to the hotel some years ago, when she was quite unknown except in the St. Germain cafés, was in answer to a telephone call from David Selznick who had offered her a seven-year contract if she would agree to be groomed by Hollywood. She refused. With chalk-white face under a raven Left-Bank coiffure, she ate her meals alone in her room, wearing an old black leather raincoat over her pyjamas. On later visits she wore jeans at all times but did not venture to drive her Thunderbird barefoot, as she usually did in Paris.

The Film Command Performances often started a chain reaction of last-minute nerves among stars normally at ease under the arc-lights. For hours they would practise curtsies and try to memorize protocol. Gina Lollobrigida had an added problem when her trunks were fogbound at Orly. She arrived in mink and tears, without make-up or even a nightdress. Hofflin soothed her with gentleness and lent her a pair of his wife's silk pyjamas. Narrowly averting a stromboli of temperament, the dress arrived barely in time for the Presentation.

Vittorio di Sica was much more relaxed. Almost as suave and debonair as his film image, he nevertheless disdained glitter and drove around in a 1930 Austin Seven. He could not resist the Port of London and spent hours talking to the dockers and quaffing pints of bitter in Wapping pubs. Equally inconspicuous was Ingrid Bergman who had come over for the ill-fated oratorio, *Joan of Arc at the Stake*, but took its failure with great calm and cycled placidly every day in Hyde Park with her children.

While Chaplin barricaded himself into his river suite and

departed with stealth to tour the South London haunts of his boyhood, Liberace beamed goodwill at the thousands of women who had greeted him at Waterloo and besieged the Savoy throughout his stay. The telephone switchboard had to be reinforced, while pageboys scurried ceaselessly to and fro with mascots and gifts of every kind, from a miniature piano fashioned in flowers to a pillowcase with his cherubic features tenderly stitched by some devoted matron. On the baby grand piano in his sitting-room stood vases of yellow and red roses replenished every day by members of his fan club.

Even this hysteria paled beside that which befell Danny Kaye who had London at his feet after his sensational Palladium season. A favourite with the Royal Family and the quarry of every society hostess, he remained the most modest of all the hotel's colony of stars. He would apologize charmingly for the added strain on the hotel's detectives, telephone operators and stenographers and give the pageboys the cakes, fruit and numerous other presents sent by admirers. The telephones in his room were nearly always off the hook. His energy on and off stage was remarkable for one who ate and drank so little. In the grill-room he toyed with a sliver of smoked salmon and salad or a forkful of spinach which he would casually aim at his eye. A meal with him was always a one-act clowning performance which would convulse the waiters and every neighbouring table. His closest rival for impromptu 'cabaret' was Fernandel who used to shamble into the Front Hall and startle guests with his lifelike caricature of an acrobatic teddy-boy. With regret he narrowly missed one epic performance in Buster Keaton's suite. The 65-year-old comedian of silent film days wound himself up like a baseball pitcher and expertly demonstrated precisely how to throw a custard pie by tossing an ashtray twenty-seven feet with bull's-eye accuracy.

George Jessel misfired surprisingly in the hotel's cabaret and on the opening night asked sadly, "The Archbishop of Canterbury can't be occupying *every* seat, can he?" However, he was consoled and idolized by people in show business and held daily court in the Restaurant. At lunch he once screwed a monocle into his eye and

271

gazed at the menu in mock terror. "Why not a simple meal at, say, $1,000?" he asked Amanda, adding, "Now, listen, I want my meat well done. I can't stand meat that looks as if it isn't quite dead yet. You might just as well be eating Sophie Tucker." He leaned forward and stage-whispered, "And don't forget to put any sprouts I leave into my car."

Waiters used to watch the Mexican film star, Cantinflas, with some nervousness. Wearing the largest sapphire ring ever seen in the hotel, he had the supple fingers of the born conjurer and liked to amuse himself by popping live baby turtles into passing plates of soup. Even more high-spirited was Curt Jurgens who had come over to film *The Inn of the Sixth Happiness* opposite Ingrid Bergman. In the American Bar he would give a hilarious impression of Sophia Loren getting out of a tiny sports car in a very tight skirt.

The crisp publicity experts were tireless in preserving the mystique of their properties who could only take off their make-up and relax behind closed doors. One star, Clayton Moore, was never seen in public or private without skintight cowboy pants, stetson and his Lone Ranger black mask. The film hero, Charlton Heston, spent hours in his suite bathing his hands, badly-calloused from the chariot scenes in *Ben Hur*. Paulette Goddard, shopping in London with her husband Erich Maria Remarque before returning to their Swiss villa, admitted cheerfully to a robust appetite and used to allay the pangs of night starvation by hoarding bread and butter, cheese and fruit in her dressing-table. Like Olivia de Havilland, who often used to greet visitors while standing on her head, she was also a yoga enthusiast. Betty Hutton, a remarkable example of perpetual motion, was in residence during her rather unhappy cabaret season at the Pigalle, and liked to unwind by shadow-boxing and doing handstands in her suite. On the same floor, writing film scripts late into the night, William Saroyan kept fit with an elaborate apparatus of chest expanders but claimed that he lost weight by fretting over his income tax.

It would be difficult to find a star who has not figured on the

272

Right, Sir Robert Menzies and his wife have long made the Savoy their home from home when they come to London on Commonwealth business or to enjoy a private vacation. *Below*, leaving a dinner with The Other Club, Sir Winston Churchill was intercepted and mobbed by eight hundred guests of the International Hotels Association meeting in the Restaurant. Standing on a chair he gave his famous V sign

The Shah of Persia and Queen Soraya receiving the Danish Ambassador
and his wife at the reception in the Lancaster Room, following a banquet
given in their honour

hotel's house-list since the war. They varied from the extrovert Rock Hudson, jiving against regulations in the ballroom, to shy monosyllabic Gary Cooper who, before leaving for his last visit to England, was asked by his studio what special arrangements he required and replied tersely, "Just hire me a Rolls, and make sure of my old room with the river view." Red Skelton was rather less enthusiastic; after paying his bill he lamented, "The guy who took the money was Sir Jesse James. When you get in an elevator at the Savoy, they want to know whether you are travelling tourist or first-class."

Simenon grumbled good-humouredly that this was the only hotel in Europe where he had to go up to his suite to enjoy his briar. Prince Axel of Denmark, who lives at the Savoy when in London, was once politely asked by a waiter to put out his pipe in the grill-room. Here informal clothes are permitted and ties provided for the open-collared, but dark suits are the only alternative to evening dress in the more formal restaurant. A millionaire cattle-breeder from Alberta took some umbrage on being turned away in his two-toned jacket. Tony Britton left his Afghan hound in the cloakroom but was refused a drink in the American Bar because he was wearing a fisherman's sweater and slacks, while Sir Alec Guinness had some difficulty in passing the front doormen when he arrived to receive his Variety Club award for *Bridge on the River Kwai*. Having come straight from the studio, where he had been filming as the disreputable painter in *The Horse's Mouth*, he was wearing shabby clothes and a four-day growth of beard.

Clifton Webb was a fashion-plate at all times and brought dozens of silk shirts which had to be tenderly laundered under his personal instructions. He was one of many visitors who returned home with ecstatic reports on the hotel's laundry service. Several guests, including one Park Avenue doctor, remain so devoted that they continue to send over their detached collars to be washed, starched and returned to them at a cost of five shillings each, air freight included. The Laundry has three machines for stiff collars; one for polishing, another for folding, and a third for curling them before they are aired and shot out into a porcelain tube for the shape and starching required by a guest.

The Spanish dancer, Antonio, always appears on the stage in frilled evening shirts which rival even Clifton Webb's. During his engagements in London he spent most of his free time being fitted for suits and shirts. Although only five-foot-five, his flashing smile and Valentino-like profile turned heads whenever he entered the restaurant. However, the place of honour on his mantelpiece was reserved for a portrait of the lovely Duchess of Alba, signed, "To Antonio—from his pupil."

Frank Sinatra liked to amuse himself and his Clan by wearing a bowler hat and swordstick umbrella. During one visit the flood of mail and calls recalled the excitement of the Liberace and Danny Kaye circuses. His telephone bill for the ten days ran into several hundred pounds. Mary Tweedy, a former journalist in charge of the Press Office, was kept busy 'screening' incoming calls and trying to outwit unwelcome visitors who became so persistent that Sinatra had to change rooms more than once to put them off the scent.

His suite was like a star's dressing-room after a triumphant opening night at the Palladium or the Palace in New York. Among those who came to wish him well on his most successful charity stage tour was Princess Alexandra whom he presented with an armful of his long-playing records. After his one-man show at the Festival Hall, he invited over thirty guests to a celebration which began in his suite at 3 a.m. and ended with a gay five-course champagne breakfast. Still as fresh as paint, he rounded off the party by going up on the roof and taking dozens of photographs in colour of the river scene.

Sinatra and his Clan have no monopoly of high spirits. A débutante's dance was enlivened by an incident which almost took one back to the frolics of the gay 'twenties. To win a bottle of champagne, the Hon. Richard Bigham, Master of Nairne, stripped off to his shorts, carefully folded his evening clothes and dived into the dark Thames. He swam to the opposite bank and back, dried off, dressed, drank his prize and rejoined the dancers.

With every room sound-proof, neighbours and the floor staff have been denied some memorable 'noises off'. Unlike Benny Goodman, who left his clarinet behind and usually took his daughter to classical concerts after a day's fishing, 'Satchmo' Armstrong liked to sit up in bed blowing his trumpet. He was one of many visiting musicians to mourn the loss of genial Carroll Gibbons who died of a heart attack in 1954 while getting out of his bath. His old friend, Sir Louis Sterling, unveiled an 'in memoriam' plaque riveted to the famous white piano which now stands as his monument in the Abraham Lincoln Room.

The film and television stars still attract the newspaper headlines but they form only the periphery of the hotel's landscape. Since the war its essential spirit has changed little from the glittering traditions of the past. Within minutes of each other's arrival, the Savoy has welcomed guests like Callas, Leonard Bernstein, Stravinsky and Artur Rubinstein. Eschewing austerity, Shostako-vitch and his son engaged a suite before departing for the Edinburgh Festival. For staff veterans with memories of Tetraz-zini, there is always a spasm of nostalgia when the enormous bouquets and beribboned baskets of flowers arrive before, and after, a concert or première by Maria Callas. As a guest she is far from being the temperamental *prima donna* and insists only on her favourite suite, with its beige and white walls, and a special huge mirror over the fireplace. She is only 'difficult' and in-accessible before a concert, due to first-night nerves when she will lock herself in her suite. Afterwards at supper, she delights friends like the Harewoods and Dame Margot Fonteyn with sprightly talk and is always first on the ballroom floor to dance the Twist or any of the newer rhythms. She slips quietly out of the hotel to avoid photographers, and spends many hours shopping, usually unrecognized. If Joan Sutherland, whom she greatly admires, is appearing in *Lucia di Lammermoor* or some other favourite, she rarely misses paying an informal visit to Covent Garden.

Operatic stars may seem less exuberant than some of their predecessors but Tito Gobbi, for one, has almost as great a sense of fun as Chaliapin. He, too, is a gifted artist and never arrives without paints, brushes and palette. Invariably he reserves a room with a river view from which he can sketch the Thames.

The old excitement and drama of a Covent Garden gala night was back when Jussi Björling drove off to appear in *La Bohème* and promptly suffered a heart attack. He had to rest for half an hour before going on stage and went straight to bed on returning to the Savoy. Within a few minutes the switchboard was overwhelmed with messages and enquiries, including one from the Queen Mother who had been in the audience.

It is perhaps a pleasant coincidence that the Italian royal family is The House of Savoy. Ex-King Umberto always stays at the hotel where he shows the firmest distaste for excessive protocol. Attended by only one aide and a valet, he stubbornly avoids the limelight. Invited to a garden party at Buckingham Palace, he had no morning dress with him and decided instead to wear a lounge suit. His aide insisted on formal dress and would not hear of his master's suggestion that it might be hired in nearby Covent Garden. The ex-Monarch's best morning coat had to be flown in from Lisbon, arriving within minutes of the garden party.

The opulent days of the maharajahs and their enormous retinues are over. When Sheik Rashid Din Saled from the Persian Gulf arrived with his bodyguard and a squad of cooks to prepare his curries, the hotel staff had brief visions of the old splendour. One night a page tapped nervously on the door of his suite to deliver a message and was startled by the sound of explosions. Expecting murder or at least some crime of passion, he saw the Sheik and his servants placidly sitting cross-legged on the floor in front of a television set, completely absorbed by Wyatt Earp.

Among today's princes is a guest like the Rajah of Faridkot who still owns huge cotton estates in India but arrives with only one personal attendant, his physician. Wearing a turban over a Savile Row suit, he admits modestly to having eleven shirtmakers, ten limousines, four light aircraft and a taste for English bitter beer. Usually he brings with him at least twenty vivid turbans, each seven yards long, which he manages to put on in under two minutes.

The Maharajah of Mysore, last of the princely rulers, is still one of the richest men in the world with a fleet of Rolls-Royces glittering with ivory and gold fittings, but unlike his predecessors of prewar days, he lives simply at the Savoy, attended by a secretary and two aides. While in England, he spends most of his time lecturing University students on Oriental art and philosophy.

However, the Aga Khan's twenty-first birthday party in December 1957 brought an echo from the lavish past, with a hundred guests for dinner and twice as many at the buffet supper and dance. The dinner was served by candlelight in the River Room which had been decorated with hundreds of red roses. Afterwards, to the strains of an eight-piece rumba band imported from Paris, the young prince led his mother on to the floor for the first dance. The party ended at 5 a.m. with kippers and bacon and eggs.

A more formal occasion was the banquet given in the Aga Khan's honour by his disciples many of whom had come from Pakistan, Persia and Africa. The festivities opened with an Ismaeli love chant by two Pakistani ladies who took an hour and a half to render its 155 verses. The banquet which followed was memorable for the first appearance in this country of *Filet de Tilapia Ngege*, a traditional dish much favoured by the old Aga Khan. His grandson offered it pride of place on the menu but tactfully intimated that supplies might be difficult. Laplanche made enquiries and discovered Tilapia to be a rare deep-bodied fish not unlike carp, but superior in taste and found mainly in Tanganyika. Telegrams were sent and 150 lbs. despatched by air from Lake Victoria. The Maître-chef then cooked a specimen portion in seven different ways before he was satisfied. He served it with a special mushroom sauce, prepared with white wine and prawns, lightly sprinkled with grated cheese. The dish was voted 'delicious' by the host and discriminating guests like the Maharajah and Maharanee of Jaipur.

This attention to fine detail has always impressed gastronomes

277

like Lucius Beebe, who has the daunting reputation of having sent back more dishes than any other man alive but has never had to do so at the Savoy which his countryman and noted guide, Temple Fielding, has classed with Claridge's as two of the outstanding hotels in the world. An editor from Illinois recently reported to his newspaper, "My bathtub is so big you can actually float in it. This bathroom has a telephone and heated racks, and one of the towels is large enough to cover a double bed." Less happy was an eccentric young American who kept praying mantises as pets. From Hollywood he had tenderly transported 6,000 eggs expecting them to hatch several months ahead but without taking the hotel's central heating system into account. He awoke one morning convinced that he had delirium tremens. His treasures were crawling all over the walls and carpet. The management took no chances when Mr. Butlin arrived with his pet leopard for a cocktail party to celebrate the opening of Billy Smart's Circus. The animal was swiftly escorted from the Savoy and chained to a no-parking sign in a side street.

No hotel is immune from human error. In the grill-room Luigi suffered one of the most embarrassed moments in his well-ordered life when a nervous waiter upset a sauce-boat over Mrs. Tina Onassis, now the Marchioness of Blandford. Her husband waved aside Luigi's distressed apology and remarked, "Poor chap, perhaps he was frightened by my dark glasses." Soon afterwards, Mr. Onassis entered the hotel arm-in-arm with Sir Winston Churchill to attend a dinner of The Other Club when the passenger lift went out of action. Roaring with laughter, they took the goods lift instead.

Many hoteliers seem to find the Savoy a natural home in London. Among those who have enjoyed a busman's holiday are Conrad Hilton who was particularly impressed by the floor service. At one time he contemplated some scheme to buy the Savoy but, needless to say, the directors were unenthusiastic. General Malcolm Beyer of New York's 21 Club used the hotel as a base for one of his European business tours. His shopping list included tons of caviare and *foie gras*; 48,000 tins of snails, 50 tons of strawberries, geese, trout and fillets of Dover sole by the thousand. Like all the other professional guests, he showed the liveliest interest in the hotel's training schemes which received a very tangible impetus in 1961 when an Educational Trust was endowed with £50,000 in Company Shares subscribed by the Chairman, Miss D'Oyly Carte, Miles Thornewill and John Hannay.

These trainees could scarcely enjoy a more varied indoctrination. On the same evening three Commonwealth Prime Ministers were being fêted in the hotel; Dr. Nkrumah in the Abraham Lincoln Room, Mrs. Bandaranaike of Ceylon in the River Room, while Sir Robert Menzies was entertained in the Pinafore Room by Prince Philip, Earl Mountbatten and various members of the Cabinet. Another night, The Shikar Club of big-game hunters dined next door to The Royal Corinthian yachtsmen; some of the world's oil kings were in secret session a wall's thickness from Europe's leading orchid growers and fanciers; and in the ballroom, members of the British Italian Society danced against a vivid background of thousands of carnations sent by air from San Remo. The Eton Beagles dined and wined in splendid isolation while, a few yards away, the *Daily Mirror* showed its usual flair for witty irreverence by giving a most successful Charladies' Ball in honour of Britain's Mrs. Mopps. One night, soon afterwards, the ballroom was the setting for ten sinuous young women from Pakistan, modelling gowns and jewels insured for £200,000. It was in the direct line of fashion shows dating from Dior's first display of the New Look to a British audience soon after the war.

The economic difficulties and slow decline of London's clubs have led to the increasing use of the Savoy's private rooms for social and business rendezvous. At a quiet luncheon party the opening moves were made for the take-over of Odhams Press by the Fleetway Publications empire. By an odd coincidence it took place in the same room where a quarter of a century earlier Rothermere, Beaverbrook and Walter Layton had met to try and persuade Elias of the *Daily Herald* to give up the free book policy which started a Press circulation war. Here some months ago, David Rockefeller, president of the Chase Manhattan Bank, held an investment forum attended by a hundred leading British bankers and other financial experts.

Sometimes, behind the closed doors of a private dining-room, matters are discussed which will never become public or not for years to come. A case in point: quite recently, Hugh Wontner received a most interesting letter from which he learned that the concept of the European Common Market first took root in the hotel. It was from Mr. E. N. van Kleffens, the former Dutch Foreign Minister, now Chief Representative (U.K.) of the European Coal and Steel Community.

He wrote:

"The other day I passed by the private dining-room in the Savoy Hotel called 'Patience'. It brought to mind a historic occasion. On March 22, 1943, the then Ministers for Foreign Affairs of Belgium, Luxemburg and the Netherlands (Messrs. Spaak, Bech and the undersigned) decided to lunch at the Savoy Hotel in war-time London with the Belgian and Netherlands Ministers of Finance and a few experts, to see whether effect could be given to a plan of these two Finance Ministers to unite the three countries after the war in a Customs Union.

"The outcome of this initial talk was positive. Some of the experts shook their heads, but they were invited to get to work and draft a plan. The first result was, that a year and a half later, on September 5, 1944, a tariff-convention was signed by the above-mentioned Ministers as a first step towards an economic union of their countries. It was this convention which heralded what is now universally known as BENELUX—virtually the economic union we had in mind, an area where goods, persons and capital flow freely without let or hindrance by customs—or other frontiers.

"So it may be said that this very successful venture saw the first light of day in the Savoy Hotel's room called Patience. 'Patience' was a very appropriate name, for a lot of patience and forbearance was needed to bring about so far-reaching a result."

Meanwhile, the 'family' tradition of club and regimental reunions, weddings and coming-out dances persists in a clientèle that renews itself in successive generations, but as Anthony Sampson has shrewdly noted in his *Anatomy of Britain*, "While the reminiscences ramble on in Pall Mall, the future is being decided in the Cabinet Office canteen, in the directors' dining-room in I.C.I. or between the T.V. tycoons at large lunches at the Savoy." Since the war the hotel has been referred to in more than one satirical revue sketch as 'the Bosses' Canteen'.

Anchored between a bustling Strand and the quieter rhythms of the ancient river, the Savoy blandly equates the old and the new. It serves crooner and caliph with the same invincible calm, ready to install a television set, an emergency operating theatre, a plugged-in telephone in the ladies' *salon de coiffure* or some esoteric spice for a special curry. Laplanche will create a new sweet like *La Mousse glacée Cleopatre* for a film première supper, while the 400th Shakespeare Anniversary was celebrated in Restaurant and Grill with contemporary dishes, including spit-roasted wild boar, garnished with potatoes steeped in sack; pot-roast swan; glazed boar's head; and a rich saffron-spiced eel broth.

The Banqueting Department remains unruffled even when asked to prepare matching drinks and canapés in vibrant pink and flame to celebrate some new lipstick and nail varnish. For a Jewish wedding it has transformed the River Room into a miniature synagogue with two rabbis officiating at the marriage ceremony under the traditional canopy of gold cloth.

As the Chairman said recently, "The management of an hotel and restaurant business such as ours does not become easier as the years go by; it requires unremitting attention to detail . . ." With a staff to client ratio of three to one of its five hundred residents, and a celebrated card-index system which records individual tastes in rooms, flowers and pillows, a guest will be greeted by his favourite floor waiter with the particular brand of whisky or gin, even the mineral water, he is known to prefer.

A special point was quickly fitted in his bathroom when it was learned that General Eisenhower had acquired a power-operated toothbrush. In the ten-roomed suite reserved for his staff at a Commonwealth Conference, Sir Robert Menzies was delighted when the management thoughtfully provided a short-wave radio so that he could listen to the early-morning commentaries on the fourth Test Match from Adelaide, and also installed a set in his car. A regular client like C. S. Forester, whose painful leg disease permits him to walk only a few yards at a time, appreciates quiet while he is reading or writing. He has top priority at all times for a corner suite on the fifth floor so that nobody can pass his door.

The same assiduity goes into the work of the Restaurant and Banqueting Department which spans a dinner-party for eight in the little Sorcerer Room to a banquet for 550 guests in the Lancaster Room where President Tubman of Liberia entertained the Queen, Prince Philip and every other member of the Royal Family at the end of his last State Visit. This was a glittering 'protocol' occasion, but at other times Royal wishes for informality are always respected by the management and fellow-guests. When Princess Alexandra brought a party to supper after the marriage of her brother, the Duke of Kent, the gossip-writers were carefully not warned in advance and therefore missed a romantic young couple who danced together almost continuously. They were Princess Sophia of Greece and her future husband, Don Juan Carlos.

Whilst the Savoy has always attracted publicity, it has been the policy of its directors to maintain a discreet silence, as far as possible, about the arrival, the activities and departure of its guests. Today there is a private hotel entrance in Savoy Hill very much where the old Parcels Office used to be. This has been used many times by the Queen and the Duke of Edinburgh, when dining privately or visiting friends, and also by the Queen Mother.

The Queen, when Princess Elizabeth, came to dine with the members of the Savoy Board. The company included the Archbishop of Canterbury, Sir Winston Churchill, Dame Ninette de Valois and General Lord Ismay. After dinner was over, Princess Elizabeth took coffee with the directors and asked suddenly if all the managers, maîtres d'hôtel and departmental heads could join the party. One by one they were introduced by Hugh Wontner, who explained the nature of their duties, and the Princess had a pleasant word with each, speaking in excellent French to the chefs. It was all entirely informal and almost like a family gathering. Before leaving, the Princess joined her other guests in the Restaurant where, perhaps for the first time in history, an Archbishop of Canterbury watched a cabaret.

On a warm summer's evening, the directors entertained Princess Margaret to dinner. The whole party, together with many others who came in afterwards, sailed down the Thames in a launch moored just outside the hotel. Among the guests were Dame Margot Fonteyn, Lord Cohen, the distinguished Judge, Lady Peel (Beatrice Lillie), Sir Ronald Howe (of Scotland Yard fame), Lord and Lady Shawcross and Captain Peter Cazalet. On their return, Princess Margaret decided to round off the gay evening by a visit to the Restaurant where she danced with the Chairman and other members of the party. Some time afterwards, Prince Philip honoured the directors by dining privately with them. Among the all-male party was Neville Duke, who was also celebrating breaking the sound barrier.

Despite all the ups and downs of history, the ancient Royal link with the Savoy remains to this day. The Queen is Lady of the Manor; the Savoy Chapel is a royal chapel and the home of The Royal Victorian Order; and the Duchy of Lancaster, a reminder of John of Gaunt, has its headquarters still in the Liberty of the Savoy.

Several years ago, when some assistance was needed in The Royal Household on matters of a domestic kind, including catering, Hugh Wontner's advice was sought. In recognition of his services, which he has continued to fulfil over a long period, King George VI conferred on him the M.V.O. In Coronation Year, the new Queen revived in his honour the ancient household title of Clerk of the Royal Kitchens, which had lapsed early in the reign of Queen Victoria.

To celebrate the first ten years of Agatha Christie's *The Mousetrap*, a thousand guests attended almost the largest private party ever held at the Savoy, with Peter Saunders as the host. They shared a birthday cake weighing half a ton which, however, lacked the ingenuity of that baked in honour of Ngaio Marsh's twenty-first thriller. The head pastry-chef studded his little master-piece with a skull, crossbones and a pistol made from chocolate icing. Another mock-gruesome party was given in honour of a 'horror film' producer. His hosts had arranged with the Banqueting Department to transform the Lancaster Room into Dracula's Parlour. So realistic were the skeletons, the death's head masks and other grisly effects that, for days afterwards, some of the waiters went about with smiles embalmed by delayed shock.

Jack Hylton, the impresario, decided to give a party to celebrate the Crazy Gang's 10,000th performance. It started at midnight in the Abraham Lincoln Room and soon developed hilariously. Arriving early, Princess Margaret was at once caught up in the Gang's uninhibited clowning. Bud Flanagan and his men had dressed up as ambassadors in full court dress, with chocolate box sashes and rows of very odd medals. The effect of knee-breeches with brown boots was startling enough, but when the 'diplomats' began to eat their carnation *boutonnières* the roars of laughter almost shook the walls.

A more formal party was the dinner given by Australia House to celebrate the centenary of Melba's birth. It was held in the Mikado Room, and her ghost may have chuckled at a memory of long ago when she was auditioned by the D'Oyly Carte Opera Company and failed to obtain an engagement! The guests at this dinner admired the unique Gilbert and Sullivan service of Royal Worcester porcelain, used since 1959 for private banquets. Kathleen Hills of the Royal Art School of Ceramics based her design on an early eighteenth-century Japanese colour print of a dancer. The plate with its border of tiny fans originally represented *The Mikado* but it was decided to extend the design to the other celebrated operas. Taken from the original costumes, the Mikado motif forms a centre to the dinner, dessert, soup and bread plates respectively. Each piece of the service retains its border of fans, the whole being carried out in tones of blue, green, turquoise, grey and gold.

On 25 January 1962 a memorable dinner was held in the River Room. At the age of 67, Alban had at last decided to retire after forty years' service with the Company. The Chairman thought the occasion merited a special tribute and invited some of London's leading hoteliers and chefs, apart from habitués of the grill-room like Sir Alan Herbert, Emile Littler and Victor Gollancz, the publisher, who for years has rarely missed his daily visit to the Savoy even though he has been known to be in and out of the grill-room in half an hour, yet incredibly with time to greet several old friends and eat his lunch, usually cold meat and pickles with a glass of wine.

Others among the sixty-five guests were the French Minister of Commerce, the widow of Alban's predecessor in the Grill, Virlogeux, and the head of the French hotel industry, who flew over from Paris. A six-course banquet was specially prepared by Laplanche in honour of his colleague. He served a remarkable menu: *Les Huîtres Royales au Pain Bis, Le Caviar Malossal; Le Consommé du Pot-au-Feu, Les Croûtons à la Moelle; Le Suprême de Sole Champenoise; La Selle d'Agneau Rôtie Renaissance, Les Pommes Nouvelles Fondantes, Les Endives Braisées; Les Fromages de France; La Pêche Glacée Bar-le-Duc, La Corbeille de Douceurs; Le Café Savoy.* The wines accompanying this splendid meal were Pouilly Fuissé 1959 (Tête de Cuvée), Château Lafite-Rothschild 1953, Mumm Double Cordon, John Exshaw Fine Champagne over thirty years old, and various Liqueurs.

During the evening the guest of honour was presented with a silver salver inscribed with the signatures of his colleagues. In tribute to him, Hugh Wontner's speech was made in French, and Sir Alan Herbert composed a poem which rhymed both in French and English. Sir Winston Churchill, who otherwise would have been present, was dining that evening with The Other Club but had the amiable thought of saluting the Maître-chef who had given him so much pleasure over the years. On the back of his club menu he wrote: "I send you my warm good wishes on your retirement and my gratitude to you for your 40 years at the Savoy."

The celebrated chef has now retired to Dijon, of which he was made an Honorary Freeman, but before leaving London he and his wife were at last able to spend a few lazy days, shopping and sightseeing. The Chairman placed a river suite at their disposal, the staff sparing no pains to give them V.I.P. service, laced with great affection.

Alban's successor in the Grill was Silvino Trompetto, the first London-born employee to become a Savoy maître-chef. Before working in the hotel's restaurant kitchens he was at Oddenino's, the Grand Hotel, Brighton and the Albany Club but had a previous link with the Savoy when he went to the Dorchester to train under Virlogeux. Among gastronomes he has already made his mark with memorable creations including *mousse de homard* and *quenelles de brochet*, adorned by a classic Bercy sauce.

Recent years have seen other staff changes. After the great General Manager, Hofflin, retired to his cottage in Kent three years ago, it was decided that, under modern conditions, the post demanded two specialists. The new joint managers were Beverley Griffin, Hofflin's deputy for some years, and Paolo Contarini who moved up from the Banqueting Department. The vastly expanding banqueting side was placed under the supervision of Evangelo Brioni (formerly Brian Evans of Swansea), who had changed his name for professional reasons. He is an outstanding product of the hotel's training scheme, having started as an apprentice in the kitchens only eleven years before.

In 1958 Amanda was succeeded as restaurant manager by his maître d'hôtel, Charles Gagliani, who has remarkable family connections with the hotel. His father was on the staff for twenty years, he has himself worked in the Restaurant since 1923, a sister joined during the war, and today his brothers and a brother-

286

in-law also work in the Savoy. Within a few months of his appointment, while on holiday abroad, he had a car accident which left him with severe injuries. The management promptly sent a doctor who reported progress daily by telephone. As soon as Charles was fit to be moved, he was brought home by helicopter, specially chartered by the Savoy, with the doctor in attendance.

Staff changes and promotion are always the result of careful planning, designed to keep the traditional rhythm undisturbed. Luigi Donzelli had proved outstanding in charge of the grill-room but his touch was more needed at Claridge's. When he took over there as restaurant manager, his place in the Savoy Grill was filled by another Luigi, Vercelli, for many years maître d'hôtel at the Berkeley Grill. Once again the traditional policy of 'inbreeding' was preserved; his first start in the hotel business had been as chef-waiter under Escoffier during his reign at the Carlton. Nevertheless, the management has become less inclined to rule-of-thumb succession and increasingly alert for promising recruits. Peter Stafford, Assistant General Manager since 1961 and one of the most remarkable finds in the post-war period, was a navigator in the Australian Air Force and later a schoolmaster before deciding to train as a hotelier in 1948. After working in various hotels, he joined the Group four years later.

"There will be a problem in the future," says the Chairman, "in finding qualified staff to replace those who today have the advantage of long years of experience, learned in an age of less speed and mechanization; but difficult though it will be, and indeed is already, we shall hope to maintain the best traditions of good service on which our reputation so much depends. This of course will include, as it does at present, a personal service on each floor of valets, maids and waiters, which is still a great feature in many of the leading hotels in Europe and appeals particularly to American visitors."

An hotel like the Savoy could never afford to become a faceless unit in an automatic chain of palaces or to sacrifice its 'house-party' atmosphere, unique in an hotel of its size. It must retain a distinctive style while remaining vigorously abreast, or ahead, of contemporary and changing trends in accommodation, banqueting and entertainment. Even within such a relatively small and compact Group, each hotel has remained so individual in character, décor and clientèle that guests are rarely aware of a central management and control.

Despite assets valued at well over £10 million and a substantial annual trading profit, the Company remains sensitive to post-war problems and the prod of competition for an expanding tourist traffic. Some time ago the Chairman reminded shareholders, "It is still necessary to bear in mind that for at least five months in every year, we are working below our apartment capacity, and that this is also true at weekends during the rest of the year. Consequently, if this pattern is the experience of others in the trade in London, the multiplication of hotels in excess of demand will have most serious consequences . . . This usually means that severe economies must be made in upkeep and in service, and gradually the hotels affected become less and less attractive and less able to recover . . . Competition in the restaurant business has continued to be extremely keen and has resulted in the adoption in some restaurants of extraordinary gimmicks in an endeavour to attract the public. In the long run, it is good food, good wine and good value for money that tell."

An hotel like the Savoy cannot guarantee survival by piping music and iced water through its arteries. Its appeal has deeper and more traditional roots. In his speech at the 75th Annual General Meeting in April 1964, the Chairman reminded shareholders of the importance of quality goods and equipment in an age of diminishing craftsmanship. "We buy linen," he said, "of a very high quality that is woven to our own specification; carpets that are made to our own design; we have applied this to cutlery and china; to taps, basins, baths and many other things, the design and quality of which we study ourselves. Today manufacturers find it more difficult to meet this kind of demand, which is much less than it was and is decreasing; but just as we are not a standardized chain of hotels and restaurants, all identical

This guest, Billy Butlin's pet leopard, was politely escorted outside when he arrived for a circus-opening party

Carved by Basil Ionides, three-foot Kasper relaxes on his perch in the Pinafore Room against a wall mirror. With a napkin round his neck he is always served the full meal at a dinner party for thirteen

Christmas lights illuminate Count Peter and the Strand entrance. This private forecourt is the only thoroughfare in England where traffic keeps to the right

This letter from Czechoslovakia was automatically forwarded by the Post Office authorities in London

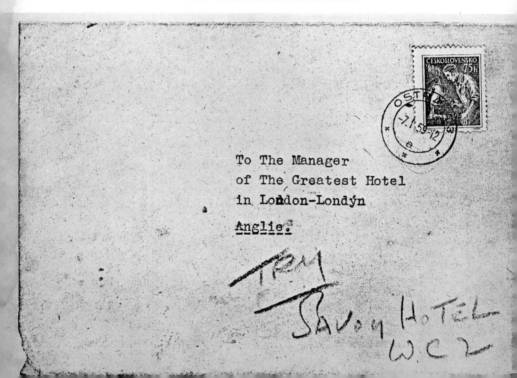

or very much alike, so too we are not satisfied with just a standardized product of lower quality which does not meet our special needs."

It has been estimated that the Group could save £100,000 a year simply by using cotton instead of Irish linen and departing from the tradition of changing bedsheets every day. No doubt additional revenue could also be secured by building and leasing boutiques in the foyers, by accepting outside banqueting and making other drastic changes in established policy. Instead, the Company has clearly decided on expansion within the existing framework. Since the war, over £10,500,000 has been invested in development. Building, wiring, decorating and other renovations produce special problems for luxury hotels which, unlike ships, cannot be taken out of service but must continue in business with the minimum of disturbance to other guests. The work has often to be done at weekends, during public holidays or at night. These abnormal conditions, apart from rising labour charges, have almost doubled the cost of building and decoration in the past ten years.

Among the most attractive post-war innovations was the new covered entrance to the hotel on the Embankment side. Aware that it was often called the Savoy's 'back door', the directors decided in 1957 that something gay and elegant was required. Designed by Eric Janes, a *porte cochère* was built of reinforced concrete, 16½ ft. high with canopies extruding over 70 ft. In the curved roof are 2,000 thick glass lenses diffusing an even, glareless light. Costing over £10,000, it now gives all-weather protection to arriving diners and dancers. While proving welcome to most, it is characteristic of an old-established, affectionate clientèle that there were also some dissenting voices. Sir Robert Menzies spoke for the minority in complaining ruefully that it robbed him of his old delight in leaning over his river-suite balcony to watch the arrival of guests!

New investments have been made. An island site covering more than an acre of Knightsbridge was bought for re-development, and part of it will become the home of the new Berkeley which will be enlarged and modernized. The shares of the elegant Connaught Hotel have been acquired and the Company's freehold property in Panton Street, Haymarket, was developed for the letting of offices and shops. Stone's Chop House, established in 1770 and destroyed in an air raid, was purchased during the war, with its surrounding property, for development afterwards. It reopened on its original site in October 1963.

Today, the London hotel scene offers a fascinating and variegated pattern. Claridge's is indisputably the Rolls-Royce among the capital's hotels; the Ritz is the Daimler, and the Dorchester not unlike a Cadillac. The new sleek and powerful hotels in Park Lane and Belgravia are still in the 'running-in' stage, but would so far seem to be international models adapted to a right-hand drive. The Savoy has the thoroughbred racing pedigree and performance of the Rolls-Bentley.

After three-quarters of a century, the hotel has retained many cherished relics of its history. There is the framed gold sovereign which Harry Rosenfeld handed over on the opening day, 6 August 1889; the original manuscript of Arnold Bennett's *Imperial Palace*; and of course countless autographed menus recalling historic banquets since the days of Escoffier. For years to come, however, pride of place may well be given to an envelope which was recently sent on to the hotel by an unknown clerk at the Mount Pleasant headquarters of the General Post Office. Someone had written from Czechoslovakia to request a luggage sticker for his collection. His letter, addressed to "The Manager of the Greatest Hotel in London", was forwarded at once with the pencilled suggestion, "Try Savoy Hotel, W.C.2."

ADVERTISEMENT FROM *THE TIMES*
2 AUGUST 1889

The Savoy Hotel and Restaurant situated on the Victoria Embankment between Charing Cross and Waterloo Bridge (opposite Cleopatra's Needle) will open Tuesday next, 6th August. The perfection of luxury and comfort. Artistic furniture throughout. Electric light only everywhere, ready for use at all hours of day and night. No gas or artificial light used. The light so shaded as to give no glare.

There are a certain number of detached bedrooms, but the Hotel is arranged chiefly in suites of rooms, consisting of one or more bedrooms, with sitting-room, private bathroom, lavatory, etc. There are no less than 67 bathrooms altogether in the building.

The Hotel enjoys the finest river and garden view in London, it has wide balconies running all along the front, commanding a panorama of the Thames, with its many features of interest from Battersea to London Bridge, and embracing St. Paul's Cathedral, the Monument, the Tower of London, the Surrey Hills, the Crystal Palace, the Houses of Parliament, Westminster Abbey and the various bridges.

There are six lifts altogether in the building, four service lifts, and two of the largest "ascending rooms" ever seen in Europe, running to every floor, with attendants working all night as well as all day, thus bringing the top floor level with the street.

The rooms on the top floor are exactly equal in height, furniture etc. to those on the lowest. A spacious and airy courtyard, into which carriages drive to get down, which is being fitted with plants, flowers, fountains etc. in the Continental style.

The building is probably the first in the world, certainly in England, the constructional parts of which are of incombustible material throughout.

An artesian well, sunk over 420 feet, gives a plentiful supply of the purest drinking water.

APPENDIX B

THE PALACE OF THE SAVOY:
SEVEN COMMEMORATIVE PLAQUES

Round the walls of the hotel's courtyard are seven plaques each of which recalls a notable stage in the history of the old Palace of the Savoy:

"Within these precincts stood the Palace of Savoy, the erection of which was begun by Peter, Ninth Count of Savoy and Earl of Richmond, A.D. 1246. Henry III, King of England, bestowed the site 'IN VICO QUI VO CATO LA STRAUNDE' on February 12th, 1246, and there was erected a palace, 'The fayrest Mannor in Europe', big enough for a large part of an army."

"Here in the palace of the Savoy, Peter, Count of Savoy, lodged the many 'beautiful foreign ladies' whom he brought in 1247 from the courts of Europe, before marrying them to his wards, a large number of rich young English nobles."

"In the palace of the Savoy lived for many months Simon de Montfort, founder of the House of Commons: This also was the home of John of Gaunt, Duke of Lancaster, who lived here in princely luxury from 1362 to 1381."

"Here, John of Valois, King of France, when brought to England as a captive by the Black Prince after the battle of Poictiers, was entertained as a prisoner of war, and died on April 8th, 1364. Also in the Palace of the Savoy, Geoffrey Chaucer, first great

English poet, came to dine many times with John of Gaunt, and here he wrote many of his poems."

"On the 13th of June, 1381, the Palace of the Savoy was burned and destroyed by rebels under the leadership of Wat Tyler. The building of the first section of the new modern Palace of the Savoy was begun in 1889."

"On part of this site in 1640 was built Worcester House, where lived Edward, Second Marquess of Worcester. At midnight on the 3rd of September, 1660, Anne Hyde, daughter of the Earl of Clarendon, was secretly married here to the Duke of York (afterwards James II), whose two daughters, Mary and Anne, became Queens of England."

"In the Savoy Palace, in 1658, by order of Oliver Cromwell, the Confession of Faith was drawn up here, also in 1661 Charles II ordered commissioners to assemble for the revision of the Liturgy, which assembly was afterwards known as the Savoy Conference."

SOME FACTS AND FIGURES

Readers with a taste for 'vital statistics' may be interested in the following details, checked at the time of writing. Allowance should be made for variation in consumable stocks, number of personnel and other figures which are inevitably approximate.

ACCOMMODATION: 400 bedrooms and 100 private suites, all with private bathrooms.

Five Banqueting Rooms, with their own entrance, reception rooms and cloakrooms. Some 1,500 banquets a year.

Eight Private Rooms, each named after a Gilbert and Sullivan opera. About 3,000 private luncheons, dinners and receptions during an average year.

STAFF: 1,600, of whom nearly 180 are employed solely in twenty-four hour Floor Service (including housekeepers, chambermaids and housemaids, valets and waiters).

The Night Service staff numbers 64.

There are 14 page-boys, maximum height five feet.

The Staff Training Scheme includes 22 management trainees and more than 30 trainee cooks and waiters.

THE ENQUIRY OFFICE: This office handles about 1,500 incoming letters, cables and messages daily. Some 6,300 telephone calls are dealt with by the switchboard every day.

WINES AND SPIRITS: The various establishments in the Group have their own cellars which draw on the main stock housed under the Thames beyond Waterloo Bridge.

Current stock, valued at over £300,000, includes 3,500 dozen bottles of vintage champagne. 100,000 bottles of Claret are on hand in the hotel, and more in reserve.

FOODSTUFFS:

Caviare: half a ton of fresh Beluga per year.

Smoked salmon: 14 tons per year.

Strasbourg foie gras: 2 tons per year.

Oysters: a million and a half per season.

Plovers' eggs: 15 dozen a day when in season.

Eggs: 14,000 per week.

Milk: 1,300 gallons per week.

Bacon: 7 cwts. per week.

Butter: a ton per week.

Vegetables: up to 14 tons per week.

Meat (not imported): 2 tons per week.

Poultry: up to 4 tons per week.

Fish: 11 tons per week.

Bread: 3,000 loaves and 45,000 rolls per week baked in the hotel ovens.

Tea: 480 lb. per week.

Coffee: a ton and a half served per month. Three-quarters of a ton mailed to customers. The hotel has its own roasting plant.

Cheeses: up to 28 varieties, according to season.

CHINA AND GLASS: Valued at over £36,000.

Working stock: 20,000 pieces of glass (90% imported from Sweden).

40,000 pieces of china.

Reserve stock: 15 months' supply of glass.

12 months' supply of china.

All china made exclusively to the Savoy's own design and is different for Restaurant, Grill, Banqueting and Private Rooms.

FURNISHING, DECORATIONS, ETC.: Each corridor uses 1,000 yards of carpet, specially designed and woven for the Savoy. Loose covers, cushions, mattresses and bedding are all made in the hotel's own workrooms, with a large stock in reserve for constant renewal.

Two thousand standard and bedside lamps, pictures, clocks and decorative china are individually selected. Each room and suite is decorated and furnished in distinctive style, adaptable to a guest's taste.

The hotel has a working stock of a million nuts and bolts.

PRINTING: Over a million items a year are produced on the Savoy's own presses, including menus, stationery, etc.

POWER PLANT: The hotel's private electricity generating station comprises diesel and steam turbine units of up to two megawatts. Steam for generation, heating and other services is provided by five water tube boilers with an output of 60,000 lb. of steam per hour. Half a million gallons of water consumed on peak days.

The system of space heating utilizes the exhaust steam to heat both the domestic and central-heating water.

Forty lifts (passenger and service), apart from the hydraulically-operated rising floor in the Restaurant used for cabaret performances.

KITCHEN EQUIPMENT: Gas, electricity and coal all used as fuel, with always an alternative source of supply in the event of failure; also, oil-fired stoves for cooking in an emergency.

Dishwashing machines, kitchen steamers and ranges all designed to specification. The specially-designed cold rooms are Savoy built.

Ice-cream mixers make all the cream and water ices on the premises.

LINEN AND LAUNDRY: 46,000 pieces of Irish linen, woven to specification, are in stock. 5,000 sheets and a like number of pillow-cases and tablecloths are in circulation at any one time, plus 18,000 table napkins.

About 7,800,000 pieces of linen a year are handled by the Savoy Laundry, together with some 42,000 of visitors' items (a same-day guest-service operates for laundry sent down by 10 a.m.).

BIBLIOGRAPHY

Books which have previously appeared on various aspects of the Savoy Hotel are:

The Savoy of London by Compton Mackenzie (Harrap, 1953). A short, stylish monograph.

Imperial Palace by Arnold Bennett (Cassell, 1930). The famous documentary novel of hotel life behind the scenes.

Meet Me at the Savoy by Jean Nicol (Museum Press, 1952). A racily entertaining view of celebrities seen from the Press Office.

The Author is also indebted to the following works for useful background data:

César Ritz by Marie Louise Ritz (Harrap).

Arnold Bennett by Reginald Pound (Heinemann).

The Frontiers of Privilege by Quentin Crewe (Collins).

The Wandering Years by Cecil Beaton (Weidenfeld and Nicolson).

The Autobiography of Margot Asquith (Eyre & Spottiswoode).

Gertrude Lawrence as 'Mrs. A.' by R. S. Aldrich (Odhams).

Tallulah by Tallulah Bankhead (Gollancz).

War in the Strand by Hector Bolitho (Eyre & Spottiswoode).

Alexander Korda by Paul Tabori (Oldbourne).

Ivor Novello by Peter Noble (Falcon).

Grace and Favour by Loelia, Duchess of Westminster (Weidenfeld and Nicolson).

I Married the World by Elsa Maxwell (Heinemann).

Gilbert and Sullivan by Hesketh Pearson (Hamish Hamilton). *Trumpets from the Steep* by Lady Diana Cooper, published by Messrs. Rupert Hart-Davis, who have kindly permitted reproduction of the extract on pages 179 and 180.

INDEX

302

303

Dolin, Anton, 176
Dolly, Jenny, 138
Dolly Sisters, 74, 117
Donat, Robert, 141, 170
Donnelly, James, 146
Donoghue, Steve, 79, 81
Don Quixote, 101
Doolittle, General James, 216
Doran, George, 75, 102
d'Orléans, Duc, 25, 28
Douglas, Lewis, 43, 246
Doyle, Sir A. Conan, 67
D'Oyly Carte, Helen, 21, 24, 34
D'Oyly Carte, Richard, 18, 19, 20, 21, 22, 31, 34, 35, 36, 158, 239
D'Oyly Carte, Rupert, 34, 36, 38, 146, 157, 158, 160, 161, 184, 199, 200, 215, 224, 238, 239, 244
D'Oyly Carte Opera Company, 116
Drawbell, James W., 191
Dressler, Marie, 139
Drury, Colonel Esmond, 250
Drury Lane, Theatre, 20
Duckworth, Gerald, 41
Dudley, Lady, 27, 31
Dufay, Emile, 227
Duff Cooper, Lady Alfred, *see* Manners, Lady Diana
Duke, Neville, 283
Dulac, Edmund 66
Dulles, Foster, 264
Du Maurier, Daphne, 133, 158, 220, 251
Du Maurier, Sir Gerald, 47, 131, 133, 141
Duncan Sisters, 101
Dunne, Sir Laurence, 207
du Pont, General Coleman, 133
Durante, 'Schnozzle', 266
Duse, Leonora, 134
Dvorak, Anton, 48

Eagle Squadron, First American, 180, 181, 190

Eckersley, Captain Peter, 107
Eden, Anthony, 173
    Lancaster House Luncheon, 265
Eden Roc Hotel, 141
Edinburgh, Duke of, *see* Philip, Prince
Edward VII, 27, 28, 42
Edward VIII, Abdication of, 167
Edwardes, George, 37
Edwards, Don Augustin, 67
Einstein, Albert, 156, 163–4
Eisenhower, General, 209, 282
Ekberg, Anita, 249
Eleanor, Queen, 15
Elgar, Sir Edward, 105
Elias, J. S. (Lord Southwood), 279
Elizabeth, the Queen Mother, 276, 282
Elizabeth II, Queen, 232, 233, 251, 282, 283
Elizalde, Fred, 113, 114
Ellis, Vivian, 135, 180
Elphinstone, Hon. Andrew, 232
Elsie, Lily, 37, 48, 59
Elwin, Maurice, 113
Embassy Club, 30, 116, 118
Engels, Jeanne, 71
Enquiry Office, Savoy Hotel, 149-50
Ervine, St. John, 63, 132
Esfandiary, Soraya (Queen), 247
Esteban, 269
Eton Beagles Dinner, 279
Evans, Chick, 74
Everybody's Doin' It, 55
Excelsior, 141

Fahmy Bey, 89–91
Fahmy, Madame, 88–91
Fairbanks, Douglas, 162, 170, 251
Fairbanks, Douglas, jun., 162
Faridkot, Rajah of, 253, 276
Farrell, Annie, 65
Farson, Negley, 166, 196
Faure, President Félix, 35

Fender, P. G. H., 77
Ferdinand, ex-King of Bulgaria, 82
Fernandel, 223, 271
Ferraro 30
Festival of Britain, 16, 243, 250
Ffrangcon-Davies, Gwen, 139
Field, Marshall, 46
Fielding, Temple, 278
Fields, Gracie, 61, 99
Fife, Duke of, 22
Fire Over England, 143
Firestone Company Convention, 254
Fitzgerald, C. J., 81
Fitzgerald, Scott, 63, 70
Fitzgerald, Zelda, 63
Flanagan, Bud, 284
Flower, Desmond, 160
Flynn, Errol, 267
Fonteyn, Margot, 249, 275, 283
Food and Wine Society, 125
For Services Rendered, 141
Ford, Henry, 76
Fordyce, Peter, 146
Forester, A., 42
Forester, C. S., 282
Fortnightly Luncheon Club, 77
Foster, Lilian, 130-1
France, Anatole, 56
Francis, Kay, 211
Frankau, Gilbert, 74, 180
French, General Sir John, 56
Frohmann, Charles, 73, 148
Fuad, King, 78
Fuchs-Hillary Expedition, 256
Furness, Thelma, Lady, 160

Gable, Clark, 210
Gaiety Girls, 45
Gaiety Theatre, Dublin, 22
Gaiety Theatre, London, 37
Galli, George, 85, 86
Galsworthy, John, 56, 63
Gandolfo, 145
Garbo, Greta, 245

Gardner, Ava, 269
Gardner, Joan, 141-2
Gates, John W., 46
Gaulle, General de, 181, 189, 195, 204
Gaunt, John of, Duke of Lancaster, 15, 39, 283
Gelardi, 64
General Strike, the, 76
Gentlemen Prefer Blondes, 99
George V, 17, 74, 87, 167
George V, Coronation festivities, 55
George VI, 167, 234, 251, 283
George II, of the Hellenes, 203, 204
Gerhardt, 105
Gershwin, George, 111
Gest, Morris, 139
Gibbs, Hon. Mrs. Vicary, 232
Gibbs, Sir Philip, 191
Gideon, Melville, 58, 79
Gielgud, John, 249
Gigli, Benjamino, 102-4, 221
Gilbert, Jeanne, 237
Gilbert, W. S., 18, 19, 20, 21
Gilmore, Joe, 236, 237
Giraud, General, 204
Gish, Dorothy and Lillian, 70
Gladstone, W. E., 31
Glenister, Mrs., 236
Gloucester, Duke and Duchess of, 247
Glyn, Elinor, 40
Gobbi, Tito, 275
Goddard, Paulette, 254
Goldsmith, Major Frank, 159
Goldwyn, Samuel, 71, 170
Gollancz, Victor, 285
Goode, Sir William, 42
Goodman, Benny, 275
Gordon, John, 191
Gort, Lord, 177
Gould, Jay, 73
Gounod, Charles, 18
Grand Hotel, Rome, 33, 49, 64
Grandi, Count, 166
Grant, Cary, 162, 260

311

Portugal, King of, 46
Power, Tyrone, 172
Priestley, J. B., 163, 166
Prince Consort (Albert), 17
Prince of Wales, Edward, 76, 78
Printemps, Yvonne, 137
Puccini, 48, 106
Pugh, Mrs., 224
Pulitzer, Ralph, 161
'Pussyfoot' Johnson, 63
Pyle, Ernie, 190

Quealy, Chelsea, 114
Quinquaginta Ramblers, 113

Rain, 71
Rainer, Luise, 172
Rajpipla, Maharajah of, 95–96
Ralton, Bert, 107
Ranjitsinhji, Prince, 86
Rattigan, Terence, 180
Ray, Johnnie, 266
Rea, Alec, 132
Reading, Lord, 78
Redding (of Chicago), 40
Reinhardt, Max, 138, 139
Reiss, Samuel, 38, 39
Reith, Lord, 109
Réjane, 45, 46
Remarque, Erich Maria, 272
Renaud, Madeleine, 174
Reszke, Edouard and Jean de, 22
Reynolds, Quentin, 190, 196, 198
Rhapsody in Blue, 111
Rickenbacker, Eddie, 173
Rigoletto, 104
Ritz Hotel, Paris, 34
Ritz, Marie Louise, 23, 25, 26, 255, 256
Roberts, Lord, 42
Robertson, Lady Howard, 258–9
Robertson, Sir Howard, R.A., 119, 221
Robinson, Edward G., 210
Robson, Flora, 139, 143

Rockefeller Center Theatre, 168
Rockefeller, David, 280
Rogers, Will, 76
Romano, 23
Roosevelt, Eleanor, 43, 46, 233
Roosevelt, President Theodore, 42, 46
Rose, Billy, 250
Rose, John, 123
Rosebery, Lord, 172
Rosenfeld, Harry, 22, 290
Rothenstein, Will, 56
Rothermere, Lord, 129, 167, 279
Rothschild, Alfred de, 39
Rothschild, Baron de, 46
Rothschild, James de, 78
Rothschild, Lionel de, 67
Royal Hotel, Guernsey, 145
Royal Marines Dinner, 234
Royal Victorian Order, 17
Royalty Theatre, 18
Royds, Admiral Sir Charles, 160
Rubinstein, Artur, 275
Rue, Larry, 190, 192, 197
Ruel, Charles, 193
Russell, Lindsay, 42
Ryder Cup Team at Hoylake, 74

St. Martin's Theatre, 132
Samuel, Lord, 78
Sande, Earl, 81
Sandow, Eugen, 57
Sanford, Laddie, 78
Sarazen, Gene, 64
Saroyan, William, 272
Sassoon, Sir Philip, 108, 166

SAVOY

FAMOUS OCCASIONS

Banquet given by President Tubman
    of Liberia to H.M. the Queen,
    Prince Philip and every other
    member of the Royal Family,
    and 500 guests, 282

SAVOY

Picehi, Wilfred, Banqueting Department, Assistant to Zavattoni; parachuted with British Commandos into Italy and shot there as spy, Palm Sunday, 1941, 183
Potts, G. B., Director, 14, 261
Pruger, General Manager, 50, 168, 224
Pugh, Mrs., Lady Superintendent, successor to Mrs. Butler, 224, 228

Quaglino, Restaurateur, 30

Reeves-Smith, Sir George, Chairman and Managing Director, *passim*.
Ritz, César, First Savoy Hotel Manager, 22, 23, 24, 26, 31, 32, 33, 34; retires from Savoy, 34; builds London Ritz Hotel, 38; break-down in health, 49, 239
Rudd, Miss Peggy, in charge of Savoy's Drury Lane factory, 244

Santarelli, Restaurant Manager, 30, 68, 96, 152, 153, 155, 175, 182–183, 222
Sayer, Leslie, Manager of Strand Power Company, 243
Schwenter, Assistant Manager to Pruger, later Manager of Maurice Hotel, Paris, 168
Schwenter, Madame, 255
Seggletz, Gustave, Savoy Hotel's General Manager, 40
Serocold, Claude, Director, 159
Somers, Debroy, Conductor of Savoy Orpheans, 76–77, 101, 107–8, 110, 111

Temple, Richmond, 108, 146, 159
Thornewill, Miles, Vice-Chairman of Savoy Hotel Co., 159, 164, 199, 200, 202, 210, 212, 224, 227, 239

SAVOY

Thouraud, 'virtuoso' de cuisine, 35, 41, 44, 45, 47
Townsend, James, Head of Gentlemen's Cloakrooms, 146, 214, 255–256
Toye, C. C., in charge of Bill Office, 175
Tweedy, Mary, Press Office, 14, 274

Victor, Reception Clerk, 147, 150, 188, 210, 223
Virlogeux, Maître-chef, 128, 145, 155, 175

Webb, Manager of Works Department, 215, 244
Williams, Harry, Head Enquiry Clerk, 30, 255
Wontner, Hugh, Chairman and Managing Director, after Reeves-Smith, 14, 148, 168, 169, 172, 182, 183, 187, 198–9, 201, 203, 204, 206, 208, 209, 225, 230, 231, 234, 238, 239, 241, 242, 244, 250, 251, 253, 256, 257, 258, 280, 283

Zavattoni, Banqueting Manager, 78, 124, 145, 150–2, 182, 183, 221

SAVOY HISTORICAL

Savoy Bailiff, Chief Clerk to Duchy of Lancaster, 16
Savoy Chapel, 16, 17, 193, 205
Savoy, Hospital for the Needy, 15
Savoy, Manor of, 15
Savoy Theatre, 19, 21

WAR-TIME EVENTS

Air-raid damage, Savoy's heavy, 215
American Bar, the Savoy's rendezvous for war correspondents, 188, 191

315

317